Displaced

The Human Cost of Development and Resettlement

Olivia Bennett and Christopher McDowell

palgrave
macmillan

DISPLACED

Copyright © Olivia Bennett and Christopher McDowell, 2012.

All rights reserved.

First published in 2012 by
PALGRAVE MACMILLAN®
in the United States—a division of St. Martin's Press LLC,
175 Fifth Avenue, New York, NY 10010.

Where this book is distributed in the UK, Europe and the rest of the world,
this is by Palgrave Macmillan, a division of Macmillan Publishers Limited,
registered in England, company number 785998, of Houndmills,
Basingstoke, Hampshire RG21 6XS.

Palgrave Macmillan is the global academic imprint of the above companies
and has companies and representatives throughout the world.

Palgrave® and Macmillan® are registered trademarks in the United States,
the United Kingdom, Europe and other countries.

ISBN: 978–0–230–11785–3 (hardcover)
ISBN: 978–0–230–11786–0 (paperback)

Library of Congress Cataloging-in-Publication Data

Bennett, Olivia, 1950–
    Displaced : the human cost of development and resettlement / Olivia Bennett
and Christopher McDowell.
       p. cm.—(Palgrave studies in oral history)
     ISBN 978–0–230–11785–3—
     ISBN 978–0–230–11786–0 ()
      1. Economic development projects—Developing countries. 2. Forced
migration—Developing countries. 3. Land settlement—Developing countries.
    I. McDowell, Chris. II. Title.

HC59.72.E44B46 2012
307.209172'4—dc23   2011040104

A catalogue record of the book is available from the British Library.

Design by Newgen Imaging Systems (P) Ltd., Chennai, India.

First edition: April 2012

10 9 8 7 6 5 4 3 2 1

Printed in the United States of America.

PALGRAVE *Studies in Oral History*

Series Editors: Linda Shopes and Bruce M. Stave

Editorial Board

Contents

Illustrations

Note about the maps: The maps show the location of the development on a national map, and the areas where displacement and resettlement took place in a more detailed map; the latter are not to scale. All maps by Julie Anson.

Series Editors' Foreword

When the United States Supreme Court decided in 2005 in the *Kelo v. City of New London* case that eminent domain could be used to transfer land from one private owner to another for purposes of economic development, a firestorm broke loose in the United States. Many throughout the nation worried about the sanctity of private property, but those most affected had to be concerned about the impact on their lives. Not only would they be affected financially, but what fate did displacement have in store for them? The issue is even more trenchant in developing societies, where marginalized people often are relocated in the name of progress.

This volume offers incisive case studies of people in developing nations when the land they inhabit is targeted for other use. Whether it be because of a mega dam project, the shifting of land from pastoral to large-scale agriculture or mining, or the establishment of game parks and conservation areas, displaced individuals frequently, although not always, suffer as a result of removal from their traditional residences. Oral histories taken in India, Pakistan, Kenya, Botswana, Namibia, and Lesotho provide a substantive base for understanding the nature of displacement, as individual accounts humanize the challenges faced by those who stand in the way of land-use transformation. The interviews attempt to stimulate communication among those most affected in an effort to help shape agendas and encourage public debate and democratic outcomes. Undertaken by Panos, a global network of nongovernmental organizations, the interviews provide an excellent example of activist and advocacy oral history whose purpose is to empower the interviewees and to affect policy. Since those conducting the interviews are from the same community as their subjects, hierarchical barriers are broken down, making for more meaningful communication.

We welcome this book to the Palgrave Studies in Oral History series and value its threefold contribution—the substantive study of displacement, an innovative approach to oral history methodology, and the global scope of its subject matter. It complements Suroopa Mukherjee's *Surviving Bhopal: Dancing Bodies, Written Texts, and Oral Testimonials of Women in the Wake of an Industrial Disaster* and Sean Field's forthcoming *Oral History, Community, and Displacement: Imagining Memories in Post-Apartheid South Africa.* Both new entries join the more than two dozen volumes already published in our attempt to bring the best in oral history to students, scholars, and the general reading public.

Bruce M. Stave
University of Connecticut

Linda Shopes
Carlisle, Pennsylvania

Preface

The firsthand accounts on which this book draws were gathered in Botswana, Namibia, Lesotho, Kenya, India, and Pakistan as part of a larger program of work within Panos London. Panos is a global network of nongovernmental organizations (NGOs), comprising seven institutes that work predominantly in Africa, South Asia, and the Caribbean to ensure that information is effectively used to foster public debate, pluralism, and democracy. Panos works with media and with other information actors to enable poor and marginalized people in developing countries to shape and communicate their own development agendas. The oral testimony program of activities, which was developed by Panos London, uses and adapts oral history methodology to the development context.[1] It works at the community level and focuses on increasing opportunities for those directly affected by development issues—people who usually lack access to channels of communication—to speak out in their own words on issues that concern them, rather than having their views defined by others.

To implement its oral testimony projects, Panos works directly with communities and local partner organizations. The interviewing team is usually drawn from those communities and/or from those working with them. They are trained in interviewing techniques and are supported to remain involved in the dissemination and discussion of the testimonies. It is hoped that community involvement in the project will act as a catalyst for further learning and empowerment, and will generate possibilities for people to articulate their own agenda for development.

The interviews are gathered primarily to publish, broadcast, and amplify the voices of the most marginalized and least heard in the development debate, and, by gathering and communicating different perspectives, to increase understanding of specific development issues. In the particular project that informs this book, the topic was the impact of development-induced displacement, especially its less visible and less quantifiable aspects. Panos London and its international partners worked with communities to record interviews for use in local language and national language publications, radio programs, and in other information activities; all narrators consented to the use of the material, with the aim of informing a wider audience of their experiences.

This book is thus slightly unusual because as an academic exploration of the socioeconomic, political, and cultural dimensions of involuntary resettlement, it draws on data that were not explicitly intended for academic use. However, we would argue that the methodology and the interviews generated provide data that stand up to academic scrutiny, and that the collection methods were robust, rigorous, and methodologically and ethically sound.

In establishing its oral testimony approach, Panos London drew on many of the guiding principles of oral history, particularly the community and public history strands, notably the value of a multiplicity of views; the inclusion of those sidelined by more formal or academic research; an emphasis on community and "nonprofessional" involvement; and the intention to reach out to wider audiences and to stimulate debate. It also incorporated other key elements of traditional oral history, such as careful documentation and archiving of interview transcripts.

The term "oral testimony" reflects Panos's belief that sustainable development demands that people participate in the debates and decisions that affect their lives and that communication is at the heart of development. It is this emphasis on the future and on the potential for change, rather than on reconstructing past history, that led Panos London to use the term "oral testimony" rather than "oral history." Moreover, the emphasis is on communication rather than research, and interviews are focused around particular themes and issues, rather than being conventional life histories.

Since Panos London commissioned and published *Listening for a Change* in 1993, in which Hugo Slim and Paul Thompson explored the value and relevance of oral history to development practice, it has worked with 50 partners in 30 countries, generating over 1,000 testimonies on different topics in many different languages, and communicating them through print, radio, meetings, video, and the Web.[2] Many of those whose words have been broadcast this way are among the poorest in their societies, with least access to education, or are excluded from power and influence by virtue of their gender, ethnic or social identity, age, or other factors. With large-scale development projects such as dams and irrigation schemes often taking place in relatively remote rural areas, many of the people interviewed for the resettlement project, which took place over several years, fitted this profile.

As founder of Panos London's Oral Testimony Programme and its director for 12 years, during which time the international resettlement project was developed and implemented, I was involved in every aspect of the work, from the in-country training workshops to supporting local communication activities. Christopher McDowell, who had first worked with Panos London in 1991, was expert advisor to the resettlement project from 1998. Although all the partners have used the interviews for advocacy and awareness–raising in their regions, this book represents the first opportunity to bring the different voices and experiences together. Our aim was to get a balance between highlighting themes and concerns common to the whole collection and topics peculiar to certain situations and communities, while also illustrating the diversity of personal experience and response. We believe the individual stories in this volume provide a richness of evidence that adds to our knowledge and understanding of complex processes of change brought about by displacement.

OLIVIA BENNETT

Acknowledgments

So many people have been involved the implementation of the testimony collection projects upon which this book draws that it would be impossible to name and thank them all, but we are particularly grateful to those people who also took the time to read these chapters: Mitu Varma, Tony Herbert, Kuntala Lahiri-Dutt, Justin Imam, J. M. Lenka, Ced Hesse, Sophia Dube, Ejaz Ahmed Khan, Asad Rahman, Gulnaz Sheikh, Willemien le Roux, Sue Armstrong, Sharon Goulds, and especially Siobhan Warrington and Kitty Warnock. Their comments and encouragement were invaluable. Olivia would like to thank Nigel Cross for involving her in the Sahel Oral History Project, which sowed the seeds for the oral testimony approach, as well as Panos London, where the ideas took shape, and which provided her with the space and facilities to write about this particular collection, and also Tim Marchant, for providing support on so many important levels.

Our book would not exist if not for the patience, commitment, and hard work of the interviewers, which included long hours of transcribing interview transcripts, often in remote locations with few modern facilities. Above all, we owe a huge debt of gratitude to the men and women who took the time to tell their stories. We hope we have done justice to them.

OLIVIA BENNETT
and
CHRISTOPHER MCDOWELL

Editorial Note

Cuts within interview extracts have been made, mainly to remove repetition or confusion. Occasionally text may have been reordered and the related sections may have been put together; breaks within and between sentences are clearly indicated by ellipses. Text inserted for clarification is in square brackets and translation and interpretations are also in square brackets. Questions have been removed.

CHAPTER I

Moving People

States, Displacement, and Resettlement

Through detailed personal recollections and reflections, this volume provides a unique insight into the experiences of people who have been displaced from their lands and are officially relocated, or who resettle in a new location without any support, as a consequence of decisions taken by governments and private interests to change the use of land. The rather mundane phrase "land-use change" conceals what is in reality a complex series of events and long-lasting processes that trigger rapid and externally enforced socioeconomic, cultural, and political change that affects the lives of many millions of individuals and communities in the developing and rapidly industrializing world annually. Central to the experiences of what is described in the literature as "development-created displacement" and "involuntary resettlement" is the exercise of power by state authorities, or by private companies with the support of governments, to remove people against their will from lands that have, in most cases, been their primary home or source of livelihood for many generations.

Although the idea of human populations being rooted in the natural environment is often criticized for positing a somewhat botanical and static understanding of human nature and society—in particular of those societies described as "traditional" and associated with indigenous, pastoralist, and remote natural-resource-dependent populations—the accounts presented in this book would strongly suggest that the rupture from ancestral lands has consequences that extend far beyond mere economic loss. The sudden and uncompromising removal from what is familiar occasions a more profound unraveling of social relationships, which compounds the risks and hazards that confront displaced populations. Those risks, and efforts to overcome them with or without external assistance, are described by the narrators in this book.

The experiences recounted are based on interviews conducted with men and women, young and old in Lesotho, Botswana, Namibia, Kenya, India, and Pakistan. The developments that displaced them took place at a variety of times, from the late 1970s to the early 2000s. The interviews were conducted as part of a wider oral testimony program, which is described in greater detail in the next chapter. The stories that are told capture not only people's concerns about impending displacement and resettlement, but also paint a vivid picture of the displacement event and of the early years of relocation and settlement. In some cases the interviewees were able to reflect on the impacts of resettlement more than a generation after the event, providing important new knowledge about intergenerational consequences of land alienation and relocation. The evidence presented in these chapters adds considerably to the body of knowledge on involuntary resettlement where, with some notable exceptions,[1] detailed ethnographies of involuntary resettlement are rare.

The acquisition of land and other resources from often marginal populations, when undertaken for purposes of "national development," involves processes that are largely remote from those most affected. People and communities who are expected and legally required to hand over their assets to the state are likely to be from the fringes rather than from the mainstream of society. In India, a disproportionate number of affected people are, as is the case in many studies in this volume, members of minority and tribal communities who live in remote areas, are largely outside the formal economy, and are unlikely to speak the official language or share the majority religion. In China, populations living in those remote places where dams and reservoirs are built for hydropower generation, where new roads are laid into formerly underdeveloped areas, and where mines excavate hard to reach ores and minerals find themselves in the way of such infrastructure. Throughout the developing world, it is increasingly marginal, "squatter," and "illegal" urban communities who are being moved to make way for the infrastructure essential for the functioning of modern and fast-growing megacities.

Whether in rural or urban areas, the decisions made to expand cities, increase industrial output, or extract mineral and other resources are made by powerful political and economic elites and are funded internationally either through private loans raised from commercial banks or through intergovernmental loans, channeled through international financing institutions such as multilateral development banks. The political and economic decision-making will, to varying degrees, have gone through domestic democratic processes; however, "development," particularly in rapidly industrializing states and on the scale that we are discussing in this volume, remains predominantly an imposed decision of the state, rather than one that is agreed on between the state and the citizen. For this reason, the accounts discussed in the following chapters go some small way towards bringing the voices, experiences, and perspectives of those most negatively affected by the development process into the political process.

The State of Knowledge

Although the academic literature on resettlement in the context of development has grown significantly since the early 1990s, the major part of that work focuses on the ongoing struggle to develop laws and policies at the national and international levels to improve the protection of and assistance available to those people who find themselves in the way of progress. This is necessary work as it challenges states and the international community to think more broadly about the protection needs, the human rights implications of resettlement, and the responsibilities of governments to balance economic growth with social, cultural, and environmental protection and wellbeing. Linked to that policy analysis work is a series of publications that have sought to explain why and how involuntary resettlement intensifies impoverishment among displaced communities.[2] This volume adds to both those strands of the literature. There is in addition an emerging literature on both the ethics and the political economy of involuntary resettlement; this volume forms part of that literature.

The displacements discussed in this volume have occurred as a result of four broad development processes that are central to current industrial and economic growth strategies: hydropower, resource extraction, mechanized agricultural production, and biodiversity protection, including the creation of game parks. They involve a range of displacement types, from direct displacement (leading to the loss of homes and land due to the acquisition and change of the use of that land) to what is termed indirect or economic displacement (see for example Jharkhand in Chapter 6), where people lose access to land and other resources that are vital to their livelihoods, which fundamentally disrupts their patterns of settlement and livelihoods. The processes of displacement and resettlement also differ. There are examples of land acquisition and resettlement organized and administered by large state authorities that were established for the purpose of building the infrastructure (see Lesotho in chapters 7 and 8, and Pakistan in Chapter 3), where the resettlement is undertaken within a proper legal and policy framework. There are also displacement and resettlement events for which the legal basis and the chain of responsibility is far less clear. In terms of time frames, the events featured in this volume took place over a wide range, from projects that have been decades in preparation (Lesotho) to those in which the displacement from land happened in a very short time frame (pastoralists in Kenya, Chapter 4), sometimes in no more than a few days, with little notice.

In order to situate these examples of development-created involuntary resettlement within wider issues that relate to the development process and its human impacts, this introduction will locate state-mandated forced relocations of populations historically and will summarize the current state of knowledge and policy. It will first discuss the recent history of state-mandated population relocation, in order to draw links between past and present motivations and to consider the role that population relocation plays in state building. Although the examples drawn on represent coercive displacement for political gain and flawed approaches rooted in a mid-twentieth-century belief in centrally planned "progress," the chapter also discusses resettlement operations that, on the surface, have proven beneficial to the populations and countries involved. It goes on to consider how the involuntary relocation of people, from mainly rural areas, plays a key role in the wider economic and social transformation in China in the early twenty-first century.

The chapter then reviews the literature on the policy situation and legal situation within which development-created displacement occurs. It considers the sufficiency of current laws and policies to provide protection against unfair and unjust displacement and the safeguards in place to enable displaced communities to reestablish their lives and livelihoods in a new location. It finally assesses the academic contribution to understanding the impact that land dispossession and resettlement have on communities, and the kinds of strategies that have been advanced to mitigate resettlement-created impoverishment.

State Evictions as a Strategy of Control

There has been a long history of involuntary planned resettlement by states, lying on a continuum from ideological and repressive resettlement (Stalinist Russia, Derg Ethiopia), undertaken for overtly political reasons, often with underpinning security motivations, to more benign "humanitarian" resettlement to remove people from situations of risk and danger. It is possible to place resettlement operations on that continuum, depending on their degree of legality, democratic process, consent, and valid justification. The majority of contemporary resettlement in the developing world is conducted by states for economic and development reasons, and the decisions taken to acquire land, locate a project, or relocate populations are always highly political. The ethical dimensions of development-created displacement have come to the fore in recent decades with the increase of land acquisition and resettlement undertaken as part of private and for-profit investments. In the following section we highlight historical resettlements to illustrate one end of this continuum, beginning with relocation and exile in Soviet Russia and looking at *ujamaa* villagization in Tanzania.

These historical episodes in state-mandated relocation are relevant to the current era because they reveal how resettlement should not be viewed as merely happenstance, or as a by-product of a particular project; rather, the moving of people is in itself a means of advancing forms of political, economic, and social change and is frequently a means to extend state control. It further reveals, as is reflected throughout the volume, that government claims that it is able to manage rapid change brought about by displacement and resettlement are very often illusory. Policies advanced to pay fair compensation, find replacement land, or to restore livelihoods rarely achieve their objectives in the absence of sound planning, consultation, funding, or political will.

The large-scale forcible scattering, exile, and clustering in new locations of populations by states for ideological and security purposes was an important feature of twentieth-century history. Applebaum has described how the Gulag system of transportation, forced labor, imprisonment, and exile became an integral part of the Soviet system almost immediately after the Russian Revolution in 1918.[3] Initially "unreliable elements" and potential "enemies" were imprisoned in newly constructed camps on the outskirts of major towns. By the 1950s, the almost 500 camp complexes, imprisoning up to two million people at any one time, were "playing a central role in the Soviet economy," producing a third of the country's gold and much of its coal and timber, Applebaum notes. Most of the camps were dismantled following Stalin's death. A few remained, and in the 1970s and 1980s, they evolved into political camps for a new generation of democratic activists, anti-Soviet nationalists, and criminals.

In the Soviet Union, as in Nazi Europe in the mid-twentieth century, labor camps, concentration camps, and political camp systems demanded the violent and forcible displacement and imprisonment of populations, which resulted in mass deaths due to starvation and disease and later ended in mass killings. These came out of what Applebaum calls the "fracturing of civilisation" created in a particular period of history, and they resulted from the ideology of Stalinism and Nazism, which was marked by a perversion of values and by the casual acceptance of violence and atrocities. We need to understand the Gulag system in the context of these histories, but it is also the case that deliberate planned displacement and the forced settlement of populations by states has been a universal feature of state formation and nation building.

James C. Scott argues that it was inherent in the philosophy of many twentieth-century states, particularly those countries emerging from colonialism and who embarked on an autarkic route to independence through socialist centralized planning, that economic and social progress could be achieved through mass population relocation. Scott is highly critical of mass resettlement schemes such as *ujamaa* villagization in Tanzania, which he believes was overly reliant on plans produced by technocrats with little connection to or regard for local conditions and vernacular knowledge, and was pushed through by the politically powerful against the wishes of the citizenry.[4]

Julius Nyerere, the first president of the newly independent Tanzania, believed that the resettlement of the country's entire rural population between 1973 and 1976 into rationalized villages functioning as cooperatives would deliver self-reliance and a Tanzanian-African course of development. It was believed that important efficiencies would be gained through the more rational use of the land, the achievement of national production targets, and the better delivery of services such as agricultural outreach, health, and education. Initially, resettlement into the new villages was voluntary, but as enthusiasm for the scheme was slow in developing and forms of passive resistance were emerging, the government announced that relocation would become compulsory for all rural residents within a three-year period, in accordance with a series of military-like "operations" to stage the enforced resettlement process.

Critics at the time and since have argued that while some temporary productivity gains may have been made, an underlying justification for such a dramatic and immediate transformation of Tanzania's society had more to do with enabling state control over the population. Resettlement permitted the accurate mapping of the population, making far easier the tasks of collecting taxes, controlling movement, recruiting for the armed forces, and, according to Hyden, reversing the process of the peasantry slipping away from government control.[5] As with other "high modernist" schemes discussed by James C. Scott (1998), Tanzanian villagization ultimately failed in its objectives; many of these failures were attributable to a lack of feasibility of the overall project, but also due to poor planning. Peasant farmers were moved to houses (built with insufficient or inappropriate building materials) near all-weather roads, often some distance from their lands, and the lands were unfamiliar to them or unsuitable for the kind of crops they were expected to grow. The distance from their fields made it difficult for them to control for pests and other damage, and the concentration of livestock and people encouraged cholera and livestock epidemics. The disruption of long-established transhumance routes was disastrous for pastoralists and damaged rangelands. A legacy of the failed *ujamaa* experiment was a deepened mistrust of government and the concentration of power in the hands of local party leaders.

Resettlement as a Political and Development Opportunity

There is however, research evidence showing that the planned resettlement of populations need not always have antidevelopment and antidemocratic outcomes. Cernea argues that impoverishment risks associated with involuntary resettlement can be anticipated, avoided, or minimized when sound planning based on comprehensive on-the-ground risk assessment is supported by legal protection and policies of recovery, involving the participation of all affected parties and backed by proper resource allocation.[6]

The resettlement in the 1970s and 1980s of river valleys in West Africa previously rendered largely uninhabitable by the prevalence of onchocerciasis (river blindness) is often cited as an example of how international collaborative action and government policy, aided by financial support, can restore land to human settlement and enable sustainable resettlement under extremely difficult conditions. The World Health Organization's Onchocerciasis Control Programme (OCP) which began in 1974 in Burkina Faso, Côte d'Ivoire, Ghana, Mali, Niger, and Togo was by the mid-1980s deemed to be the most successful disease-control undertaking of all time. Resettlement was at the center of the control program and was undertaken with the help of large amounts of foreign aid and political support, following a prolonged drought and famine in the Sahel region, It was also triggered by demographic pressures within states in the region to open up new land for settlement to ease overcrowding elsewhere. The resettlement program itself was made possible because the planners and politicians viewed the vast underpopulated areas as an opportunity to counter food insecurity and drought through the OCP and an integrated rural development and livelihood reestablishment program.

The Burkina Faso government established a body to closely manage the resettlement and the ensuing productivity, setting targets and laying down strategies for production in the Volta Valley. The authority recruited households on a voluntary basis to create agricultural smallholdings and allocated land randomly in order to avoid ethnic clustering. D. E. McMillan undertook a longitudinal study of the Volta Valley resettlement sites and found that *dirigiste* tendencies of the authority and its desire to control resettlement activities from the center were only partially realized. Formal planning in fact gave way to local adaptation as farmers, rather than intensifying their agriculture (the preferred strategy of the Volta Valley Authority), opted instead to extensify by pushing out into surrounding land; they further adopted strategies to diversify the source of income available to the household through off-farm activities.[7] McMillan found that settlers adopted a wide range of coping and adaptation mechanisms, reestablishing institutional networks to provide mutual support and knowledge to fellow farming households, and particularly new farming households, and did not always comply with the plans of the centralized authority, which often proved inflexible. The resettlement program provides guidance as it shows that future resettlement programs will benefit from international cooperation and political support; the commitment toward financing; and integrated planning approaches in which resettlement in itself is a driver of development, but where planning is sufficiently flexible to permit individuals and communities to marshal their vernacular knowledge and expertise in pursuit of appropriate strategies.

Resettlement as a Catalyst for Transformation

The significance of involuntary resettlement in the transformation of China to a socialist society built on market principles has thus far been underestimated. The Three Gorges Project, involving the construction of the world's largest hydropower project, inundating more than 1,000 square kilometers of land and forcing the direct displacement and relocation of more than 1.3 million people (and the projected indirect displacement of an estimated 4 million additional people due to reservoir-linked erosion and flooding) over a ten-year period is perhaps the highest-profile mass resettlement in China's contemporary transformation. However, according to the Chinese government's own statistics, land "acquisitions" by the state led to the displacement and compensated resettlement of between 2 and 4 million rural Chinese annually in the first decade of the twenty-first century. Resettlement in China is often viewed as merely an unavoidable by-product of processes of industrial modernization that are led by power production and transportation. It is argued here, however, that rather than being peripheral to the transformation of the Chinese economy and society over the past three decades, the mass resettlement of largely rural people, but increasingly of urban residents, has played an important part in that transformation.

Resettlement, it is argued, has contributed in important ways to the key processes of transformation, namely, the reform of the state-owned sector, the creation of a market-based "stakeholder" society, managed urbanization, the restructuring of agriculture, and the gradual and as yet unrealized establishment of new land markets and institutions of property rights. Resettlement has provided the Chinese state with a series of opportunities to initiate transformations in a far more efficient and speedy way than might otherwise have been accomplished. To a large degree, this has been possible because the state continues to own the vast majority of rural land and, unlike other large industrializing countries such as India, it is able to take far-reaching decisions on land-use conversions at a fraction of the cost incurred by democracies, which have an established land market backed by property rights exercisable through the courts.

At its simplest, resettlement permits transformation by taking very large numbers of people off tracts of less-productive lands, thus enabling the dismantling of agricultural communes and the shifting of that labor through resettlement-linked financial support into the rapidly growing market economy. In some cases, new workers are provided employment in factories where a proportion of jobs are set aside only for those resettled. Resettlement further functions as a cushion against the inevitable unemployment, with the risk of social and political unrest that results from such a rapid contraction of the state sector by planning in advance the redeployment of labor. Within rural areas, resettlement, as a result of the Three Gorges Project and many other infrastructure schemes, has increased demands for the granting of new property rights over agricultural land, and related demands for greater accountability and democracy at the village level. Resettlement increases the volume of land transactions and encourages diversification into farms and nonfarm activities. This is a central strategy of the modernization process, because it is believed to promote efficiency and act as a stimulant for economic growth.

In this way, resettlement is contributing at a critical time in China's reforms, accelerating the downsizing of the state sector, moving people to where markets can be established, and creating through rapid social change a cultural shift in those moved from a horizontal, often subsistence life in village houses, dependent on the state for public goods, to a vertical life in the newly created or newly modernized towns and cities of the East, where self-reliance replaces dependency and accelerates incorporation into new systems of social relations. While reform takes place at the level of government and ministries that are creating a policy and legal environment for transformation, that transformation is in itself an expression of human relationships and resettlement through the dismantling and restructuring of human relationships in a compressed period of time and provides an important dynamic for change, in which social liquidity is a modernizing force.

Displacement Policy and Impoverishment

The displacement and resettlement of populations in the developing and rapidly industrializing world will increase in the coming decades as a result of population growth, the rising demand for power and managed water linked to industrialization and urbanization, and the shift to large-scale agricultural production. Predicted climate change, or at least states' adaptation and mitigation of such change, is also likely to result in additional resettlement as a consequence of:

- significant new infrastructure projects (in pursuit of hydropower and water diversion and storage and the construction of sea and river defenses);
- biodiversity enlargement and protection (the creation of new forests, grassland, and wildlife reserves);
- increased biofuel production;
- the proactive and responsive relocation of communities from land under threat of flooding or salination.

Such involuntary displacement and resettlement will unfold in societies where migration, both internally and internationally, and in particular rural-to-urban migration, will continue to be a significant feature of economic, social, and political transformations, both spontaneous and state-directed, which in turn are influenced by patterns of national and international investment.

The displacement and involuntary resettlement literature, supported by operational evaluations of emergency and longer-term responses by states, international organizations, and NGOs (nongovernmental organizations), points to a strong correlation between the processes of land and resource loss and alienation, displacement, and resettlement, and the impoverishment and political marginalization of those affected both immediately and over generations.[8] Michael Cernea's Impoverishment Risks and Reconstruction Model, which emerged out of his time working on social safeguards and involuntary resettlement programs at the World Bank and from many years spent advising governments and companies on resettlement, identifies a number of key impoverishment risks associated with displacement and resettlement. The risks, which should be understood as being in addition to the "background" risks that shape the lives of people in the developing world, are homelessness, landlessness, joblessness, loss of common property resources, the risk of declining health and mortality, and social and psychological marginalization affecting individuals and groups. Cernea argues that these risks are not inevitable and can be anticipated and overcome through proper planning, knowledge, and the investment of resources. McDowell has subsequently argued that these risks need to be understood in a far wider analytical framework, taking into account historical, political, and economic processes and wider government policies beyond the immediate resettlement context, and looking at them in relation to the functioning of formal and informal institutional arrangements and how these affect people's access to and control over resources vital to their livelihood opportunities, an important factor.[9] McDowell's adaptation of the concepts of sustainable livelihoods to better understanding has been applied by various scholars.

In studies that have compared the outcomes of displacement and resettlement across and between the displacement domains (where the proximate cause of displacement was either conflict, a natural disaster, development, or was the result of a state-mandated relocation scheme), the creation of new forms of impoverishment or the deepening of existing forms of impoverishment and the distancing of displaced and resettled people from full participation in society are indeed marked features of the displacement–impoverishment nexus.[10] The largest and most comprehensive body of evidence of this relationship has emerged out of studies on development-created forced displacement and resettlement over the past forty years, since 1971.

Cernea estimates (as of 2010) that more than 15 million people annually in the developing world lose their assets and are likely to be involuntarily resettled as a result of land acquisition for infrastructure projects in both the public and private spheres. This marks an increase of 5 million people displaced each year, when compared to World Bank estimates produced in the mid-1990s. A large body of research suggests that the majority of those displaced and resettled remain impoverished for at least seven to ten years.[11]

Community disarticulation is arguably the most complex part of the displacement and reconstruction process. The term is used to refer to the tearing apart of social structures, interpersonal ties, and the enveloping social fabric as a result of forced resettlement. Cernea and McDowell have described the main elements of community disarticulation as the scattering of kinship groups and informal networks of mutual help. The unraveling of spatially and culturally based patterns of self-organization, social interaction, and reciprocity represents the loss of valuable social capital that compounds the loss of both natural and manmade capital.[12] Although these components of impoverishment were identified in relation to involuntary resettlement induced by planned development processes, evidence suggests that the same risks—though in different combinations and with different intensities—are critical in other domains of forced displacement.

The United Nations guidelines on internally displaced persons call for such development displacement only to be undertaken for "compelling" public purpose development. However, the line between public and private development is increasingly blurred, as governments are faced with limited public funds to meet the demands of infrastructure development. The establishment of special economic zones in India and China has led to continuing conflict as people protest against the acquisition of large swathes of land. Even purchase by the private sector is considered risky to land-based rural farmers who, once divested of their land, have little skills with which to turn cash into sustainable livelihoods.

New forms of particularly pernicious impoverishment have been identified in which political disempowerment coupled with marginalization—both within displaced communities and between the displaced and the wider society and the state—is creating new vulnerabilities and social unrest. Pieke recently described land acquisition as "the most important source of discontent and exploitation in rural China at the moment."[13] In India, increasing social unrest or the fear of unrest prompted the government of India to approve in 2008 for the first time a Resettlement and Rehabilitation Policy that focused on both public and private sector investments. The adoption of the policy is a clear indication of the importance of this issue to one of the world's major economies.

Particularly vulnerable are tribal and indigenous populations, and those rural and urban dwellers unable to prove ownership of the lands they occupy or depend upon for subsistence. These populations have been historically at greater risk of summary eviction in the development process. In October 2007, for example, thousands of landless peasants marched to New Delhi to protest against the threat posed to their livelihoods by industrial development, special economic zones, and supermarkets.

The growing and immediate challenge of managing the development process while protecting the rights of citizens in situations of displacement and land acquisition has five main drivers:

- inadequate available unoccupied public land for development purposes
- increased forced acquisition of both private lands and public lands occupied by the landless
- the nonavailability of alternative land for replacement to ensure that those who lose their lands to development are able to regain sustainable livelihoods
- increasing numbers of private-sector investments that have no regulatory oversight by the state
- a rise in public–private investments with state involvement in expropriation, but where investments are profit-oriented rather than in the public interest

The Management of Displacement and Resettlement

There have been a number of important policy developments over the past decade to improve the response to development-forced displacement and to provide more effective safeguards for those most negatively affected. A number of governments, particularly in Asia, have adopted—though have not always fully enacted—national and regional resettlement policies and laws (for example Vietnam, China, India, Sri Lanka, and the Lao PDR), and have acknowledged past damage (as the Chinese have recently done in paying reparations to some of the 23 million people displaced by dams in that country since 1949). This might suggest that states are gradually accepting their responsibilities and understand that development and economic progress cannot best be achieved by disenfranchising and leaving behind populations who by happenstance live in the path of progress.

For the main lenders, most notably the World Bank and the Asian Development Bank (ADB), there were strong pressures from staff within those institutions in the 1990s, and also from NGOs on the outside, to strengthen safeguard policies to ensure that development funded in part or wholly by bank loans did not have the perverse counterdevelopment impacts of increased impoverishment, marginalization of indigenous population and women, and accelerated damage to the environment. Consequently, there was encouraging dialogue between the international financing institutions and lender governments on new legislative frameworks within which land acquisition and involuntary resettlement would be conducted. There was encouragement also that the banks' oversight role was being strengthened.

However, in recent years the development banks would appear to have backtracked from this commitment and the initial momentum in improving legislative frameworks has been lost. Despite operational improvements in calculating and making reparations for assets lost as a result of land acquisition, the record remains bleak and impoverishment remains the dominant outcome for the majority displaced from their lands and communities as a result of development investments. There are a range of new uncertainties in the coming decades that present even greater challenges for policy makers, civil society, academic researchers, and the affected populations. For example

- the fast-evolving *shift towards commercial development,* for example in highways and energy development, particularly in the construction of dams for power generation;
- with *conflict-related internal displacement* on the increase (see International Displacement Monitoring Centre, 2011, Global Report), it is more commonly the case that development-forced displacement is intermeshing with conflict population displacement; this dynamic has clear protection implications;
- *disaster-related displacement* is on the rise (International Federation of the Red Cross, 2010, World Disasters Report), and again there is a dangerous intersection of types of displacement that raises complex response and protection challenges;
- the rise of new investors, such as China in Africa and in the Mekong Region, raises potential social risks that have not been documented.

Research continues to show that development displacees in unstable countries, and particularly in undemocratic countries in conflict, are very susceptible to human rights violations and to multiple displacement.

In private-sector projects, the market is the preferred mechanism to establish justice in the acquisition process, through willing buyer, willing seller negotiations aimed at achieving a fair price, planning a time frame for vacating land and resources, and setting the conditions under which the transfer of ownership takes place. Many commentators have rightly questioned willing buyer, willing seller arrangements as a just basis for land and resource acquisition, particularly where, as is the case in South Africa, it is the basic principle for wider land reform programs.[14] A number of authors have highlighted the clear power imbalances between the buyer (likely to be a multinational company backed by the state) and the seller (typically marginal populations, distanced from the centers of power, politically unorganized, and who are demonized as NIMBY-inspired opponents of progress). It has also been highlighted that most private-sector land acquisitions are undertaken in a framework in which the project has been identified as being in the national interest and therefore the buyer is able to resort to expropriation if the potentially willing seller is not willing. Critics have also highlighted the failure of cash compensation to provide for long-term restitution for people whose livelihoods are dependent on land and on access to other natural resources. Large parts of the financial industry that invests in projects in the developing world that include land acquisition and involuntary resettlement have adopted the so-called Equator Principles (2003), which seek to ensure that any projects are developed in "a socially responsible manner." Other companies, in mining and construction, for example, have adopted their own similar "statements," setting out social and environmental commitments. However, the scale of private-sector involvement in investment projects that displace populations is unknown, and corporate reporting, beyond the typically vague commitment to social responsibility, is far from extensive in raising questions about transparency and regulation.

In public-sector projects, land and resource acquisition is governed by national legislation—where such legislation exists—that frames the state's right of eminent domain and often dates back to the colonial past (see for example India's Land Acquisition Act or LAA of 1894, with limited modifications in 1985). Such legislation sets out the state's entitlement and the process it must adhere to, but says very little about the rights and entitlements of those who lose their land and other assets in the process. Eminent domain powers are frequently granted to private companies, enabling them to acquire land and resources and displace communities for projects that are for-profit, rather than being in the public interest, as is intended but is not adequately defined in most land acquisition laws. Disputes over land and resource ownership and the unpicking of complex and overlapping tenurial arrangements are major factors in the development process, and some in government would argue that they are a significant obstacle to economic growth and industrial progress. Land acquisition laws, asset valuation, and forms of compensation are widely thought to be ill-suited to resolving such disputes in the interests of all parties. Various governments (for example Ghana, Vietnam, and Indonesia) are now seeking to formulate new land policy development frameworks to respond to the increased demand for land and to navigate between customary systems of land and resource tenure and state systems that are compatible with the demands of export-driven, market-oriented economies. It should be noted, however, that in most developing countries domestically financed projects proceed in the absence of national resettlement laws.

Personal Accounts and the Broader Picture

The personal narratives that form the core of this book are explored in six case studies (chapters 3 through 8). These accounts of land acquisition, displacement, compensation, resettlement assistance, and the experiences of rebuilding lives and livelihoods in a new location can be read against the knowledge and analysis set out above. Together, the case studies illustrate the current scope and scale of state-mandated land acquisition in the developing world as a consequence of national development plans that demand increased hydropower production; the turning over of large areas of land to tourism and to biodiversity protection; the conversion of land for food production on an industrial rather than a subsistence scale; and the accelerating extraction of valuable natural resources to aid industrial growth. The resettled populations featured in this volume are therefore a part of economic and political processes that are global in nature and are linked to patterns of international trade and investment, and to market-driven demands for goods, but these are global processes that have very local and personal impacts. The detachment of affected communities from the global decision making that results in projects that demand land-use change and changes in ownership permeate the interviews and reinforce a strong sense of powerlessness and inability to alter or control events.

The interviews provide a commentary on resettlement policies and their implementation. The research evidence outlined above suggests that current policies are designed principally to enable governments to facilitate land acquisition as a national priority, rather than to protect and assist those people who live on land that is scheduled for acquisition. The experiences of the affected populations detailed in this volume disclose the consequences of such policies and include: poor preparation and planning for resettlement, a lack of consultation and an absence of consent, flawed asset valuation, a failure to secure appropriate replacement land, the unjust use of force against resettlers, administrative malpractice, and an overreliance on insufficient and mismanaged cash compensation.

The Case Studies

Each case study has an "Introduction and Background" section with an overview of the projects or interventions that are the cause of displacement and, where applicable, an overview of the compensation and resettlement policies, but the majority of each chapter consists of the words of the displaced themselves, with commentary on the range of responses, experiences, and memories featured. Details of each testimony collection, such as the number of interviews and the languages involved, are contained in the notes to each chapter.

The first case study (Chapter 3) looks those displaced in the late 1970s by Pakistan's Tarbela Dam. With many people recalling events of nearly 30 years before, this chapter highlights the enduring impact of resettlement and its effect on different generations, as well on the varied income and occupation groups that made up the long-established rural communities inundated by the reservoir. Chapter 4 draws on a set of interviews with pastoralists in Kenya. They were displaced at different times, and by a range of development interventions, including government-sponsored large-scale agricultural schemes. Displacement brought about a rapid and almost total loss of livestock for most of those interviewed, and this in turn forced them to take up other occupations to survive. Because livestock were so central to their way of life, there were powerful social and cultural ramifications to this change, made even more distressing, as many narrators compellingly describe, because the new occupations were traditionally seen as low status—even shameful—ways to make a living. Chapter 5 takes the case of another group for whom displacement has been linked to significant changes to their way of life. It is based on interviews with small groups of San in both Namibia and Botswana, whose people have experienced a long, gradual process of exclusion and removal from their traditional lands. These particular accounts highlight how resettlement has continued to be shaped by their generally negative experiences of competition with others for resources, whether for land or, as now, for education and development opportunities.

The tribal belt of Jharkhand in eastern India is the focus of the Chapter 6, which draws on interviews with men and women who since the mid-1980s have been displaced by increasing numbers of open-pit coal mines in the Damodar Valley and surrounding areas. The fields and forests from which many of the displaced lived have been torn apart for coal or have become so polluted that agriculture is no longer possible. Many are reduced to making a precarious living on the fringes of mines and coal dumps. The nature of the displacement, which has encroached on the land piece by piece, mine by mine, has undermined opportunities for united resistance or protest against unfair or inadequate resettlement policies.

The last two chapters both concentrate on Lesotho, in Southern Africa, but draw on two different collections of interviews. Chapter 7 features a set of interviews that, unlike the other collections, was gathered before any of the narrators were displaced. They were still living in their highland communities in the Molika-liko river valley, aware that in six months or so construction of the Mohale Dam would begin and they would be removed from the land. They describe their current way of life and also reveal much about the difficulties of the negotiation process and how uncertainties and misunderstandings can trigger a process of disempowerment long before people are actually moved. The final case study (Chapter 8) draws on interviews recorded in Lesotho between 2001 and 2002, three to four years after displacement, with some of those previously interviewed in Molika-liko as well as with other men and women. This continuity allows us to track the fortunes of some narrators and it reveals to what extent their fears and hopes about resettlement proved accurate, while others provide different perspectives, among other things, highlighting the complexity of designing compensation packages that can take account of and respond to different needs and personalities. Many of the displaced expressed frustration that the compensation arrangements had stifled rather than stimulated individual agency.

Marginalization

These accounts add weight to academic evidence that for the majority of those resettled against their will in the development process, the outcome is one of marginalization and deepened impoverishment. This is not the case for all resettlers, and there are data from China that point to limited success where "resettlement with development" has been achieved in those relocations where the resettlement project was pursued as a development project in its own right.[15] In this book, we hear of some individuals and families who, by virtue of their assets and status prior to resettlement, or as a result of their ambitions, were able to markedly improve their livelihoods and life opportunities after resettlement. However, the majority of those interviewed describe their social and material lives as being worse off than in their original location, and Cernea's Impoverishment Risks and Reconstruction Model captures well the multidimensionality of risk. The loss of land and the failure to replace land, which results in a loss of production, food, housing, income, security, status, and the untethering of social bonds, has proven the key risk, compounding other losses (access to health care, education, and common property resources).

These and other threads describing the processes of change, continuity, and adaptation from the interviews are discussed in greater detail in the Conclusion (Chapter 9). The methodology employed in gathering the interviews, the challenges and issues raised by its use, and the value of taking account of personal narratives in the context of development are explored in Chapter 2.

The Individual Voice

The Challenges and Benefits of Listening to Personal Narratives

The people whose experiences inform this book spoke out because they wished to tell the wider world what resettlement had meant to them, to their families, and to their communities. They were not the subjects of a conventional research assignment, but rather participants in a communication project that aimed to give voice to people who had found themselves unwilling experts in the complex effects of displacement.

This chapter explores some of the issues and challenges that arose from the methodology employed, which was community-based and used nonprofessional interviewers working in local languages, and from the aims of the project, which were primarily awareness-raising, and which reflected the need of people to speak out and represent themselves: to be the ones who framed questions as well as answered them. Although it draws upon the multicountry oral testimony resettlement project that gathered the interviews that inform this book, this chapter also reflects experience gained and lessons learned during similar international testimony collection projects that explored different themes, such as women's experience of armed conflict, desertification, and poverty reduction. This chapter looks, for example, at the relative advantages of using insider or outsider interviewers, issues to do with translation, concerns when working with people with low levels of literacy, and power relationships. It then explores some of the ways in which personal narratives can complement and illustrate other forms of development research and can help to produce a more nuanced and realistic picture of development initiatives and their impact.

The Importance of Process

As explained in the preface, the resettlement interviews and other testimony collections were gathered by Panos London and its international partners. One of the differences distinguishing these projects from pure research is the emphasis on process, following on from the belief that in the development context, the processes of information collection and communication are as important as the product. One of the objectives is to strengthen the capacity of communities to undertake such work themselves, articulating and communicating their own concerns so that they can increase their influence over development planning and decision making. To this end, oral testimony projects incorporate a significant degree of training and a commitment to involve local people at all stages. Working in partnership with a local or national organization, usually over several years, Panos provides training in interviewing skills and support in other aspects of testimony collection and dissemination.

The one-to-one interviews are undertaken in local languages, between people who share some, but not necessarily all, aspects of each other's background and experience. Interviewers are usually selected from the community concerned where literacy levels permit, or from local organizations' field staff who live and work with the local people and share some of their background. Interviews are recorded in the local or national language and then are transcribed by the interviewer, word for word. The emphasis for interviewers is on openness and willingness to learn, and there is an assumption that the process of listening, as well as narrating, is of benefit. Past experience indicates that development fieldworkers who become involved in conducting interviews can benefit significantly from taking time to listen and to learn from individuals' different experiences, priorities, and concerns.[1] They often gain greater understanding of and sensitivity to the communities' needs and priorities, as the following comment from a group of Oxfam Hong Kong fieldworkers who participated in an oral testimony project in southwest China suggests. "In the process [of testimony collection], we realized that the village women are much more capable than we previously thought," admitted one. "And our understanding of the issues is better... more realistic."[2]

The partner organization, which may be an existing development, environment, media, women's, or community group, keeps the local or national language recordings and transcripts and uses them to raise awareness of the particular issue being explored. Panos London works with English translations and communicates them to a wider international audience through publications, specialist articles, radio programs, online, and through dedicated websites. As well as for advocacy, the testimonies have been used by local groups and partners to document certain traditions, livelihoods, or lifestyles; for education and literacy work; and to bridge the gap between generations in rapidly changing societies. Local groups communicate their collections through exhibitions, community meetings, booklets and more substantial publications, literacy and educational materials, radio programs, and occasionally television programs.

Once a partner organization has been identified and it has selected a team of interviewers, the next step is a training workshop, a key element of which is the discussion of the topics to be explored within the interviews. The "topic guide" that results builds on the knowledge and experience of the participants and reflects their particular concerns and circumstances, as well as exploring broader aspects of the issue—in this particular case, the impacts of displacement. Interviewers are not expected to cover every topic in every interview, but are encouraged to use their judgment and initiative to develop in depth those themes that seem most fruitful with individual narrators, and which best reflect the narrators' interests and experiences. The overall aim of the interviewers and the project is not to advance a particular theory or argument, but to record a range of experience that might yield fresh insights and build up greater understanding of the topic.

During the workshop, participants also explore the value and techniques of open-ended interviewing, and undertake and review practice interviews. They discuss how to get as representative a range of viewpoints and experience as possible, by carefully selecting the individuals they want to interview, and they explore some of the pitfalls of being an "insider" interviewer, such as assuming particular kinds of knowledge. Participating NGOs and their staff may have a particular agenda; for example, they are usually on the side of the displaced and fighting for better treatment and compensation. Part of the training is to get NGO staff to leave behind some of their preconceptions about the issues and people's experiences.

For the resettlement project, as with similar ones, most interviewers had no prior experience of open-ended interviewing, and few had university-level education. In most cases, interviewers were themselves displaced; several were both interviewer and narrator.[3] In Jharkhand, India, for example (see Chapter 6), eight of the ten interviewers had themselves been displaced by coal mining.

Education levels occasionally limit how many members of a community can become interviewers. In the Lesotho collections (see chapters 7 and 8), the low literacy levels of Molika-liko's residents meant they could not undertake the interviewing task, which involves lengthy amounts of transcription. As a consequence, the interviewers were all local NGO staff working with the displaced. Most were from the Transformation Resource Centre (TRC), a national NGO concerned with social justice and human rights.

At the time of both collections, many of the narrators in Lesotho were under considerable stress. They had been "interviewed" by Lesotho Highlands Water Project staff on several different aspects of relocation, to little positive effect, as they saw it. The process of measuring their fields for compensation purposes had been an unhappy one, with some people intimidated by university-educated officials. They had become wary and suspicious of those they didn't know, so it was important that these interviews were done by people who knew the narrators, had worked with them, and had won their trust. The narrators also used many locally specific expressions, so familiarity with the narrators' cultural and physical environment was crucial for effective follow-up questions. TRC fieldworkers met all these criteria. Although literate, they had already shown their empathy with the displaced by living and working with them for several years in often difficult conditions. In most cases, the rapport between narrator and interviewer was excellent.

Since this work, nonliterate community members have been involved as interviewers by having them work in partnership with a staff member of the partner organization, who managed the transcription.

Compromises

Given the circumstances in which these projects are undertaken, the importance of trust and local knowledge, and the commitment to build communities' communication skills, the practice is to use mostly insider interviewers. Using professional researchers might achieve a higher percentage of "successful" interviews, in which the majority of subjects are covered, and interesting topics are skillfully pursued and teased out. The training and support of inexperienced interviewers does mean that the quality of all interviews cannot be guaranteed. Some interviewers prove ill-suited to the task, and most testimony collections contain a few transcripts in which good leads were ignored, or in which the interviewer focused on his or her own interests and didn't allow the narrator to develop his or her own perspective, or remained fixed on documenting facts rather than on evoking reflection.

Nevertheless, by training people whose educational or professional experience would otherwise have excluded them from such an information-gathering exercise, the interviewers learn new skills and gain in confidence. For some, such as the young San men and women for whom resettlement had meant a significant dilution of their parents' and grandparents' way of life, becoming interviewers helped them to renew links with aspects of their past (see Chapter 5). In these projects, the fact that participation may enrich the skills and experience of those involved justifies the process adopted. Interviewers gain in understanding and respect for values and experiences they may not share or from which they have become distanced, and people denied a public voice gain channels of communication. At its best, this approach produces extremely powerful material and a productive relationship between narrator and interviewer, based on mutual understanding, respect, and rapport.

Translation

Conducting interviews in local languages, although important for a relaxed and informative discussion, means translation is required for the international, and sometimes even national, work undertaken to communicate the material.

The Right Words

Translation issues begin at the training workshop, emerging as part of the sensitization of interviewers. Sometimes the mother tongue in which the interviews are being conducted may be commonly used for ordinary family concerns and for locally specific cultural and historical matters, but the interviewers are accustomed to using a national language (or even English) to express other concepts. Thought and practice may be necessary to find the best ways to describe certain topics in the mother tongue. In southwest China, in an oral testimony project with five minority groups with their distinct languages, there was concern about the word used for "gender." The first word (the literal equivalent might be "women's power/rights + ism") was viewed as rather militant and, it was felt, might invite suspicion or defensiveness. The other, favored term (more akin to "femininity + ism") was seen as "softer," more academic. "Information" was another potentially loaded word, with one version carrying suggestions of "spying" or surveillance.

Understanding and respecting these nuances and getting them right can be crucial to establishing an atmosphere of trust and common purpose. It was through such a discussion in some early oral testimony workshops that the practice was adopted of referring to those interviewed as "narrators," stressing their active role, rather than the more passive "interviewees."

Since there is a commitment to communicate narrators' words to a wider international audience such as the planners, policy-makers, and media who influence development decisions, interviews need to be translated. In *Listening for a Change,* Nigel Cross examined some of the pitfalls inherent in translation, taking the case of the Sahel Oral History Project (SOHP).[4] For various reasons, most of that project's interview tapes, although recorded in a local language, were transcribed directly into French or English, the official international languages of the Sahelian countries concerned.

The main dilemma in translation of these first-person accounts is whether to go for fluency or fidelity. For the SOHP, two translators were tried out. The better educated translator—a university lecturer—produced a more fluent version, but it lacked some of the detail of the original and, as the lecturer admitted, he had included some interpretation of what he thought the narrator meant. The more faithful translation was by someone with less formal education but with more local experience, as he came from the same area as the narrator. His version was not so polished, but the verdict was that it more truly represented the spirit and meaning of the original interview.

Cross acknowledges that both versions are likely to be "corrupt" in some ways, and that ideally one would spend considerable resources on this particular process, cross-checking transcripts with tapes and narrators. Cross-checking does take place, both of the original tapes and transcripts and later of the English translations, but financial resources are stretched, distances between offices where transcripts can be processed and the communities concerned are often huge, and there are many literacy challenges, so the process is not exhaustive. In line with Cross's conclusion that transcription into the original language before translation would have greatly helped the SOHP, Panos's usual practice is for interviewers to transcribe the recorded interview in full in the original language. They are asked to note areas of confusion or ambiguity and as far as possible resolve these soon after the interview. Translation into any further languages, such as from Oraon to Hindi in Jharkhand (see Chapter 6) is done from these transcripts, with guidelines on how to deal with local expressions, phrases, and proverbs. In our choice of translator, Panos favors local knowledge and a willingness to sacrifice fluency for fidelity to the spoken word where necessary.

For the English-language versions, once again word-for-word translation is encouraged rather than literary flourish. This means, however, that the English texts do not always do justice to the richness of the original recordings. There is a detailed and lengthy process of reading the translations, highlighting areas of ambiguity or possible misunderstanding as well as local and other specific references that need unpacking by those in the field. Much exchange follows between the local coordinator, the interviewing team, relevant specialists, and those working on the English transcripts. Where local words do not have English equivalents, such words and phrases are kept in the original language and explanations put in brackets afterwards. A glossary is built up, which is continually added to, and the meanings are refined whenever possible. Interestingly, in the case of the Lesotho collections, the post-relocation interviews that feature in Chapter 8 had far fewer locally specific references than those gathered prior to displacement—it seemed the narrators' new worlds were already less rich. Some cultural traditions were being diluted, and few of the plants, herbs, and wild vegetables of Molika-liko flourished in their new environments.

In searching for patterns and themes in these interviews, which have been through various levels of translation and interpretation, we accept that some omissions and misunderstandings will have crept in along the way. We have tried to guard against making too much of passages where the presence of ambiguity warns against overly definite conclusions. But the process followed acknowledges the pitfalls inherent in working with translations and is an informed attempt to minimize them.

Advocacy and Awareness-Raising

The resulting testimonies may be communicated for a variety of reasons, although primary among them is the desire to raise awareness of the narrators' concerns and experiences among a wider audience. To give one example, Prerana and Panos India, the NGOs working in Jharkhand with people displaced by open-pit coal mining in the area (see Chapter 6), disseminated the interviews in a number of ways. During 2002, a booklet containing edited versions of many of the interviews, *Kali Haryali* ("Black Green"), was produced in Hindi and was distributed among the displaced themselves and the wider community in Hazaribagh, the district town. A roundtable meeting took place, attended by government officials, coal technologists, academics, activists, and representatives from the displaced communities and from the mining sector, including Central Coalfields Limited Ranchi and Central Mine Planning & Design Institute, Ranchi. As a result of the discussion, a set of recommendations for better policy and practice was developed by the participants. The roundtable generated media coverage in the local and regional press, with prominent local daily newspapers carrying the findings of the testimonies as well as the discussions at the roundtable. All India Radio produced two 15-minute programs based on the testimonies. Two of the displaced were interviewed on local TV channels. Panos India has continued to work on the issue, in 2007 publishing a book on mining issues in India titled *The Caterpillar and the Mahua Flower,* followed by *Alchemy of Iniquity: Resistance and Repression in India's Mines, a Photographic Enquiry* in 2008.[5] The interviews have also fed into and have generated further academic research on the issue.[6]

Representation and Community Identity

For some groups, the fact that they were the interviewers of their own people, and that together they could explore the issues of importance to them, was crucial to the project. For example, the testimony collection from San people in Botswana (see Chapter 5) coincided with growing resentment among the San at the continuing interest of academics and journalists in their communities and what they saw as the persistent failure of "outsiders" to represent the San and their concerns as they would wish themselves to be represented. They welcomed the opportunity to become their own interviewers as well as narrators and to decide what they wanted to explore in the interviews. A group of younger people were selected by their own San organization to be trained as interviewers; this decision reflected a concern among the San that there was a growing gap between the generations and that younger people had become almost ashamed of their past and traditions.

Indeed, a breakdown in understanding between generations is an important facet of the social impoverishment that some San described in their interviews; older men and women who had never been to school expressed sadness and anxiety about the alienation of the younger generation. So powerful were the processes of dispossession that some of the younger participants at the workshop initially seemed unsure that their past was worth exploring and documenting. Anthropologist Hugh Brody describes well the profound effect of continuing discrimination: "The anger of tribal people is intense, but often directed inward. And they fall into a deep silence...[having] absorbed the lessons of their oppressors: indigenous customs, history and ways of speech are matters of shame...Shame and grief, accumulated from generation to generation, can tie the tongue tight."[7]

Since the mid-1980s, however, a number of San organizations have been founded all over Southern Africa to articulate what they want from development. With so few San representatives at any significant level in any of the professions or in government service, these organizations have had to fight to be heard. "We have no voice in this country," said a spokesperson for First People of the Kalahari in December 1996, at a seminar organized by the Media Institute for Southern Africa. Some of the barriers to communication in the modern world—with its focus on the written word—are slowly being broken: appropriate orthographies for some San languages are now being developed. As Brody points out, part of the process of breaking the silence of "shame and grief" experienced by some tribal groups is their assertion of the value of their own language(s), as a means of identity as well as expression. A theme that emerged strongly in the San interviews featured in this book was the importance to them of mother-tongue education, and how the system of education they had experienced, which largely ignored their language and history, had left many children alienated from their own culture.

The project with the San was a small one, but it triggered a much larger community-led oral history movement. As training progressed and the first practice interviews were completed, the enthusiasm of the young participants grew. As one said, "At last, we'll be writing our own history, rather than outsiders."[8] The accounts they gathered in 2000 and 2001 were full of detail and together represented the beginning of an important record of their past, not least because it was gathered by the San for themselves. The resulting testimonies were discussed and debated at community meetings and were edited by the interviewers and their supporters into local language booklets for their community. Several orthographies existed for some of the San languages used but no literature, except for academic works inaccessible to the speakers themselves. These booklets added accessible material that could be read and listened to by the communities. They were used in language development workshops, and as the San involved began to feel more at home with the orthographies, using texts they had been responsible for creating, they were even able to suggest some changes to the linguists.

With the participants now identifying with the project and its purpose and using the material in ways that seemed valuable to them, the Working Group of Indigenous Minorities in Southern Africa (WIMSA) started more projects using these interviewers and the local coordinator. They eventually developed a region-wide testimony project, which fed into San conferences and negotiations with government agencies and other organizations throughout Southern Africa and formed the basis of the illustrated book *Voices of the San: Living in Southern Africa Today,* which was published in 2004 to mark the closing of the Decade of Indigenous Peoples.[9]

Power Relationships

While these oral testimony projects emphasize the value of the process as well as the product, and are attempts to democratize information gathering and dissemination, it doesn't mean that they escape some of the dilemmas inherent in such work. Power relationships are still present, and more often than not they are tipped in favor of the interviewer and project organizers. The interviewer's role is not neutral: the questions they ask, the leads they choose to pursue or abandon, these and other factors influence the final shape of the narrative. As already discussed, interviewers may be more educated than the majority of the narrators, and, through their involvement in the project, have more control over the way the testimonies are used.

In traditional life-history projects, narrators are often asked to read, and if necessary to amend, the transcript of their interview. In many of the communities where Panos works, low levels of literacy render this impracticable. This constraint is also why narrators' consent to use of the material, in ways specified and explained by the interviewer to each narrator and at public meetings, is verbal and is recorded at the time of interview. Experience shows that most narrators welcome the all too rare opportunity to relate their own perspective on development issues, and to participate in a project that values their views and that aims to convey them beyond their own physical and social worlds. A major advantage of the community-based approach is that, since most projects do include members of the community as interviewers and narrators, with some people being both, it reduces potential power imbalances and generates a greater sense of ownership of the project. This in turn means there is a strong vested interest in honoring the commitment by project participants to use the testimonies only for the purposes explained, and to respect any restrictions, such as the occasional use of pseudonyms, that have been agreed.

Extracting Meaning

Nevertheless, however correct our intentions, difficulties remain in regard to achieving equal power over process, content, and outcome. And in writing a book such as this, the extracts we have chosen to highlight reflect our sense of what is important in an interview and involve decisions that are not taken by the narrators.

Translation is again an issue. Unable to speak the multiplicity of languages, we cannot use the tape-recordings to better understand inflection, nuance, pace, and mood of the speaker, although we do our best to minimize misinterpretation. The emphasis on the value of process also has implications for the analysis or interpretation of the testimonies. Variability in the quality of the interviews has to be accepted. At their best, these interviews are vivid, full of human detail, powerful, and even poetic—despite caveats over translation and transcription. At their most disappointing, they are studded with lost opportunities and tantalizingly spare answers. The style of interviewing may vary in any collection, and there may not be much consistency in the questioning. Most interviews have some questions in common—about family life and history, for example, and key questions related to the main themes, or questions to start off the discussion on certain topics—but they do not necessarily follow the same pattern. Indeed, since everyone's experience is unique, it should not be possible to compare "like with like," but it does mean that it is not possible to analyze answers to exactly the same questions across a whole collection.

Similarly, the selection of narrators may not be ideal. Getting the required spread of age, social identity, occupation, and other relevant factors is discussed at the workshop, but interviewers—working in remote areas, often at distance from each other, seeking extended conversations with narrators whose time is tight at the best of times—sometimes find it hard to achieve the balance or profile required. And not all those identified make good narrators. Thus, for a variety of reasons, Panos's control over the data collection itself is less than tight.

The Development Context

The Importance of Perceptions

The aims of this oral testimony resettlement project were to support displaced people to articulate their experiences and perspectives, and in the process raise public awareness and debate. Its aim was also to complement more academic, scientific, or quantitative research on displacement by gathering and disseminating material that is unapologetically qualitative, produced by nonspecialists, and offers insights, perceptions, emotion, and anecdote, as well as more factual information. We hope that the experiences and views gathered may provide fresh perspectives on development-induced displacement, especially the social and cultural impacts, and that these may help modify and improve resettlement policy and practice.

Above all, both process and product highlight the need to take account of people's perceptions in order to gain understanding of motivation and response. A key part of the training workshops that begin each testimony collection is to get interviewers exploring the meaning and significance of events for people and to prompt reflection, rather than merely accumulating detail and description.

Memory is of course "faulty" and personal accounts are subjective. People rearrange past events to suit present needs, and collective and personal myths inform people's recollections. But just as oral historians argue that these are not so much flaws in reliability as vital clues in the search to understanding a society's past, so it is these characteristics that give oral testimony its value in the context of development. What people believe to be true can be as important as what may be true in a more factual sense, in terms of exerting influence upon their hopes, fears, priorities, and choices.

Getting Away from Sectors

Listening to community history and individual narratives can place current priorities and views in a wider context. People don't think or act in the neat sectors in which specialists work. They don't make economic decisions in a vacuum, so taking account of personal and collective memories and history can illuminate the values and past experiences that underpin social and economic structures, relationships, and patterns of decision making. Such information can help communities and development practitioners plan more effectively for the future. Yvonne Orengo, director of the Andrew Lees Trust, wrote of their experience of an oral testimony project in Madagascar: "The [interviews] give dimension to our understanding of how a person's life is weaved in and around the resources and external factors in their environment, as well as the twists and turns of 'fate' in that mix. As development practitioners this can help us understand the balances that have to be considered when we make decisions, and to acknowledge how everything we do can have unexpected impacts that we need to better anticipate."[10]

Another important use for the methodology is in evaluation, where it is well suited to explore the complexity of the different contexts in which development initiatives occur, and to understand influences coming from outside of a particular project. It can help identify what is important to beneficiaries and, as "formative" evaluation, it can identify valid "domains" of change—the kind of things a project expects to have an impact on—which can then be tracked with other evaluation methods.

Experience and Expertise

The use of oral testimonies can also help to shift the balance whereby, to paraphrase John Gaventa, "Technical, expert knowledge [has] predominated over the knowledge derived from experience [and] common sense."[11] Specialists in the effects of displacement have a huge role to play in improving policy and practice, but there are also lessons to be learned from the unwilling experts in resettlement who have experienced it firsthand. The fact that their views are "subjective" is part of what makes them valuable. They need to be assessed with care and sensitivity, but as Gaventa points out, the value placed on "objectivity" is questionable and can sometimes be a way of protecting professional mystique: "The claim to the superiority of science lies in its related claim to objectivity... In practice objectivity is translated in scientific method to mean a sharp bifurcation between expertise, based on the study of a problem, and experience, the subjective living of that problem."[12] To challenge the dominance of expertise over experience means challenging the view that institutionally validated knowledge has the monopoly on "truth" and objectivity. Indeed, one key value of working with oral testimonies is that it should encourage recognition that all accounts of past and present and forms of knowledge—dominant or marginal, individual or collective—are partial and subjective.

Scientific quantitative research has an essential role to play, but it can be complemented and sometimes challenged by more qualitative evidence, such as that which emerges in personal accounts. Otherwise, a rich source of knowledge is ignored. One leading authority on resettlement, Ted Downing, acknowledged this gap: "The literature on displacement is...rich and expanding, but...displacement theory itself is in its infancy—barely beyond classificatory schemes of phases and identification of risk factors. And the rich experience of peoples, including those who have survived forced displacements, is untapped."[13] Our book is one attempt to bring this "rich experience of peoples" into the debate on resettlement and its impact.

The Power to Complement and to Challenge

To what extent have researchers and policy-makers within the development context utilized this methodology? Nearly two decades after Panos London published *Listening for a Change,* which called for greater use of oral history tools and skills in the development context, there is evidence of increasing acceptance of the potential of using in-depth personal narratives. In 2000, for example, the World Bank published its *Voices of the Poor* study, which it said differed from all other large-scale poverty studies because it "presents very directly, through poor people's own voices, the realities of their lives."[14]

The study used many quotes to illustrate the different themes covered, though it did not present interviews in depth. It confirmed the centrality of non-economic factors, such as social and kinship networks, to the poor's survival, and revealed the oppression, humiliation, corruption, or simple irrelevance that they encountered in the range of institutions—state and nongovernment—intended to support them. It highlighted their vulnerability to exploitation by employers and traders; their extremely negative experiences of politicians, elites, and the police; and the psychological dimension to poverty that all this implies: the endless experience of powerlessness and dependency.

Robert Chambers, a member of the study team, wrote that while many of the findings were not exactly new, "living and working with the evidence brought them home with a stark sharpness."[15] And this, he said, is where one potential for influence lies: it is the power of the poor's own words to move people that can reduce the gap between them and those in power. He continues to promote "the crucial importance of the personal dimension" and its potential to help "those in power to be more realistically informed and persuasively influenced."[16]

The World Bank's work signaled a greater acceptance of the importance of nonquantifiable factors in poverty dynamics, and of the need to learn more about them. Some academics specializing in poverty have looked specifically at the value of using life histories, notably Uma Kothari, who wrote: "The study of poverty dynamics has been dominated by the quantitative analysis of panel datasets. These can clearly identify patterns and correlates of economic and social mobility, but have found it difficult to explain why these occur."[17] One criticism of poverty reduction policies is that they take an oversimplified view of the poor and ignore the variety and complexity of experience. Kothari and David Hulme argued that the use of life histories can counter this tendency, by deepening understanding of poverty dynamics.

It would be hard to gather enough personal accounts to match the huge samples of quantitative research. But a collection of say 40 personal narratives—while highlighting the complexity and variety of experience, and the conflicts and contradictions within and between accounts—does allow one to abstract dominant themes and concerns. Kothari and Hulme agree with others using this methodology that it is possible to draw from a series of individual accounts common themes, patterns, and processes, for "oral testimonies are not simply a personalised account of events and experiences but simultaneously reflect the wider context in which they take place."[18]

Kothari and Hulme argue for the use of multiple methodologies. By including life histories, the undeniably valuable large-scale aggregates and datasets can be complemented and countered. "Life histories can challenge hegemonic versions of poverty and in so doing inform the formulation of policies which are more cognisant of dynamics and processes, as well as the interconnectedness of people's lives" they note.[19] And while they agree that personal accounts can bring issues to life and break down barriers between narrators and readers, Kothari and Hulme also argue, as did Chambers, that the impact can be more significant and long-term: "Life histories are not simply 'tales,' they are narratives than can help motivate public action and influence policy."[20]

As academics, Kothari and Hulme are able to use insights gleaned from personal interviews to inform their research conclusions and recommendations. Panos works in the context of the media rather than in academia, but its interview collections, like this one, have informed and stimulated researchers, highlighting ideas that merit further exploration. And firsthand accounts and direct voices have become more central to development literature. In 2010, for example, the International Fund for Agriculture and Development (IFAD) commissioned Panos London to undertake a series of testimony collections in rural areas of China, Egypt, Madagascar, Pakistan, Peru, and Senegal to inform and feature in the 2011 Rural Poverty Report. IFAD's president wrote that the interviews provided "vital insight into . . . the changing reality of rural poverty."[21]

The rise of blogs and other social media outputs that relay personal experience and opinion to a potentially massive audience are all part of the greatly increased opportunities for the use and influence of direct voice.[22] Nevertheless, despite the increasing acceptance of the value and power of "voice," there remain limits to the extent to which such material can be incorporated into development knowledge and programming, and institutional learning.[23] Sometimes the concerns are still about its nature: the material is too anecdotal, contains prejudice and inaccuracies, and is likely to exhibit conservatism and nostalgia. There are parallels with the criticisms aimed at the early oral history movement by traditional documentary historians: that their work, was among other things, motivated by politics rather than scholarship; that it elevated faulty and subjective memory over precise examination of data; and that far from correcting bias in traditional history, it opened up new areas of distortion, stemming from the personal agendas of both interviewer and narrator.[24] Other hesitations are because the amount of material gathered in a testimony project can seem overwhelming and even though immersion in people's own words is powerful and motivating, policy-makers understandably protest that they do not have the time to wade through pages of text. Sometimes road maps are needed to negotiate the wealth of material, and a book such as this is an attempt to provide one such map.

The Importance of the Wider Context

One of the strengths of personal narratives, identified by Kothari and also by Faraday and Plummer, is that they can "locate the individual in the wider context of their overall experiences and the socio-historical framework in which they live."[25] In the interviews that inform this book, it is clear that most narrators' scope for action was determined by a number of factors, some highly personal, but others relating to the roles with which their own society had invested them. Birgitte Sorenson discussed the relationship between the national and the local context for people resettled in Sri Lanka by the Mahaweli Dam.[26] Her work sheds some light on the differing degrees of agency to be found among the resettled whom she studied, and some of the groups who speak out in this book.

The Mahaweli project was a massive infrastructure development of the mid-1970s and was at the time symbolic of Sri Lanka's move into a modern future alongside other newly industrializing countries. But it was also based on ancient irrigation systems, so at the same time it incorporated pride in Sinhalese history. In the opening ceremonies for the different settlements and engineering structures, speeches and press coverage emphasized how glorious a project it was and how the settlers were an integral part of it. They were positively encouraged to identify themselves with the progressive nature of the scheme.

Two other factors were significant. Most of the settlers Sorenson studied were landless laborers, just managing to meet basic needs. They were therefore more than willing to be moved to an area that, however agriculturally difficult, offered them land, homes, and support for development. Even though the element of choice involved was limited, since the alternative was chronic poverty, the fact that these settlers were motivated to resettle puts them in a fundamentally different position to, say, the residents of Molika-liko in Lesotho or those in Pakistan's Tarbela Valley, who had no desire to leave. In addition, the group that Sorensen studied was resettled alongside an established village, whose residents they regarded as being of a lower caste and more primitive in their agricultural and cultural practices. The settlers saw themselves as the "civilizers," bringing in new methods of rice cultivation, for example. This contrasts with the settlers in Lesotho (see chapters 7 and 8), who found their old skills redundant in the new environment and had few opportunities to gain new ones. The authorities' management of their compensation further constricted or frustrated agency and initiative, rather than encouraging them.

The contrast between the cases confirms the value of exploring the extent to which the resettled may identify positively with a development undergone for the national good—or may simply feel as though they are obstacles to progress, who have to be swept away. The latter perspective corresponds more closely to the views expressed by the narrators in Lesotho: "We are nothing, the planners planned and we are not part of the planning" (Lipholo Bosielo).

Ambiguity and Contradiction

Annabel Faraday and Ken Plummer also point out how the oral histories and their "focus on process and ambiguity" highlight the fact that most lives are in reality far more ambiguous, problematic, and chaotic than most social science research acknowledges. As they say, "the life history technique is particularly suited to discovering the confusions, ambiguities, and contradictions that are displayed in everyday experience."[27] This makes life history a valuable counterbalance to policy making that does not allow for such ambiguities. Indeed the interviews that follow in chapters 3 through 8 are full of examples that demonstrate how people's circumstances do not fit neat compensation and valuation categories, and that illustrate the need for flexibility in policy implementation.

The Resettlement Interview Collection

In the resettlement project, some 300 individuals were interviewed, in 8 countries and 15 languages.[28] The first interviews were gathered in 1997 and the last in 2003. Just under 200 were translated into English. The size of the different collections range from 60 interviews gathered in Pakistan to 18 in the second Lesotho collection. Details for each collection—the number of interviews, the partner organization, the languages involved—are contained in the notes to each case study (chapters 3 through 8). All the translated interviews were read in detail and inform this book; some 75 of those 200 narrators have been quoted. Necessarily, a smaller sample is quoted at length, since this book can only reproduce a limited proportion of each long and detailed account. Large chunks of text had to be cut and difficult decisions were made (see the editorial note in the front matter).

The process of extracting meaning from this range of individual accounts has been one of being steeped in the interviews and reading them many times, until certain themes, patterns, and concerns come insistently to the surface, as well as variations in response and experience. This reading of individual interviews, summarizing content, and identifying key themes began as the English translations came in; Panos London worked with the in-country partner to clarify the transcripts and also to assist in the development of local publications and communication activities. Coming back to the material, sometimes after several years, the original summaries and notes on content were invaluable, yet as the testimonies were read again and again and understanding deepened, these were annotated, challenged, and expanded.

Grieving for Lost Places

It is clear that these personal accounts, characterized by variety, detail, and strength of feeling, shed valuable light on the multidimensional nature and psychological impact of displacement. And they reveal that the sense of loss that individuals experience when forced to leave somewhere that is full of personally significant memories is profound. Peter Read, an Australian historian, has written on forced relocation in the "first world." In *Returning to Nothing: The*

Meaning of Lost Places, he looked at Australians' reactions to losing their homes, which lay in the path of dams, motorways, and national parks. Losing a home, he argued, can be as emotionally disturbing as losing a close friend or relative, and can inspire a deep and long-lasting grief that is insufficiently recognized. The Australian authorities, he points out, are not alone in "ignoring the psychological effects of place deprivation."[29] Chapter 3—the first case-study—features the stories of men and women who were forced to leave their communities to make way for Pakistan's Tarbela Dam. In many cases, the villages had been their families' homes for generations. Although they were interviewed nearly 30 years later, the enduring nature of their grief is striking. Many said that after three decades, they still felt like "visitors" in their new locations; to them, "home" remained Tarbela.

Another key feature of all the resettlement interviews was people's sense that they had lost control over many aspects of their life; their accounts were studded with examples of the slow, steady, and cumulative effect of powerlessness. But there was also evidence of agency, adaptation, and resilience. The following chapters are an attempt to represent the whole range of concerns, perspectives, and experiences present in the interviews and to highlight common and contrasting threads, rather than to showcase those extracts that are the most articulate or compelling. We have tried to do justice to the narrators' concerns and experiences, but the resulting text is inevitably partial and has been filtered through many layers since their words were first spoken.

Awkward Individuals

This volume demonstrates that oral testimony has a role to play in development and resettlement practice. The rich detail of personal narratives can do much to challenge the tendency of policy-makers to treat communities as homogeneous. Perhaps one of its greatest strengths is that it reminds policy-makers of the awkward individuals on whom development ultimately depends. To quote Paul Thompson on the value of oral history: "Above all [students] are brought back from the grand patterns of written history to the awkwardly individual human lives which are its basis."[30] The social cost of displacement continues to be underreported; the stories that unfold in the next six chapters are a crucial reminder of the psychological burden of resettlement, and of the individuals who are bearing the cost.

CHAPTER 3

"We had a set way of life. All that has been disturbed"
Tarbela Dam, Pakistan

A public meeting was going on in the school. The Tarbela Dam was being constructed. It was some [politician]. The dam, he said, would destroy our future generations. I still remember his words: "It will ruin your coming generations." I was at a loss to understand. I was young. I wondered what that man was saying. I couldn't get the hang of it. But now, at the age of 47, I clearly understand the wisdom in what he said...We are all scattered...if one uncle is in Punjab, the others are elsewhere...having no communication with one another...and our generation...it's badly affected, and our next generations too...That man was right.

—Noshad Khan Tareen

Noshad Khan Tareen was in his late teens in 1976 when he and his family were forced to leave the village of Jattoo located in the Tarbela Valley. Situated close to the banks of the Indus River, in what was formerly Pakistan's North West Frontier Province, Jattoo was one of about 120 long-established agricultural communities that were submerged by the reservoir of the Tarbela Dam. Around 96,000 people were displaced as a consequence of the dam, reservoir, and associated infrastructure, which was 20 percent more than originally estimated.[1] Most were subsistence farmers—tenants or landowners—with a small percentage working as artisans or semi-skilled workers, often following hereditary occupations such as blacksmiths, barbers, potters, cobblers, and musicians. Fishermen and boatmen—boats were the main form of local transport—worked the rivers.

The Indus also provided a living for those who stored or transported mountain timber downriver to the cities, and for the *zarkash,* who panned the riverbed and sifted out and sold the flecks of gold found in the sand. Some of the higher land inundated was in more remote tribal areas, with particular patterns of land ownership and governance.[2] About 45 percent of the displaced population was, like Noshad, under 20 years of age.

The interviews in this chapter represent a small sample of those displaced as a result of the construction of the dam; however, the overall collection of interviews from which these are drawn covered a range of occupations, locations, and economic status.[3] Although people were interviewed 25 to 28 years after resettlement, their memories were extraordinarily vivid. Many older narrators relished the opportunity to reflect in detail about daily life in Tarbela and the special events and festivals that punctuated it, as well as their relationships with others in the village and the social institutions of the *hujra,* the traditional meeting place for men, and the *jirga,* the decision-making assembly or community court.

Most described a well-ordered world, built around agriculture, in which everyone had their place and particular occupation. Because whole communities were moved, mostly to specially built townships, the resettled included people from across the social and economic spectrum. In common with involuntary resettlement more generally, communities were not resettled together, so extended families were separated and the old social order and relationships were disrupted.

The majority of those quoted in this chapter came from the same area; they constitute both the landless and landowners. Their individual accounts are not the whole story, but they do provide a glimpse into some of the far-reaching social impacts of this displacement. In particular, they show how enduring the impact of resettlement has been, still reverberating in some families nearly 30 years after the event.

Introduction and Background

The Tarbela Dam on the Indus River, in Haripur District, Khyber Pakhtunkhwa Province (formerly North West Frontier Province) is about 50 kilometers (31 miles) northwest of Islamabad and is the third largest dam by volume in the world. The contract to build Tarbela was signed in 1968; the operating authority was Pakistan's Water and Power Development Authority (WAPDA). Designed to store water for irrigation and flood control and to generate hydroelectric power, the dam was constructed in phases, with the final river outlet completed in April 1976. It was during this final phase that the majority of people were displaced.

The criteria for compensation were set by the government in 1967. Approximately two-thirds of the affected population, specifically those who could show ownership of land holdings greater than 0.2 hectares (0.5 acre) of irrigated land or 0.8 hectares (2 acres) of rain-fed land, were eligible for replacement agricultural land in Punjab or Sindh province. Those with holdings of less than these limits were eligible only for cash compensation. People with houses in the affected area were to be paid cash compensation at 1968 market values, and new townships for the resettled were built: Khallabat Township, Kangra Colony and New Darband Colony, Pehur Hamlet, and Ghazi Hamlet on the fringes of Ghazi town (see Map 3.1b, which shows the new settlements).

Resettlement was on a massive scale and was fraught with problems, including the refusal by the Sindh government to release 65 percent of the allocated land.[4] In 2000, nearly 25 years after displacement, the World Commission on Dams (WCD) found that many grievances over failures in the consultation and compensation process had still to be addressed. This was despite the fact that in 1996, in response to criticisms by the "Tarbela affectees" of their treatment by WAPDA, the World Bank made the commissioning of an independent survey and action plan for the many outstanding claims part of its loan agreement for the Ghazi-Barotha hydro-power project, downstream from the dam.[5] Grievances included corruption, long delays in receiving alternative land and payments, which resulted in significantly reduced real value due to the devaluation of the rupee, and lack of employment and training opportunities.

In addition to the experiences of the displaced, this chapter is informed by the accounts of several people employed by WAPDA. Their strikingly honest accounts confirmed many of the criticisms. Among the failings one official identified was the lack of involvement of those affected: "I think public participation is very important. We were deficient in it at Tarbela."[6] He acknowledged too that the strict rules disadvantaged smaller landowners whose property didn't exactly fit the criteria, and that the negotiations and discussions excluded women and the landless. Also severely disadvantaged were those whose livelihoods were directly tied to the river: fishermen, boatmen, and *zarkash* (gold panners).[7] It was the World Bank's intervention, he said, that "enlightened us on the issue of affectees' rights in 1996. We didn't have this in mind. We had ignored women . . . 50 percent of our population." He also confirmed that the failure to provide replacement land in Sindh was never satisfactorily resolved.

This former WAPDA official believed the affectees were victims of the government's lack of experience: "The government is not to blame because it was the first mega-project of its kind involving evacuation on such a large scale." In his view, the displaced "sacrificed everything for this project." These narrators might dispute whether the cause was lack of experience or lack of political will, but their stories illustrate the extent to which the displaced and the next generations agree that they did in fact "sacrifice everything" and, at the time this interview

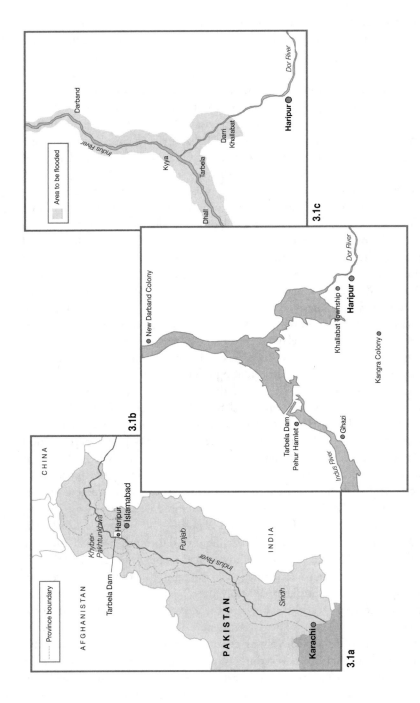

Figure 3.1 a. Pakistan and neighboring countries, showing Indus River and location of Tarbela Dam. b. Present-day Tarbela Dam area. c. Pre-inundation Tarbela Dam area. Maps by Julie Anson.

collection was completed in 2003, they continued to lack adequate acknowledgment or recompense. So many issues remain unresolved at the time of this publication that the Samaji Tanzeem Mutasireen Tarbela (Social Organization for Tarbela Affectees; SMT), founded in 1996 to fight for the rights of the displaced, is still active some three decades after the resettlement occurred.[8]

"We Will Always Remember That Place"

We had our own culture and customs. We had a set way of life. All that has been disturbed . . . I still dream of those orchards, streets, and fields. We are living in this township for more than 27 years now but we never dream about this area. We will always remember that place.

—Ahmad Saeed Khan

Ejaz Ahmed Khan, president of the Social Organization for Tarbela Affectees, was 20 years old at the time of displacement and was interviewed in 2001. He described an event so traumatic that 28 years later he remained determined to fight for the rights of "each affected person of Tarbela Dam."

The resettlement process first started around 1968 to 1970. Some people from WAPDA came here and started taking measurements . . . But they took no one into their confidence . . .

The simple people of our region thought that theirs was a fertile area and that the government wanted to acquire it and might establish mills and factories there, or start some fishing project—that was why they were there, and why they wanted to evacuate the local population.

"An atmosphere of uncertainty"

"There was no participation," said Ejaz, and the lack of consultation fueled anxiety. "It was a project of international status. As soon as it started an atmosphere of uncertainty emerged, as the WAPDA authorities had not realized the necessity of taking local people into their confidence."

As well as lacking clear information, many villagers—whose communities had hardly changed in decades—said they found the concept of such a massive dam and loss of land almost unimaginable. They could scarcely believe it when evacuation began and the waters first encroached on their villages. Ejaz explained why so many stayed until the last minute:

The authorities had deliberately not informed the people, because they were not giving them their full rights. When they were evaluating the houses they favored those who had bribed them. In case of those who did not bribe, they gave a very low price for their houses...then they released water without giving them proper compensation. How could people believe it would happen without compensation having been given? True, they did know that the dam had been built. But unless one receives the compensation, who would agree to leave a place?

The shock and chaos of the evacuation was recalled by many, who described people weeping, clinging to the graves of their forebears, and struggling to gather their belongings in the face of rising water. "I will never in my life forget that scene," recollected Ejaz.

> My [widowed] mother was there; one sister and four brothers and the family of my maternal uncle...I was standing in the courtyard...The water had even approached there, but my mother was saying that we would not leave...Then came the trucks to carry the luggage. The water was coming up so fast that we could not lift [onto the trucks] all of the most necessary of our belongings...People were trying to load their cattle onto the trucks...[but] we could take only what was most important and left the rest of our belongings, submerging in the water.
>
> Let me tell you, my eyes were moist. I was totally baffled, unable to understand what was happening. Our belongings, that house, that *hujra* [meeting place for men], and the banyan tree...that we used to climb and in which the bees used to make honey...I couldn't understand whether it was really water coming up or just a dream...
>
> Very strange things were happening...I saw that on the roof of the mosque were dogs, cats, snakes, and other animals trying to save their lives. [Yet] the cat was doing no harm to the rat; the snake was not stinging anyone. Every creature was baffled. I have no words to describe it.

Ejaz, like many of the narrators who feature in this chapter, previously lived in Jattoo, a village within Tarbela, the community after which the dam was named (see Figure 3.1c, which shows some of the original communities before the dam's construction). He explained: "Tarbela was divided into certain sections. The one we lived in was known as Tarbela Jattoo, and was the very heart of Tarbela. Tarbela consisted of about 1,000 houses. And Jattoo, the village that was ours, had four hundred houses."

Ejaz's family were landowners, and their replacement agricultural land was in Punjab province, 400 kilometers (248 miles) away from Khallabat Township, where they had settled. The majority of the displaced, whose roots were in agriculture, were moved to specially built townships. The largest was Khallabat, near Haripur, which over time absorbed people from more than

80 of the submerged villages. Settlement was haphazard and communities were broken up.

> Many changes have taken place. The structure of the population [in the township] is not the same as it was in the village...People have shifted to various places. Our own family has scattered here, there, and everywhere...people do not mix with their neighbors. Their relationships have not developed in the nearly 30 years [since displacement].

Ejaz's comment about the lack of neighborliness in the township was echoed time and again by other interviewees. Some of the strongest themes in the accounts are how life in Tarbela was distinguished by strong community relationships, and regret that these did not survive resettlement. Ejaz and others described bonds that stretched back for generations. They were between landlords and tenant farmers, as well as between those who worked the land and those who followed hereditary occupations, from potters and blacksmiths to musicians. For the landowners interviewed, the loss of those bonds also meant a loss of identity and status and it is clear that this has been one of the harder adjustments for them

Figure 3.2 Ejaz Ahmed Khan, former Tarbela resident and president of the Social Organization for Tarbela Affectees. Photo by Siobhan Warrington.

to make. "The family identity we used to have is no more. Now no one knows where any one comes from," Ejaz commented.

The World Commission on Dams' case study on Tarbela devoted much of its extensive report to technical aspects, acknowledging that "the human dimension of the Tarbela dam is the least well understood."[9] These accounts show how powerful the less quantifiable and visible human dimensions are; the dismantling of social relations and networks, the loss of identity and status, combined with personal feelings of grief, anxiety, and powerlessness, seem to have undermined the ability of some individuals to recover from displacement. More than one elder narrator said that, even after nearly 30 years, they had never felt "at home" in their new locations: "We feel like guests here, who are bound to return home after a few days," Makhan Jan said.

"Joblessness has taken away peace of mind"

Several narrators commented that, soon after relocation, a significant number of older people died prematurely. The causes of these deaths cannot be known but the narrators made a direct link between the experience of relocation and the trauma of losing their land and home. Noshad Khan Tareen, whose words open this chapter, had personal experience of this:

> I tell you those who were 55 or 60 years of age at that time couldn't survive beyond two to three years after they left that place. I can quote examples from my own family...I lost [five relatives] because they couldn't adapt to the change forced upon them. The sources of their earnings were gone; there was unemployment; they had lost everything.

Noshad was a student who also worked in his father's shop at the time of resettlement. The family had in addition a milling business and owned land farmed by tenants:

> We had a mill with three different machines, first for spinning cotton, second for chopping animal feed, and third for grinding wheat. We had a lot of work chopping fodder. The population was growing fast and the existing watermills could not meet the demand...Our business flourished as it was ideally located among various villages...The shop also gave us a lot of business.

He remembered life there in fond detail, including the fertile land and rivers full of fish, and he emphasized its simplicity:

> The food was simple...It was farmyard manure that was used, not chemical fertilizers. So the people were healthy. They had maize, milk, yogurt, buttermilk,

and butter…They lived long: my paternal grandfather died at the age of 105 and the maternal grandfather at the age of 100. Even my father died at 80. They were farmers; life was austere.

It was his view that as a consequence of resettlement people died at a younger age than would normally have been expected. While he believed a less healthy diet and the township's poor quality drinking water were contributory factors to the ill health he saw around him, Noshad stressed the psychological element: "Everyone is uneasy. One or two of every family are mentally upset." Much of this unease he observed stemmed from the lack of occupation:

> Today there is unemployment. Life is full of worries…joblessness has taken away peace of mind. They had land [before], which was a blessing. Now they have lost their lands…and they die at the age of 50 or 55, even 45. It has happened within 30 years.

The mills and factories to provide work for the displaced proved "false promises," he argued, and in the absence of proper employment many men could only get intermittent casual labor. Only those with financial resources could raise the funds necessary to acquire documentation required to work abroad. This was seen by many narrators as a key reason why drug addiction had become so widespread among young men, especially in Khallabat. Noshad continued:

> This is a very different world, with unemployment as the major problem…It's like throwing a man into a deep well and making it impossible for him to climb out of it. We're all left without any resources. Compensation money has been consumed in building a home…
>
> One can [look around] here and see how unemployed young people are taking drugs; most of them are using heroin; some are using *chars* [hashish]. We have no words to describe their plight. Pay a visit to this place late at night and you will find them in groups of five or six, busy using drugs of various kinds.

Noshad's family were given land in Punjab as part of their compensation.

> We were allotted lands at Kamalia where the canal water was inadequate [for irrigation]. The land at Tarbela was fertile. Here it was hard…To develop 100 *kanals* [1 *kanal* equals 506 square meters or 0.125 acre] of barren land a lot of capital investment was needed…We had no resources.
>
> The second problem was that time was needed to understand the nature of the new land. The limited amount of money [the resettled] had in their hands was wasted in their futile attempts to cultivate these lands. For instance, they ploughed these lands in the same fashion as they did at Tarbela. But the

Punjab land being different, they lost their limited capital. Thus our people went on going downhill financially. After five or six such attempts they lost heart and started selling their land. Many of them decided to come to Khallabat Township. Here again problems waited for them.

Noshad's family also "lost heart"; they moved to Khallabat and leased out their land, but the income it brought was insufficient for Noshad's generation to live on:

> One of my brothers is making his bread and butter in Japan in the capacity of an illegal immigrant; the other has married a girl of British citizenship and lives in England. They had to, as it was not possible for our family to make ends meet. You can understand the constant torture one undergoes staying illegally in a foreign country, because this is a crime. His children are here and we have to look after them. My brothers support me. I have no other source of income.

With his brothers "scattered" outside Pakistan—one living apart from his children in constant fear of deportation—Noshad said ruefully that he understood the meaning of the warning he heard all those years ago: "It will ruin your coming generations."

The Loss of Family and Role Models

A strong concern voiced in the accounts was the declining contact with the extended family, in particular how this had diminished the role of older relatives as guides or mentors. Rafaqat Ali Khan was in his late teens when the resettlement took place. He described how his family were relatively well-off, owning land that was cultivated by them and their tenants, while his father had a job in Karachi, where he owned a small plot of land on which he planned to build a house. The family relocated to Karachi from Tarbela, and Rafaqat and his brothers worked as laborers for many years. Interviewed when he was 48, he had become the owner of a small shop and he recalled that one of the strongest memories he retained of life at Tarbela was its communal nature, something he believed was difficult to recreate.

> [To create] an alternative to Tarbela is not possible. The people there followed a collective pattern of life. They would work the whole day but in the evening you would see them in the *hujra* [traditional meeting place for men] sharing information with one another, and one another's problems, too. Here we don't have it; everybody is part of a machine...they have to work as laborers...No one has time to share the problems of others...There is no such thing [as the *hujra*] here...These institutions were very important in that society...

We had our own distinct culture and an identity of our own that we lost on account of the construction of the dam. Our village families had their separate *hujras*. Every family had its identity. But the dam has scattered us [to different resettlement sites]. Families have disintegrated. And now our children, because of the distance, do not recognize their nearest and dearest. It is the greatest of the losses we have suffered.

He particularly regretted the loss of the "disciplined family pattern":

All our family were dispersed and scattered. Some of them settled here in Karachi, some in various parts of Sindh, and some in Punjab. Now it is not possible to attend one another's weddings and funerals. Our children have had no introduction to one another... In our earlier pattern of life a child would grow up into manhood within the environment of a disciplined tribe. He knew his kith and kin. Now we don't have that. Relationships do exist but physical distance has destroyed that disciplined family pattern.

This lack of family discipline and structure was similarly lamented by Makhan Jan. She was in her early thirties at resettlement, and had just lost her husband. She had also moved to Karachi, where a few members of her husband's family lived, but was separated from the majority of her extended family. "This abominable dam has displaced all of us and thrown us at such diverse and far off places, the way grains of rice fall and disperse on the land. This is how we are scattered."

Makhan Jan described how one of her two sons had become a heroin addict. Although he eventually stopped using the drug he remained "idle." She acknowledged that the lack of employment was a key factor in young men's vulnerability to addiction, which had affected so many displaced families. But as a widow, and no longer part of a close-knit community, she also believed a lack of older role models had contributed to her sons' difficulties as they grew up. "It was not possible for me to go outside to keep watch on his activities," she explained. Like many of the women narrators she observed *purdah,* which restricted her activities outside the home. Her sons may have had better formal education in the city, she said, but they lacked the guidance that a network of relatives would have provided:

They studied up to ninth and tenth grade. They would perhaps not have studied this much in the village. But there are a number of ways in which their upbringing would have been better... At least some uncle, paternal or maternal, would have been there to look after them, or a senior member of the family could have acted as a guardian [so that] the children would have remained disciplined.

"Who knows us here?"

Makhan Jan continued: "I don't feel adjusted [to life] here, even after a stay of 30 years."

> The sweet memories are still not gone. I just close my eyes and find myself in my village, where I see that it is evening time. I sit under the roof and watch the children playing, and men ploughing the fields. I also see the games in the street among the children. I watch women baking bread in the oven at sunset. Then I see at nightfall all my friends absorbed in listening to stories from an elderly woman.
>
> The next moment I open my eyes and find myself in this rotting city of Karachi, the same that people call the "city of lights." I could not, though I have been looking, find light anywhere in this city of lights.

The interviews reveal that for many of the resettled, in particular those who left in their middle age, Tarbela remained their "home" some 30 years on and their attachment to it was undimmed. Makhan Jan's interview also suggested that a significant element in her continuing distress was that she was not reconciled to the change in her social status. Once a member of one of the most prominent families in her community of Jattoo, she found this meant nothing to her new neighbors: "The respect that we lived with there is non-existent here."

> Who knows us here in Karachi? Karachi respects a person who owns a large bungalow, or a car. Who is going to respect people like us here? Our respect was great in the village. Our family was much esteemed as my father was a very big landlord. His property was unlimited. He was held by all in high esteem. Then I was married into a family with vast lands and huge property. It is the memory of all this that keeps me sad. Wealth is not that important, as money is round and rolls away. A good name is better than riches.

For 55-year-old Ahmad Saeed Khan, Tarbela also meant so much more than simply a home. He was fully aware that the high status enjoyed by his land-owning family, including the positions they held in the Muslim League, was to a large extent a consequence of them living in the same location for many generations. This history was not something that could be recreated: "The love and affection that we found in that area is not available here." He explained:

> In the villages, hundreds of landowners would keep thousands of tenants who thus earned their living honorably... We had a set way of life... Our family was very established. Now if we work hard for even one hundred years we will not be able to achieve the status which we had at that time.

Rafaqat Ali Khan similarly recognized that his family's identity and status had stemmed from the relationships they had established in the community: "We had an identity of our own at Tarbela. Even our *halis* [tenant farmers or servants] used to eat their meals at one place with us...Where could we get that identity from now? Impossible indeed! That identity one cannot buy from a market."

One woman, Gulnaz, a 50-year-old teacher, felt the only identity that they had now was as the displaced: "Now we cannot say that this area belongs to us...Our ancestors were born and raised in Tarbela, so we used to love that area and said it was our own...we have lost that. Now we can only identify ourselves as affectees of Tarbela Dam."

Paradise? A Different Perspective

Compared to the landowners interviewed, former tenant farmers displaced to make way for the Tarbela Dam appeared more accepting of the changes they had experienced. Excluded from WAPDA's resettlement negotiations and ineligible for land compensation, tenant farmers were seen to be some of the worst affected at the time of displacement. However, research commissioned by the World Commission on Dams found that some 25 years later many members of this group were "much better placed now than in their previous life."[10] Although the interview material represents only a small sample, the accounts given by the landless do suggest a willingness to take up new occupations and the gradual achievement of economic independence.

Taj Boro, a woman in her fifties, came from a landless family previously living in Kyya and subsequently resettled in Ghazi. Her memories of life as a tenant farmer were generally positive and she felt the local landowners took good care of them. The landowners in the Tarbela region were largely Pathans, Pakistan's second largest ethnic group, within which there were different *khels* or kin groups, such as the Khans and Tareens. In their interviews, tenant farmers tended to use the words Pathan and Khan interchangeably.

> Our house was *gharran,* which means that it had been built on land owned by someone else. It [belonged to] the Pathan family, who had permitted us to build our house...Later when the dam was constructed people received payments but we got nothing, as we had no land. As compensation for the rooms we had constructed, we received only 1,100 rupees [approximately US$111 at 1976 rates]...[so] we could not buy any land...It's only now, after this much time that we have purchased a small quantity of land.

Her father and uncle worked on "the land of rich people who gave it to us for cultivation...We passed nice days there. The only problem was that land was not ours."

It was customary that such land was given to the poor so that they could construct a house. Sometimes the house itself was built for them by the Khans...And then all such people, including us, worked in their fields. Besides, we women worked in their houses when needed. When any of our children grew up they would start working on their land.

The Pathan family would help us in every possible way. They would always come to our aid...They took great care of us. They gave us not only land but also employment and besides this every facility. In contrast, the government gave us neither a place to construct a house nor any employment.

[But when] the dam was constructed, even the Pathans didn't bother to think of helping us. We were from the poor. Everyone took care of only himself.

Almost all of the tenant farmers interviewed emphasized a strong bond that existed between the landed and landless and described how this bond was broken following resettlement.

Taj Boro's husband was able to secure a job in the Frontier Constabulary; with his salary and by borrowing some money, they bought land in the new settlement at Ghazi and over time were able to build a small house and give their children some education. However, when interviewed in 2002, she described some deterioration in their circumstances. Now widowed, her health was poor, but with only one of her two sons working, as a laborer, they could not afford the operation she needed. The family had no room to grow crops or keep livestock, and there were no farmers for whom they could work. She contrasted these travails with her previous life in Tarbela:

Our men would go to the river to catch fish. We would also catch the wood floating downriver. It was used as fuel...Our village was in a beautiful location, with the river on one side and the mountain on the other...Boats were used to travel between villages. Such fun it was being there; there is no such charm in life now.

Opium was produced. It was loaded on camels and sold at Tarbela. It was a source of great income. Two-thirds of the crop was the right of the owner; the remaining one-third was kept by the tenant. But even that one-third share used to be a lot. We were quite well off in the village...Here everything has to be purchased, even water.

A Hard Life

Not all the landless interviewed viewed life in Tarbela as positively as Taj Boro. Nazeer Mohammed was in his fifties when interviewed and, in common with many of the narrators, he originally came from Jattoo. He acknowledged the landowning Pathan family had been good to them and "helped us in difficult times." However, despite their patronage,

> Life there was substantially different from life here. That was a very hard time. It was marked by perennial hunger. There were financial hardships...The land belonged to other people. We lived in a house owned by Pathans. They were the influential people of the village.

He explained that his family wasn't obliged to work for their landlords, although they were asked and often agreed to undertake certain tasks. In return they received occasional gifts of food, but living conditions were tough, especially as from a young age Nazeer had to support his family including two older sisters:

> I was left fatherless when I was only one. My mother became the breadwinner, and brought me up. [At ten] I had to drudge at a restaurant for just 2 rupees a day, and my mother had to toil in the same way. She would go to [a richer] house and bake bread, or she would plaster the walls with mud, or would do some household chores, and earn 2 or 4 *annas* [16 *annas* to one rupee].

He later secured employment with WAPDA at the dam site, but resigned after seven years: "They would not increase my salary, and it was not possible for me to [survive] on that. Casual labour was a better choice."

Nazeer identified the different occupations in the village, including weavers, blacksmiths, carpenters, and cobblers:

> All of them worked for the landlords [who] gave them wheat or corn at the harvest...People of all professions were helping hands in agriculture...The cobblers would prepare the shoes of the farmers for six months and in return they were given a couple of *urris* [a traditional measure equal to approximately 10 pounds] of grain...Wages for six months were just one or two *urris* of grain. Just imagine! Such were the times then.

He described life in the village as being "not easy for working people" but "easy and comfortable for landowners." However, he was on balance positive about the relationship between the Khan landowners and those who to some degree relied on their patronage:

> They respected us very much. They would not be harsh. Never did they insult us. Never did they quarrel with us. Never did they scold us. They were affectionate and considerate, and treated us like brothers.

"Everyone was busy saving himself"

As a consequence of resettlement, however, this relationship broke down: "It was in the end that the Khans spoiled that atmosphere. Since the situation of everyone looking out for himself had arisen, they said, 'Arrange each for yourself!'" At the time of moving, Nazeer's family had no money for a truck and they recalled receiving no help from the government or the Khans: "The Khans knew that...we needed the trucks. They did not help us. They did not do well by us. They did not offer and we did not ask them for help. They knew that we needed their help, so...why should we ask them?"

Despite his anger, he recognized that the intensity of people's distress at resettlement forced them to focus on their own situation rather than seeking to help others. He described how he felt when they reached the new township:

> When we came here we were so seriously mired in our own problems that we didn't see how others behaved towards us. We could not perceive what others were doing, who was ruined and who survived. Everyone was busy saving himself.

Almost all narrators agreed that the mutual support systems that had previously functioned, particularly at times of stress, could no longer be relied on. As Taj Boro put it: "That was a time when everyone was grinding one's own axe. No one bothered to take care of others."

Nazeer managed to secure work as a mason and carpenter in Khallabat and after many years he and his wife were able to buy a small plot and, piece by piece, constructed a house of their own. "Today we have settled in this township and by the grace of God we are not in as much trouble financially as we used to be in our village. Here God has been so kind to us."

Displacement: "A Blessing in Disguise"

For Nazeer, displacement brought economic independence. For Maqsoodan Jan, the independence gained was less material, but no less significant. "Thanks to God, we are now free people," was her verdict on what she saw as the only positive impact of resettlement. She was 80 when interviewed, also from Jattoo and from a family of *meerasis,* hereditary musicians, dancers, and singers who perform at weddings. Her husband also took up music as a profession and the land they cultivated as tenants was fertile, allowing Maqsoodan Jan's family to live off their harvests and her husband's low income. Despite this she felt the family was "oppressed" by their Pathan landlords and said the men in her family were "at their beck and call."

She described life since displacement as being hard, with the death of two sons and her husband. Nevertheless, being free of what she termed the "repressive attitude" of the Khans proved a significant consolation:

We cultivated our own land [in Tarbela] but it was in the hands of the Khans…The Pathan families were prosperous. How could we be a match to them, with our land limited to no more than 3 or 4 *kanals?* [about 0.375 to 0.5 acre]

"Yet our Tarbela was a great place to live," she continued. "I was 50 when we resettled here…I still wish the land of Tarbela were not covered by water, and [we could] go back and start living there once again…When we left the village our hearts bled." Despite its restrictions, she remembers life there "was so good":

One would purchase two to three *maunds* [1 *maund* equals 40 kilos, so equivalent to 176 to 264 pounds] of onions in season and the whole family would use it throughout the summer. Tarbela was rich in all kinds of vegetable…meat was not expensive.

She described her husband's work and the other social occasions that they enjoyed:

The marriages used to be so wonderful and so ceremonious…the men danced the traditional Hazara dance to the drums beaten by the *meerasi* in the *hujras* and we watched their performance from the roof of the house without any restriction.

My husband performed with a group of eight to ten artists. They were generously rewarded in the form of *beilein* [small sums of money thrown by the spectators]…His share was usually 200 to 300 rupees. The group didn't receive any payment from the host family.

The Eid ul Fitr festival at Tarbela was really a great festivity, which continued for eight days. Women wore the veil to go the fair…they would have *samosas* and *pakoras* and enjoy themselves with the swings without any interference by men or boys. Every care was taken.

Besides this there was a great fun at the times of sowing and harvest. Everyone in the village would come to the venue of the harvest where the host whom they had helped would serve them a feast of *dhal* [pulses] and *desi ghee* [clarified butter].

The narrator's nostalgia was however tempered:

We have fond memories of our time passed at Tarbela—except the memories of the treatment meted out to us at the hands of the Pathans are bitter…we could not sleep in peace due to fear of them. So there was one improvement [since resettlement]—we got rid of the repressive attitude of the Pathans of the village.

> The Khans were the elected leaders. At election time... the leader would
> threaten the people and direct them to use their votes in favor of a person that
> he named. The people had no choice. We lived in their houses and had we
> resisted we would have had to vacate them. So we cast the vote as they asked
> us to.

In common with a number of the landless interviewees, Maqsoodan Jan singled
out the *jirga,* the decision-making assembly or community court, as particularly oppressive: "The *jirga* of the Pathans was very effective. It held its meetings at Tarbela at the stipulated dates whenever a dispute arose. They upheld
the principles of justice—but what they did with poor people were blatant acts
of highhandedness." Nazeer Mohammed said something similar: "In the case of
disputes, the matter was ultimately carried to the *jirga.* Pathan and Syed families
both gave verdicts. We were not consulted... They were feudal lords, and we were
poor people. Who would have consulted us?"

Maqsoodan Jan was particularly critical of the demands made upon the men
in her family:

> Early in the morning they would ask us to go to one place or the other to do
> this or that... they would send us on various errands or to carry messages con-
> cerning their marriages or deaths... The men were paid a paltry sum in return.
> There was no regular salary for the services they did.
>
> Once, three men from our family were sent ten miles away at night to
> communicate a message of someone's death... If they refused they would hold
> them captive in the *hujra* and beat them. Once, my son took one cob of maize
> from their fields. They chained him up at the *hujra* and gave him a severe beat-
> ing. My husband went there and offered to pay the price of the corn and then
> they released him.
>
> Thank God we are now free people! We had to leave our homeland with
> our hearts broken. Yet we say it was a blessing in disguise as we got rid of their
> bondage.

"The needs of the people were very limited"

Makhan Jan, who was interviewed in Karachi, was a member of a landowning
family in the same community as Maqsoodan Jan, and remembered the relationship between the landed and landless as being less exploitative. She recalled the
role of *meerasi* families such as Maqsoodan Jan's:

> These people performed services at weddings or funerals. Their women would
> wash dishes, clean the houses, and do all work at the weddings. They would pass
> on invitations... They all belonged to the same family. Some of them worked

inside the houses and some performed outside duties. We also treated them well...flour, rice, money...what was there that we didn't give them?...even dresses to wear.

Although she acknowledged her family's fortunate position in the community, she believed the poor had few problems:

The needs of the people were very limited. Everyone was content with whatever he had. The grains of wheat and maize were used at shops for bartering...Even a child would go to a shop with just a handful of grains and get any of the eatables he liked. Cash was something unknown there. Life was very simple. People preferred to live within their means.

As a woman who had to observe significant restrictions on her interaction with the world outside her family, she may have been unaware that wealthier families like hers were not universally appreciated. As described earlier, she believed her family "was much esteemed." But these two women also agreed on many things. They both mourned the loss of the social activities of the weddings and the fairs at Eid and other religious celebrations. As Makhan Jan explained, although she and her female relatives "would sit together at the house of any one of them in the evening and remain busy, gossiping and joking till late, listening to stories from one another," there were boundaries that were not crossed. "The older women of our family would not let us speak or laugh loudly lest our voice should be heard outside the house."

However, during the fairs, certain days were reserved for women only; almost every woman interviewed recalled these as occasions of great pleasure and social interaction:

Get-togethers were confined to weddings and the village fairs. On the occasion of Eid, a fair lasted eight days, held in different sites. It used to be great entertainment! Participating women used to be not only from the village where the fair was held but also from far off villages...Male visitors were not allowed.

Both women also expressed appreciation of electricity, access to transport, and health facilities in the new locations and above all, they welcomed the greater acceptance of education for women, something that all female interviewees cited as one of the most positive things to come out of being resettled. "That she should be educated is something extremely important in case of a girl. If I myself had been educated to a higher level I wouldn't have been exposed to this many difficulties after the death of my husband. I would have faced our circumstances more successfully," commented Makhan Jan.

Ultimately, though, the most far-reaching impacts of displacement for these two women were not material: for Maqsoodan Jan, it was the gaining of independence from the local landowners; and for Makhan Jan, it was the loss of a privileged position and the "respect" this had brought her.

"We wished all to remain unchanged"

Similar to Makhan Jan, Akhtar Bibi regretted the change in her family's status and circumstances since resettlement but also welcomed new attitudes to female education: "A girl was no better than an animal at that time. It's a healthy development that daughters have become important in their families." She had lived in Phooldar, close to old Khallabat village, after which the new township was named.

A recurring theme in her testimony was the contrast between the settled order of village life—which she admitted was virtually her Pathan family's "own state"—and the fragmented nature of their new life, living close to people they barely knew and separated from family members resettled elsewhere. She remembered "the grim atmosphere of silence and sadness" before they left, "casting a last glance at everything in the village as there was no possibility of seeing it again...We wished that all that were not true. We wished all to remain unchanged." She described the relationship her family had with the rest of the villagers:

> We would help the poor in the village by giving them grain. Most of the people in our village, I mean the poor, used to be in need of wheat or maize, which was their staple food. If one were in need of some money we would also give her money. But the needs of the people at that time, when they lead a simple life, were so limited that they would meet their requirement by simply the grain or flour that we gave them. Besides this, 50-100 rupees were sufficient to meet their requirement. We would also give them assistance in the form of milk, butter, or butter oil.
>
> At that time the major problem of the poor farmers used to be the annual payment of *maalia* [land tax]. They would often come to seek some financial help, as it was not possible for them to save, after toiling for a whole year, enough money to pay the tax. In case of illness, we the landlords would help a person.

Her one major regret about life before displacement, she said, was the lack of education for women; she was "ashamed" of her own lack of literacy:

> I am not educated at all...our elders didn't believe in female education...They would not even allow the opening of schools in their village. They thought

that girls from the lower level of society would go to the schools and would be influenced by the change and thus the pattern of life that existed would be disturbed.

The elders thought that it was sufficient for a girl to be able to recite the Holy Quran and to perform routine household activities...That was, in fact, a time when the more a girl was ignorant and illiterate, the more she was worthy of praise.

In her youth, Akhtar Bibi was unable to challenge the prevailing attitudes but she was clear about the value of education:

I think it is very important for a girl to be educated because if she finds a respectable teaching job, she would contribute to the prosperity of the family. An educated girl can expect to find a job in any organization, such as a mill or factory.

When interviewed at the age of 50, she had three daughters and two sons, all of whom had been educated and were working: "I didn't even consider whether we could afford their education or not. My husband had a job in the telephone factory. All that he earned we have spent on these children."

After displacement, she said, she lost the sense of security that had characterized her early life: "There was no certainty." She talked at some length about the troubles faced by the resettled, and how unemployment and drug addiction can tear families apart, further strengthening her belief in education for girls: "It prepares them to withstand any difficulties that they may come across. Supposing a girl is married to a man who happens to be, at some stage of life, unemployed or becomes a drug addict...The girl could, in such circumstances, support herself and her family." Some of the younger women interviewed had faced exactly this situation.[11]

Sharing Memories

Akhtar Bibi was in her early twenties when the resettlement took place, and had lived longer in Khallabat Township than in her original village. Like many of the older narrators, she welcomed the opportunity to relive her past. She expressed sadness that these memories were not shared by her children:

I often tell the details of the past events to my children. They listen to this tale sometimes with keen interest, but show indifference to it at other times. Obviously, of what interest should all this be to them? They have not witnessed all this with their own eyes. That's why I feel some relief today. At least there has been someone to listen to all this with such care and interest.

The importance of memories of life in Tarbela and being able to share them with others came through particularly strongly in the interviews with those narrators who were in their thirties or more when resettled. Makhan Jan said that, even after three decades, to lift feelings of sadness she sought the company of those neighbours in Karachi with whom she could recall the past.

> When I feel a bit depressed I visit relatives or other residents in the neighbor-hood and would like someone to talk with me about my village, but there is rarely any time with anyone these days. Your coming here [to interview me] is like gaining my heart's wish. I have given vent to my long pent-up feelings. I feel happy and relaxed and shall certainly have a peaceful sleep this night. Otherwise, no one likes the company of old people like us. No one wants to listen to us.

Many of the older narrators were aware that their stories had less and less meaning for new generations growing up with no experience of life in Tarbela. Mushtaq Ahmad Khan, interviewed in his sixties, was one of those who moved to a different province rather than a local township. On arrival in Punjab from their home in Dhall, the family faced many obstacles: "It was a new place, with new people, an unfamiliar language, different social setup, and different customs and practices." In a detailed and thoughtful interview, he stressed the lack of continuity and cohesion within the extended family and between the generations that had been brought about by resettlement. His children, he said, had absorbed "local influence" and spoke Punjabi more than their mother tongue of Hindko.[12]

> We had a respectable place in the village, with our own *hujra* and a mosque in our name. But having come here we are all only "Pathans" in the eyes of the local people. We have been driven from pillar to post. Brother is separated from brother, and son from father. Every one of us is in trouble. We retain neither that identity nor that prosperity that once we had . . . Our children are not famil-iar with their close relatives and their children.

He talked with sadness of the fact that the younger generation will never see the land which meant so much to those who were displaced:

> We have at least some traces of our identity, but it is diminishing. After 10 or 20 years we would lose even that. It's a matter of great concern for our children. We have seen our lost place; they have not seen even that.

However, there is evidence from the interviews that the retelling of the stories about Tarbela did have an effect on the younger generation, even those who

were born after resettlement, such as Qurat ul Ain Shah. She was 22 when interviewed. Her family had relocated from Kyya to Handkia, a more remote location
than most resettlement sites, many hours by road from Haripur. She explained:
"I could describe all the events [in Kyya] as if I myself had been there. I can feel
all that. What I have heard, really, runs like a film before my eyes, even now."

The Next Generations

Sultan Ahmed is another whose account suggests that stories of life in Tarbela
were repeated so many times by the older generation that they became internal-
ized by some of the next. His family came from Darri, which he described in
great detail, yet he was less than four years old at displacement. He recognized
the subjective nature of such representations: "Our village was a paradise on
earth... [but] everyone loves his own land. That's why everyone exclaims that his
village is a paradise on earth."

Sultan's family moved to Khallabat Township and he described tensions emerging soon after relocation, as different communities got "mixed up"
together:

> The government had only sorted out the plots, it had not [designated] the hous-
> ing with a view to settling the people of Darri at one place, and those of old
> Khallabat village at another... people took up the plots haphazardly. [Yet] each
> village had its own language and dialect, and its ways and customs...
>
> In the earliest days there were rows. Children would quarrel; it was not a
> friendly atmosphere... People of different villages [were] mixed up everywhere.
> It became a real problem for us.

As soon as he was old enough, Sultan became a carpet weaver, but the factory
closed down and he fell back on casual labor before finding work in Saudi Arabia.
After some years he returned, prompted by concern for his young son, who was
unemployed: "Drugs are paralyzing our new generation... because of unemployment." Interviewed some three years after returning from Saudi Arabia, Sultan
was himself without work and he traced back the problems faced by his family to
their displacement from Tarbela:

> If we had been in our own village... we would have cultivated our own lands;
> shepherded our own sheep. I was three or four years of age when the dam was
> constructed and have passed my whole life suffering misfortune ever since. I
> could never finish building my own house. If we build the bathroom, we can't
> afford to build the kitchen; if we build the kitchen, the living room cannot be
> built... At the new location they did nothing for us... they were supposed to
> install some industry [to create jobs].

In desperation, he had returned to the mountain slopes above the Tarbela reservoir, hoping to make a frugal living from rearing and selling livestock.

> When I came to this mountain to settle here, all my relatives asked why. I told them that I was jobless and that my son, too, was not going to get any job. If I had some hope of a job in a factory, I would have never opted for a life on the mountainside. But it is fear of tomorrow that has forced me to take refuge here. I wanted my son to get himself set here for the future...
>
> No government has looked after us; our problems have remained unattended... It is not easy to live here. Had we been satisfied [with the resettlement deal] we wouldn't have come here at all.

"Their hearts are full of frustration"

The interviews with younger people, even those too young to have experienced or fully understood the social networks and collective activities that their parents mourned, suggested that subsequent generations did feel a distinct sense of loss. Many expressed sadness about the unraveling of extended family support systems, but they also regretted having moved out of a largely self-sufficient rural economy. Obliged to pay for food and utilities, it was essential that in the new location they were waged, and the lack of employment left many feeling deeply frustrated and in some senses "cheated." Sultan Ahmed's response was to move back to the mountains, whereas Aslam Hayat remained in Khallabat Township; his subsequent experiences bore out what many older narrators had said about life in the resettlement site.

Aslam was 16 when his family had to leave the village of Murti, near Tarbela. Interviewed in his forties, he expressed his anger about the "inadequate" compensation, which he said was used up just surviving the first difficult years: "We were illiterate and had no skill; the land allocated was not sufficient. How could one plough a plot of land as small as 10 *marlas* [2722.5 square meters]?" He admitted that he had sought comfort in drugs: "We were not addicts in the village... After coming here, unemployment and frustration has shoved us into addiction."

> Work? Young people have none. In the morning...they join their idle friends. And then they behave like hooligans, use drugs and, intoxicated, lie on the beds. Young as they are, their hearts are full of frustration. What should they do? A burglary or a robbery? You may yourself visit these houses and see how many have jobs. There may be certain houses where one family member is in Japan or Canada and their old mothers have some relief. But most of them are unemployed. There are no permanent jobs...

Feeling such frustration one cannot enjoy even happy occasions... Everyone is lost in his own world... After coming here it seems one's whole life is but duty. I am a driver and before this I have worked in ten different mills and factories. I also worked as a laborer. Because of unemployment I went off to Karachi too. Had we all stayed here what would my family have eaten?

The perceived need to concentrate on their own survival appeared to have strained relations between family members:

A distance with our relatives is growing. When we were settled in the village, we were well off... and mutual respect was there. [Now] one brother has gone to Hyderabad, the other is in Sukkur, and the third is in Khallabat. That one is in real trouble with four children and two old parents to feed. The job brings him 1,800 rupees and it is uncertain. It may be there today and not tomorrow. The one in Hyderabad is also in trouble, inhaling cotton in a mill.[13]

Family relations are gradually losing their warmth. Everyone is engaged in fighting their own hardships. If one person is starving, even relatives avoid him.

Life in the village was different. One could survive for a year there even without a single rupee. Here you cannot pass a single day... here the wheel of life doesn't move without money...

There was a time when God had given us the gift of canals of water. Now we pay 100 rupees for a water supply that we know not when it will come... There used to be simple lamps in the village. No one wanted an electric connection. Now we receive a bill of 1,000 to 1,500 rupees. The firewood we used to collect has been replaced by gas; another expenditure...

Simple people with a farming background received compensation, but they spent the whole amount here. I'm speaking of those who knew no skill other than farming. They were 75 percent of those who came. The other 25 percent were people who were clever or had some skill. Such people started doing different jobs, in business etcetera. The literate joined some service. Some took the chance to go abroad. They are well-off. Their sons are studying at [expensive private schools]... But my son goes to the government school and when he returns it is as if he has spent the day in a quarry mining coal! So in our system it is only the [well-off middle class] that reach the top positions.

Aslam described having work but no economic security. In common with others who began resettlement with limited resources and "no skill other than farming," it had been a struggle to survive and family support networks had been stretched to breaking point. In his view, this was compounded by the fact that there was no relationship or reciprocity with those in authority such as that which existed with the old landowners:

> All these parliamentarians are but gangs of thieves. They are those who have received [funding] to construct sewage lines and have built their own gardens while the sewage work lies unattended. The roads are also in a miserable condition. They collect the taxes from us to provide these facilities... It's a very different world [to Tarbela]. Better not ask about it, as my heart bursts with grief as I speak about these things.

Acceptance: "We Are a Part of This New Life"

Gul Bibi was about 11 when her family left their village of Darband. They were given little notice of the resettlement date and had to stay in various locations, spending precious compensation money on rent, before they were allocated land in Kangra Colony, near Haripur. Her family had considerable status in their community; her father was a respected *maulvi* (Islamic scholar) at the mosque and other male relatives used to deliver the judgments in the *jirga*. They owned some shops and land. She recalled the "calamity" of their departure:

> I had a great emotional attachment with my village... How could we accept having to vacate that land that was ours? That was our home... It was a catastrophe; everyone was weeping... What was going to happen to us, everybody was asking? You can just imagine the state of mind of a person with no place to move to... If one willingly leaves a house, and shifts to a new place after making all important arrangements, that's something different.

Nevertheless, she believed that part of the reason she remembered village life so fondly was because it represented her childhood, and "the real hardships, one feels, start after marriage." When interviewed in 2002, she was in her late thirties, with three sons and a job in a factory. She took her secondary school certificate after marriage, and had become the family breadwinner. Her disabled husband's health had deteriorated and once he was no longer able to work, she had been forced to look for a full-time job: "If I had been better educated I would have got a much better position than working in a factory. In our society women need education more than men do." Fortunately, she said, hers was one of the best employers: "The factory has a very good working environment. At the time we report for work, a proper assembly is held; the Holy Quran is recited... They give every respect [to women workers]. They have given us all kinds of facilities, a dispensary…a staff bus."

One of the difficulties for Gul Bibi was that her need to work compromised family tradition: "I am the only person in my family to go out to work. Our family observes the restrictions of *purdah*. In our family a woman is not supposed to meet an outsider unless that person is closely related…but I have to deal with men…I have no choice." She was proud of her family's reputation for piety and clearly still struggled to reconcile going out to work with their high moral standing.

Like others, she regretted the loss of self-sufficiency in the old village: "Grains, vegetable, fruit, everything. All these things were available in Darband." Now, she said, everyone in her colony was obliged to compete to find work, otherwise they didn't have the income to feed or educate their children.

> The people here have both skills and education. They have qualified on different courses but all this is meaningless, as they can't find jobs. There are many such people: girls who have done teaching courses and boys educated up to graduate and post-graduate level…Getting a government job today is nothing less than a Herculean task.
>
> Unemployment is the worst thing. In my opinion it promotes crime. It's the very root cause. Take the example of poor people. They can't afford to educate their children, so they find no other solution but to send their small children to work. These children are attached to a *suzuki* [taxi van] on which they work as a conductor, hanging in the rear of it; or they become cleaners on the buses. They start smoking and keeping bad company. The next thing they achieve is addiction to drugs, and begin to move into the world of crime. But how does all this start? Unemployment.

The strain of being responsible for all domestic work and stretching her salary to cover food, utilities, and school fees, even with support from her wider family, was evident in her interview:

> I am most of the time surrounded by worries and anxiety. You can understand my position: I am the one in the family to take care of everything. And when there are such responsibilities one's mind is preoccupied all the time.

Indebtedness was widespread among the resettled communities and this was something Gul Bibi felt the relatively privileged villagers had found particularly hard to come to terms with: "Obviously, when a person has lots of money and helps the poor, and then all of a sudden he loses all that and becomes a debtor to others, his grief must be much more intense."

"Now we are adjusted"

There are many things that Gul Bibi said she missed about Tarbela, particularly the warm and supportive relationships within and between families, and the natural environment: "In the beginning the new place had no attraction for us at all. Not for a long period of time could we accept it. Obviously it is difficult, very difficult." She admitted it was hard to find the words to describe the distress of resettlement, concluding that only those who undergo it can really understand the experience. It took years to complete their house, and they still lacked what they believed to be their full compensation.

However, despite the strains of life, she said that even if it were possible, she would not return to old Darband.

> Now we would like to live here...Now we are adjusted...We are used to this new place. In the village we had had no facilities such as transport...[now] we have amenities like electricity, water, and gas. We are a part of this new life.

Her answer partly reflected an acceptance that had developed over time: "In the beginning we were [particularly] sensitive on the issue of leaving behind the family graves. But gradually we accepted it. Still, a feeling of sadness is there because those graves are at such a far off place now." However, there are two positive reasons underlying Gul Bibi's approval of her "new life": the availability of education and changed attitudes to women.

"Education...teaches us humanity"

Of all the facilities and amenities she appreciated in the city, education was the most important: "There are very few who do not benefit from this." She didn't see education just as a passport to employment, but valued its "civilizing" effect: "After coming to the cities people have become comparatively liberal. Now they allow their daughters to go out of their houses for jobs or education." The change has been substantial:

> I think many of them have worked a great deal after coming here. Some of them received education, and on completion have even started teaching. The girls, some of them, work in the factories. Some work indoors on embroidery or sewing...Some girls are learning to use computers. Women, generally, prefer to be teachers.

Although many narrators regretted the breaking up of the social order, particularly those such as Gul Bibi who came from more prosperous families, she believed "the social change that has occurred is in the positive direction." While she remembered fondly the mutual support systems and social order of the village, including the respect given to elders, she also recalled aspects of her life that were less attractive:

> An order given by an elder was always obeyed; no one could even think of refusing him…That was something good. But there was another aspect, too. Those children's minds were curbed by restrictions. Even boys were subject to restrictions. Children were subject to a great deal of pressure. I think it was not something healthy…
>
> Respect for parents is important. But…young people should also learn to communicate their problems…It should not be that as soon as a child comments on something the parents react harshly to discourage him and tell him that they must not speak when their elders are talking. His personality fails to grow.

There were other ways in which village society oppressed people, especially women, and in her view education has been the key to changing this:

> The family of a husband used to be very harsh upon a woman, although it was not so in our village but in the [mountainous] area behind us…They were too harsh upon any girl they brought as a new bride…Now the social environment has certainly improved. Education, you know, is the main factor that teaches us humanity…
>
> People have developed better understanding and wisdom…Good education teaches us a civic sense and manners, to respect elders, the rights of others, all these things. Now a woman is given her rights. She is now an equal partner with man and is serving in every department of life.

She acknowledged, "The life I am living now is certainly full of greater hardships. We used to live a peaceful and comfortable life when in the village." But, she said, "Hardships are a part of life." For many of the displaced, the yearning for "paradise lost," the weakening of family ties, unemployment, and addiction were negatives to be weighed against an opening up of educational opportunities, especially for women, and the breaking down of restrictive hierarchies and attitudes. For Gul Bibi, the social changes brought about by resettlement had made her new life acceptable.

CHAPTER 4

"I have lost status in my community"

Conservation and Agricultural Production in Kenya

We were moved in 1992...I had over 200 head of cattle and by 1993 I was left with only five...[So] I started doing something contrary to my culture to earn a living. I became a farmer. This made me become a very inferior person in my community because I had violated its norms and culture...I am not called or invited to any of the community's festivals or gatherings...[Those] who still have livestock have no respect for me, irrespective of how close we were in the past. Even their children...they used to greet me like a parent, but nowadays they...pretend that they are not seeing me.

—Roba Dokota, Orma pastoralist

Roba Dakota is an Orma pastoralist who has spent most of his life grazing the dry lands of Kenya's Coast Province with herds of livestock. Interviewed in 1999 at the age of 50, he described how five years earlier his whole world changed when his community was forced off their dry-season grazing area in the floodplains of the Tana River. The land had been taken over for a large-scale rice irrigation scheme by the Kenyan government's Tana and Athi Rivers Development Authority (TARDA). Roba Dakota and others interviewed explained how there was minimal warning or negotiation about what was to come. His community went from disbelief to defiance until they were finally evicted by the state: "Soldiers were brought to evict us forcefully...There was no way we could ask for compensation because we were just chased away."

He described how families hurriedly collected together their children and animals and trekked west for some 25 kilometers (15.5 miles) to an area known as Dida Ade, where many settled. The new area was dry and dusty, far from the river delta, and the lack of pasture soon took a toll on their livestock, which were also vulnerable to unfamiliar tick-borne diseases to which they had no immunity. Many of his fellow pastoralists suffered catastrophic losses; Roba Dakota himself went from owning over 200 head of cattle to owning 5 in just one year.

To pastoralists, animals are not simply an economic resource but are at the heart of their identity and way of life. The loss of livestock brought about far-reaching social, economic, and political changes among the Orma and Boran pastoralists interviewed, affecting their diet, relations between men and women, and served also to challenge powerful taboos linked to their sense of identity. What these stories reveal is how displacement sometimes is not so much about loss of place as about the changing of a whole way of life. And because survival necessitated taking up work such as farming and charcoal burning—occupations traditionally seen by many pastoralists as low-status and shameful—most of the narrators also found themselves ostracized and humiliated by their wider community. Such occupations are seen as undermining pastoralism, since farming takes land, often the best, while charcoal-making necessitates cutting down trees, which are critical sources of highly nutritious fodder for livestock in the dry season. Those pastoralists who had not been displaced and who, against many other odds, continued to live with large herds, began to draw a line between themselves and the displaced, who had "violated [their] culture" and whom they no longer regarded as their equals.

Introduction and Background

The narrators in this chapter are members of the Boran and Orma pastoralist communities of Kenya.[1] They share a common ancestry, being closely related to the Oromo of Ethiopia, but around the sixteenth century they, along with the Rendille, began to move from southern Ethiopia to northern Kenya. By the nineteenth century they were firmly established in Kenya, competing for grazing land with Somali pastoralists. The Boran tended to concentrate in what is now Kenya's Eastern Province and the Orma in the Coast Province, around the Tana River.

These pastoralists identified not so much with one distinct site but with a large area, and above all with a way of life that involved moving herds of livestock between distinct sites with specific functions, such as forested areas and salt licks, and particular grazing areas. During the dry season, they spent time at specific areas that still had pasture and water for their animals.

Their animals represented their wealth and were their main source of food and milk. Animals and their products were traded for cereals, tea, sugar, clothes, vegetable oil, and so on. The pastoralists followed a seasonal migratory pattern that could vary from year to year, timing and destinations being primarily determined by the availability of nutritious forage and water. The main reason for mobility is to maximize livestock production levels, and it requires years of experience and knowledge to track the best-quality pasture, since its timing and distribution is variable and short-lived.[2]

Loss of Land

Over the last few decades, a significant number of pastoralist families in Kenya have experienced resettlement and a change of lifestyle and livelihood. These displacements have some similarity with those of the San in Chapter 5, in that they are not always isolated events stemming from one specific development activity, but rather are connected with wider political and economic processes. In this case, influential factors included long-standing farmer–pastoralist tension and competition, political and ethnic violence, the preference of governments for settled rather than nomadic populations, the aftermath of armed conflicts, drought, and increasing restrictions on mobility.

Mobile populations are frequently regarded with suspicion because of their falling outside of bureaucratic control, and pastoralism has long been seen by a number of African governments and policy-makers as "archaic," economically inefficient, and environmentally destructive. According to drylands specialists at the International Institute of Environment and Development (IIED), "these perceptions are not evidence-based, yet drive much regional policy;" they argue that pastoralism has been chronically undervalued as land-use system.[3] As a result, until recently the Kenyan government has consistently failed to support the sector, and has often taken control of pastoral land for commercial farming, ranching, and conservation. The situation for pastoralists, excluded from political power and largely unprotected by Kenya's land laws, has been bleak. More recently, the government formulated a new Land Policy and has identified pastoralists as some of the people most vulnerable to dispossession.[4] It also acknowledged that pastoralism has "survived as a livelihood and land use system despite deliberate efforts from successive governments to replace it with other land use systems."[5]

Such shifts in perception have not yet been enforced through legislation and have come too late for the pastoralists whose experiences inform this chapter. They were primarily displaced by large-scale irrigation schemes, wildlife parks, and other development projects. Many were forced to move from their dry-season grazing areas in the Tana River flood plains, prized by the Kenyan government for their agricultural potential. Often unable to find new sites suitable for their animals before they started dying on a massive scale, these pastoralists found that displacement was the cause of far-reaching social and cultural change.

The accounts in this chapter are few; they are drawn from a larger collection of interviews with pastoralists from 1999 to 2001, who had undergone

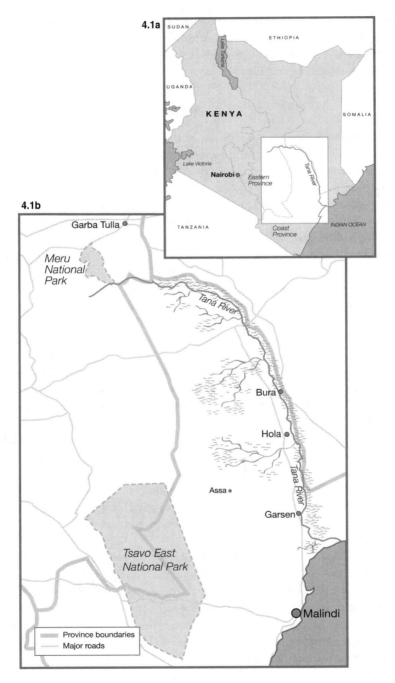

Figure 4.1 a. Map of Kenya, with Tana River area highlighted. b. Detail of Tana River area. Maps by Julie Anson.

resettlement for a variety of reasons. Most of the women interviewed in the original project were refugees displaced by conflict, not by development, and so the accounts in this chapter are primarily from men.[6] Nevertheless, although the story that unfolds is partial, it does highlight how the loss of their way of life has had far-reaching effects. It also illustrates how adjustment to new circumstances has for many been made much harder because it has been accompanied by shame and isolation, as a result of deep-seated negative attitudes among pastoralists to other occupations.

"Nobody Will Visit the Home of the 'Soil Diggers'"

Haji Kuno Galgalo, 61, is Orma; at the time of the interview he was living in Assa, in the Tana River district, in Kenya's coastal region. He was evicted from his land in the late 1970s by the government to make way for the Tsavo East National Park. He described there being no negotiation; after some initial resistance, the arrival of soldiers prepared to use violence left the families no choice but to leave. They moved to Assa, an area with insufficient water and pasture to sustain their large herds. Many lost most or all of their livestock:

> The government one day came and just told us to shift—to any other place—as the area has already been set aside as a National Park... We were told the Kenya Wildlife Service would occupy Kungu [where we lived]. They also told us that the area had been gazetted as a park for a long time and it was only that we were not aware of this.[7] Now the time has come, we were told, to pave the way for the game department to take care of the wildlife...
>
> We resisted and took the issue to our divisional and district offices but all in vain. Nobody was willing to assist us... We resisted by stopping the tractor that was clearing the area, arming ourselves with arrows, *pangas,* and clubs.
>
> The District Commissioner, who [was brought from Hola] addressed us in a *baraza* [public gathering]. We said we could not move because it was a dry season and there was no water in nearby places—so in the event of mandatory movements, we could only do it when the rains came. It was after these complaints that heavily armed soldiers were brought to evict us forcefully. So we moved... What else could we have done? He did not tell us where to go. We were not given an alternative site.
>
> The majority of us moved to Assa... where some few wells were available.
>
> The journey was terrible. Our assistant chief requested a vehicle from the soldiers and ferried children and the elderly, who were unable to walk to Assa. The rest of us shifted with our livestock. There was no water. Some people died

on the way, because of the terrible beatings [by the soldiers]. I found resettlement in Assa to be terrible...

[With our arrival] the livestock in the area increased tremendously. I started digging wells that were very deep in order to water my cattle and goats...Besides the water shortages, pastures were deteriorating...and after a month there were signs of over-grazing...And in two-and-a-half months the animals were starving...

I had about...900 head of cattle, but when I came to Assa I lost my animals and I now have about 50. Yet I have 15 households to take care of. I have four wives and 25 children.

"Since we were evicted we have become beggars"

In Assa's unforgiving environment, Haji Kuno admitted that it was virtually impossible to rebuild a herd.

In the past if someone was left with only five cows due to some calamities, after five years that person would be self-sufficient again. But now, even if you are left with five animals, you will never progress or improve because you don't have anywhere to graze; there is no water and there is no suitable grazing land, therefore animals don't increase in number and one will never become self-sustaining again...

This is a fundamental change, because in the past we have been wealthy. We have never asked anything from the government, we have never begged—not even from the colonial government. But since we were evicted we have become beggars. We beg for food, water, and almost everything, including our land. This is a big problem. The government does not bring enough food...about 30–40 bags of maize for four sub-locations to divide and share. The population is about 4,000 families. How can it be enough?

"My heart feels so bad"

Those such as Haji Kuno, who were left with a few animals, were able to some extent to maintain their pastoralist way of life, but in order to do so they needed the support of others with larger herds. Even so, he had lost the status he used to enjoy and, as he was seen as a man who no longer had the "interests of livestock at heart," he was no longer invited to the community's twice yearly meetings.

Despite his own experience, Haji Kuno was stern and unyielding in his condemnation of the pastoralists who had lost all their livestock and had turned to farming. "Farming is the work of inferior communities in our culture...Nobody will visit the home of the 'soil diggers,' no one will marry into that family and no one will call them Orma anymore," he explains. "They have gone astray...Yes, the Orma have split into two different groups."

The interviews reveal that those who resorted to charcoal burning and unskilled work such as being night watchmen were equally looked down on. For Haji Kuno, those with a few animals and a desire to hold on to the pastoralist life, however precarious their livelihood, were accorded respect and any support that was available:

> They are assisted by others who have more livestock than they do. Their relatives, in-laws and friends will give them a few animals. For example, if they are left with three they can be given two more or so because people will say, these people have not turned to farming and they should be assisted. They are treated on an equal basis with any others in the community...because they are still pastoralists.

Yet a deep sadness at their situation surfaced in his interview, especially when Haji Kuno explained how the poverty and shame associated with giving up pastoralism had greatly increased divorce and family break-up: "Even relatives distance themselves from a poor farmer. This has greatly affected family relations."

> The farmers' boys cannot be given girls [from our families] in marriage because then they will take the girls to farms. No way—both the girls and their fathers will not agree to this. [So these boys cannot marry] unless they go elsewhere...
>
> In fact there are so many affected people who have felt so bad and isolated, they have moved away to other places, outside the district...They go looking for unskilled work such as being a watchman...In fact if you ask me about this, my heart feels so bad. Please don't ask me about that. They have moved to big towns like Malindi, Mombasa...All those whose boys were unable to marry and whose girls are not married have moved to those areas.
>
> They don't find much work but they look after the animals of those staying in the towns. Some do the milking; others work as security guards. Herding is what they prefer because this is what they are used to [but] they are generally working for "enemies," by which we mean anyone who has no resemblance to our community and has a completely different lifestyle from us.
>
> Some move with their families, while others abandon their families completely. The latter are followed to wherever they are and are brought back to their families, though some refuse and opt to divorce their wives rather than come back. This has caused a lot of family break-up.
>
> Oh, terrible things have happened, many people have divorced their wives. Two of my daughters have been divorced...and I am now taking care of them with their children. So this change is a terrible cause of family break-up.

Many women also ran away from their husbands who have become destitute and turned to farming and charcoal burning as a source of livelihood. The women are accepted back [by their families] because they understand the situation—they would not like their daughters to be staying with such poor people or those who have gone to the extent of changing their lifestyle.

Haji Kuno's description of the fate of those struggling to make a living outside the pastoralist community revealed something of the complex Orma attitudes to occupation, which magnified the distress and marginalization that those without livestock felt:

They just engage themselves in jobs such as watchmen, waiters in hotels; others undertook charcoal burning and firewood collection...The income they get sustains them for a night or two...

[Charcoal burning] is bad in our culture. Anybody who depends on fire to earn a living is seen as an outcast...in our lifetime no Orma son has ever engaged in this...It is therefore very bad [for these families] because even before as farmers they were considered a low-class group, but charcoal burning has even more far-reaching effects—because this is a sign of total outcast.

A few were able to secure work on the rice irrigation scheme that was developed later and which in 1992 displaced Roba Dakota, whose words open this chapter:

They only employed a few to scare birds from [eating] rice and a few who serve as watchmen...but to us that is not a job...because it is a job for the stomach only [meaning, just enough to buy food]. Nobody can buy a cow from that job, a goat or even a sheep because the salary is so meager, so we don't consider it to be a job if it will not enable you to buy any kind of livestock.

"Farming Was Not Their Culture"

Pastoralism is a strategy to support a population on land with fragile and limited resources where the pastoralists' mobility allows arid regions to support life. However, fierce competition for scarce resources in these areas has long created tensions and competition with settled farmers, and some of this is at the root of the stigma attached to agriculture. And in the most marginal environments where pastoralists live and produce, the land can be severely and swiftly degraded by cultivation, further increasing their suspicion of those who farm.

A further factor is the association of digging the soil with death, since for many pastoralists, the only time they "turn the soil" is to bury their dead. Elders like Haji Kuno Galgalo remained reluctant to let go of such attitudes, even though it became clear that he too was suffering some discrimination as a result of his greatly reduced animal wealth. As already explained, he was no longer involved in important community decision-making:

> The Orma community has its own system of administration. Twice a year live-stock owners meet, and discussions are held for three days on issues affecting the community at large. During such occasions people with no livestock or few animals are not allowed to attend because they are assumed not to have the interests of livestock at heart.
>
> In fact I am one of those. [In] Kungu I was among the key people who could make independent decisions on behalf of the community and such decisions were binding. But nowadays I am not invited to any meetings or weddings simply because I don't have enough animals, as I used to.

In the end, he said, those like him struggled on, keeping their few livestock going with limited movement, but causing friction with settled farmers in the process:

> We just graze them near rivers and around the farms. When the owners are not there we sometimes graze the animals in the farms...If you are unlucky you get caught. There are those who were caught and paid fines and sometimes were detained at the chief's office, but it has become a day-to-day happening. We graze on the farms both at night and during the evening. If we are caught, we normally tell the farmers the grass and the rice look similar and we cannot differentiate the two!

"I am looked down on as an outcast, someone... of no value to the community"

Haji Elema Guyo Barissa, an Orma elder a decade older then Haji Kuno Galgalo, was displaced from the Tana River delta by the huge TARDA rice irrigation scheme.[8] Both these men, as the title "Haji" indicates, had made the pilgrimage to Mecca but since displacement, neither they nor anyone else in their communities had been able to afford to make this important Muslim pilgrimage. They lamented that religious festivals were only rarely celebrated following their resettlement, in part because animal slaughter was a key element of feasts and celebrations and without their own herds they could not afford to buy animals in for this purpose. A further source of distress and cultural change, borne out in many of these accounts, was that few were able to afford religious education for their children.

Haji Elema was displaced along with his community, which according to him numbered about 2,000 people, in 1992. Like Roba Dakota, who was displaced at the same time, he said they were given little notice: "It was early one morning while people were milking the animals that we saw some tractors were clearing the bushes next to us and they continued moving towards our villages." They were not provided with alternative places to settle so they refused to move, following which "some trucks full of soldiers were brought to clear us from the area. They came very early in the morning and brought the men together and beat us up to evict us by force."

He believed the government viewed them as little better than the animals that roamed the land. Lacking education or political influence, he said, "We had no alternative but to move."

> We were not given any room for negotiation, so we followed their orders...we knew [that the] government did not have any regard for us, so any further resistance could have been very harmful...
>
> Why we did not ask for compensation is because we are already seen [by the authorities] like wild animals on that land—because our community is not educated and there is nobody to lead us to the necessary offices. Because we all fear the government we did not ask for any compensation and of course none of us knew that we were entitled to any.[9]

The pastoralists who were forced to move along with Haji Elema settled in Danisa, near Garsen, where their children became sick and their livestock died. By the next year, their herds were a fraction of their original size. Overgrazing and lack of water were the main problems: "Wherever we took the animals for watering along the river is said to be somebody's farm." Like others, he refers to agriculturalists as "riverines" and "the enemies."

> We did not adapt to the Danisa environment at all. Children became very sick because of the many mosquitoes...We were the first to settle in this area— human beings and animals found it hard to adapt...we encountered different types of ticks and disease that were not known to our animals. They did not have any resistance and coupled with the lack of pasture, the animals started dying in their masses...
>
> I can personally say I lost all my herds, something I cannot forget...I have only ten cattle remaining...I have been a herder since childhood and so I am much used to animal products. Since we came here to Danisa, I am not getting milk, I am not getting meat. We are now feeding on maize, which brings us another complication altogether.

Unlike his fellow elder Haji Kuno Galgalo, Haji Elema turned to other work.

> [Now I live] a kind of life which the Orma has never experienced before. For instance, cutting down trees and making charcoal out of them and selling it to earn a daily living...I am looked down on as an outcast, someone of very low status and of no value to the community. I have lost my identity in my community together with my family.

"Nobody even comes to greet me"

Haji Elema, responsible for 3 wives and 18 children, still left his home early each morning to find wood, although his offspring did much of the charcoal making. His first three children were educated in the Islamic tradition but the loss of their animals and dramatic decline in income meant none of the other children had received any schooling and only 3 of the 18 had married, into "riverine" farming families. The lack of livestock was thought pivotal in their failure to secure marriage partners among those Orma who continued a herding life. His humiliation was extreme:

> During the day, when the animals went to graze, elders used to gather at my house. They discussed with me different issues. But now nobody comes to me, no elder comes to me—nobody even comes to greet me. Everything has changed.
>
> We used to discuss the fortunes of our animals; we used to look at the stars and asked those well-versed in such things: how things are going to be? We used to talk about the stars [which could signify] rain, or drought, or conflict, and other factors affecting livestock. And after looking into all these things, there are ways that we used to pray in order for a bad thing not to come our way and so on.
>
> For instance there is a star for rain. At night, after the cows are milked, we went to the *kraal* [animal enclosure] and we looked for this star. If it was in a good place, we used to pray to God and then we waited for rain.
>
> They used to ask me about the appropriate time of weddings...According to our culture it has to be looked [in the stars] since there are good and bad times—these stars foretell if couples will have children [and] if the fortunes of the woman and the bridegroom may not correspond and whether or not they may prosper in their lifetime...
>
> I don't [interpret the night sky now] because I spend the whole day felling trees for charcoal so that I get home very late at night; I can't look at it. I have to look for food for the family—I have to prepare charcoal.

He didn't even look at the stars for his children's weddings because "nowadays as they intermarry with these foreigners...they don't know about it."

"Nobody remembers one another now"

He admitted there was some division within the Orma even before the far-reaching changes brought about by displacement: "Those with wealth were considered to be superior to those without any." And now, "because I have no wealth, I have to accept that I'm among the inferior."

But at least in the past, he said, the community did its best to assist the poor: "We used to help these people by collecting animals from everybody [and] we gave them to him and so he starts rearing [more animals] and depending on himself again." He agreed with Haji Kuno Galgalo that such support systems are now under strain, partly because it is hard to rebuild herds in the new environments but also because everyone's resources are stretched: "Nobody remembers one another now."

He couldn't provide anything when his son and two daughters married: "They just went ahead themselves and did the wedding from their own wages." He said he felt so demeaned by his family marrying out of the Orma community that had he had his old wealth, he would have killed the "foreigner" and paid compensation to the family, rather than let him marry his daughter.

Haji Elema gained nothing from the rice farms developed on the land they had to leave, which had anyway failed by the end of the 1990s.[10] According to him, no one from his community was employed there: "They said that we were illiterate." They denied them jobs such as watchmen: "They told us that [our sons] didn't know how to open gates and used their own boys to do that. The other job was protecting the farms from birds that eat the seeds; this time they told us that we didn't know how to throw stones using catapults."

"A Man without a Culture Is Like a Tree without Roots"

Roba Dokota, 50, was also displaced in 1992 by the TARDA rice irrigation scheme. His family had returned to the same location every dry season: "I was born and brought up in Gamba." He recalls how little notice they had of their removal:

> As we continued to live in Gamba in comfort, without any disturbance or interaction with outsiders, we started seeing small vehicles running up and down, taking some measurements and surveying our grasslands. When we asked our local chief, we were told they were doing a survey for a rice scheme that was to be established in the region. We just kept quiet and continued staying there. After some time we saw some big machines, tractors, clearing the bush in our flood plains. We decided to ask as a group why they were destroying our grazing land, only to be told that we were supposed to shift

elsewhere to make way for the rice irrigation scheme. We felt they were just joking...After a month or so they officially came to our home and asked us to move from the site.

We told them that we were born there and that we were not moving unless they gave us an alternative place to live...we did not know where else to move. They then came with several soldiers. They gathered all the men in the village together and started beating us...I was beaten terribly and my houses burnt down. My children ran away and my wives started collecting things and running. Some of my boys opened the calf enclosure so that calves could find the mother cows and move off fast...Some people just grabbed their children and ran off without caring about their animals...In terms of villages we were about ten, if not more. In terms of household numbers, every village had about 50 households or families.

Although these events occurred more than seven years before his interview, the memories remained fresh:

I remember it was a Monday [when] they first came and told us to move. Then they came back three days later and asked us why we had not moved. We then told them that we had discussed among ourselves and found that we have no alternative suitable place to go to and therefore it was difficult for us to move. It was on the fourth day that the soldiers were brought...

We [moved that same day]...virtually running away from the brutal solders...in the process we ended up at Dida Ade [30 kilometers or 18.6 miles east of Garsen]. It was an area that could only be lived in during the rainy season, when the pastures were green. [And] it was dry...

Besides the scarcity of pasture, Dida Ade was infested with ticks that were not found in the flood plains of Delat and Gamba. The ticks started infecting our animals and they started dying...

We were moved in 1992. By 1993 we...had lost all our animals to the ticks and starvation. I had over 200 head of cattle when I was moved from Gamba and by 1993 I was left with only 5.

Within a year of displacement, he said, "I started doing something contrary to my culture to earn a living."

Because everyone does what he can [to survive]...I became a farmer. This made me become a very inferior person in my community because I had violated its culture...I am not called or invited to any of the community's festivals or gatherings for any kind of consultation. No cattle owner comes to my home whatever the situation.

The loss of respect from others had been dramatic and painful; it was as if his past had been wiped out:

> [Those with livestock] feel that since I have changed to being a farmer, my knowledge has also changed, and just washed away. Nobody comes to me and asks me anything. I am only respected by the ones who are [in the same situation]. But the others who have livestock like before have no respect for me, irrespective of how close we were in the past. Even their children . . . in the past they used to run to me and greet me like a parent, but nowadays they don't even greet me. If we meet they pretend that they are not seeing me, and just pass by.

Having decided he had no choice but to farm, he had difficulty getting land:

> Because there are those riverine communities who have always been living along the river, unlike the pastoralists, [they] always claim that anywhere along the river is their grandparents' place or someone's farm, so this gave me a lot of problems. Wherever we cleared the land, they kept on claiming it to be theirs. So I kept on begging one of them who was a friend of mine and eventually, after giving him one cow out of my five remaining animals, I managed to acquire a small piece of land, which I am still working. I acquired it towards the end of 1993. [Do I grow enough food?] Not really, just some little to sustain us. I get no other assistance.

Roba's story bore out the view of others that poverty and prejudice had affected their children's marriage prospects:

> My girls are not married to anyone from my Orma community and my boys cannot marry from my community because they belong to a family of 'soil diggers' . . . Only two of my daughters were married when I used to have some cattle, but the rest are just at home: one of them is 30 years old and the other one is 27. One of the other girls was married at 16 and the other at 15.

"It is the younger generation who are the ones mostly affected by this change of lifestyle," Roba concluded. "They are the ones who have completely lost their culture and way of life." Because of these taboos, some have married into other communities: "Some of the younger generation have already married some Christians and have become Christian themselves, including my son and daughter. I have personally not gone to see where they live, but I am told they have both become Christians." Like others who mentioned this, the change of faith had broken the bonds between parents and child.

His own marital status had changed:

> I used to have four wives but now I have two. The other two disowned me when
> they found things were too difficult for me. When they saw that I had lost all
> my cattle and had become a very poor person, resorting to farming as a way of
> earning a living they...went to the Khadia office [Islamic magistrate] and told
> him that I was not taking care of them properly—because I did not have the
> money to buy them enough clothes or even hoes, they demanded separation.
> [They wanted] to be able to go to their old family homes, who still had enough
> animals. And to avoid the cost of going to the Khadia office in Hola, which
> required bus fares that I could not raise, I decided to divorce them. They are
> now married to other men who have enough cattle.

"A horrible, miserable change"

Other family relationships also weakened as a result of the taboos attached to his
occupation:

> My relationship with my relatives has become very poor. Even my brothers—
> who were not living in Gamba during the eviction and therefore still have
> some animals like before—have ceased coming to my home. My own broth-
> ers think little of me and treat me like someone not known to them. That
> element of blood relationship is fading and no one is concerned with one
> another except for those who own cattle. They don't visit me at all. Except,
> when problems become too much on my part and I decide to send some of
> my sons to them, then they sometimes send me a little money that can buy me
> some clothes or so.
>
> In the past, hardly a month would pass by without us visiting one another.
> This is terrible—a horrible, miserable change that has never in our lifetime
> befallen us.

Roba Dokota pointed out that the speed of the changes he described had been
particularly traumatic. Not only was there no period of consultation or negotiation prior to displacement, many of them had lost virtually all their animals—
their source of income and the resource in which they invest—within a year.

> This situation is something very difficult to describe [yet] something that has
> happened to us very abruptly. Imagine—I was a rich person and within a period
> of months I became so poor that I resorted to farming. Now the only thing I am
> doing is looking for ways of bringing up the children by doing all I can to find
> something for them to eat and wear.
>
> I have not asked for any assistance...I am getting about four kilos of maize
> every three months, but I don't think this is worth mentioning. This is the only
> kind of so-called assistance I am getting from the government.

"We have lost a whole world of a culture"

The shame of not having enough to contribute to religious ceremonies had resulted in a weakening of important community events:

> In the past during the month of Ramadan we used to build a small *boma* [enclosure] to enable us to pray together and break the fast together in the evening. Every one of us used to buy something and bring it to such a gathering in order to seek God's reward. But now that we are all depending on maize, in which case some may have it and others may not, we have completely stopped coming together. Even those who would have liked to take something to such a gathering, what they have is so little that they feel ashamed... Everyone breaks the fast at his own place... We still come together to pray, but as soon as prayers are over everyone goes to his own home. Nobody invites anyone to his home to celebrate together the end of Ramadan...
>
> Our children don't come together and perform the traditional games [and dances]. Everybody is busy working on the farms, nobody even talks about [doing such things]... everybody is tired. We have lost a whole world of a culture.

Like others, he noted that the Orma community had fractured into two groups, with those who had significant herds setting themselves apart from those without livestock: "Those of us who lost our animals have deviated from our culture, while the others who still have their animals maintain the Orma culture and this therefore makes us two distinct groups."

He expressed deep sadness at not being able to pass on Orma knowledge and tradition to his own family: "None of my sons are in Islamic education and I am not teaching them Orma culture."

> In the past we used to go and spend [time] under the same tree as the elders, discussing community issues and teaching our children aspects of the Orma traditions, including teaching the eldest sons how to interpret the stars. Every elder would talk of what he had heard and seen, and people would learn from one another.
>
> But nowadays we don't come together and there is no teaching of one another because of this terrible change of lifestyle. Normally the elder sons are called and taught about the culture of the society and all other aspects of the community. Yes, I was the eldest son of my father. He has really taught me a lot and I have benefited much from it.
>
> How can I teach [my sons]? In the first place, where are they? I have eight sons and only two of them are around with me. The rest are always in the towns, some of them working as watchmen and some looking after the animals of people in the towns.

Roba was unequivocal about the damage that displacement had brought: "The change has affected our culture terribly—it has eroded it. Many of us have turned to practicing something against our culture to earn a living. And a man without a culture is like a tree without roots."

He mentioned a few practices now being adopted that were previously quite foreign to pastoralists: "Imagine, some of my sons leave very early in the morning looking for wild bees in order to harvest the honey...they also hunt for antelopes and giraffes to meet the food needs of the family. Our children are behaving like the sons of Wata [hunter-gatherers]."[11]

"Women Have More and More Work to Do Nowadays"

Roba Dokota also mentioned a shift in the position of women. Their burden of labor had increased but so had their role and influence on family matters:

> Women have more and more work to do nowadays because they are doing virtually everything. In the past they were only milking the cattle, building the huts, and taking care of the children...Nowadays, they also do the farming, the charcoal burning, and the selling. Oh, yes. Nowadays women have a lot of powers. They have to be involved in all decision-making processes, unlike the past when women were not informed of anything.
>
> [My wives and I] do everything on agreement after consultation now. Yes, I have to inform them of anything I intend to do because we are basically equal.
>
> Sometimes we go together to the farm and at other times I remain at home and send my wives to the farms with the girls. At other times I go and my wives stay behind. [When I am at home] I do the work that would have been done by my wives. I cook food for the children and take care of them until the mothers come back. This was something very shameful for men to do. Even now, those who have cattle don't do it. But with us, we are seeing it to be very normal.

The elderly Haji Elema Guyo Barissa also described these changes:

> Now women are doing more work than men...they are the breadwinners nowadays. They are even called [to meetings] and informed about issues that were only discussed by men. According to our culture women were not even invited in [to places] where men are. Now I have to ask the women [about every decision] because we have become the same; I don't have the superiority I used to have.

As a result, his own responsibilities altered; on those occasions that his wife "spends the day in the bush...I look after the children...Yes, I do what women used to do. I never did such things before; it was a taboo."

"I do what is done by the women when they are at home"

A similar story was told by Haji Abashora Galole, a 47-year-old Orma who was displaced by the same TARDA irrigation scheme in 1992. He spoke in more detail about the changes in men's and women's roles, particularly the adjustment in attitudes:

> Long ago I was the family breadwinner, since I had cows, but now [my wife] has more responsibility for she does a lot of work to bring in food...Now she cuts down firewood, she gives time to the farm, so she is much busier than me...
>
> Now that the cattle are no longer there, men and women do the same kind of work. When I remain at home I normally do the work done by the women when they are at home. [This] includes taking care of the younger kids, cooking...
>
> [Today] we agree to share and assist one another regardless of the nature of the work. In the past, according to our culture, if men were even seen near the fire, let alone cooking, it used to be regarded as very shameful!
>
> Even your fellow men, when they spend the day together, they will be talking about such men...[And] such wives whose husbands are found near the fire [doing women's tasks] are normally despised and abused by other women. But now women actually enjoy it. This is because our culture has changed...Now nobody even comments about [men cooking].

In spite of the fact that he thought people were getting used to the changes, his account revealed underlying discomfort. His wife had assumed responsibility for getting their eldest son married; something that in the past would have been his decision. "Yes, my first wife has done so. She told me all about it and said she was the one to be responsible since the money is hers. The fact is that she is the one who works. And also the boy has his part to play as he also brings some small amounts [of cash]. That is how all it is—in fact I can't help but just agree to whatever I am told."

In less than two years, Haji Abashora went from owning 500 cattle to owning no more than 4:

> In the past, I had many steers, I was recognized in the community, I was known by old and young, I was known by my relatives. But now, since I lost my animals, nobody knows me, nobody comes to me. Why? Because I am a charcoal burner, I'm the same as the blacksmith. Because I'm overpowered by my wives,

they are the ones who arrange the marriages of my children. These are the things that I have really hated in my life.

In common with other interviewees, after his exclusion from the grazing lands and the loss of his herds, he was unable to give his children any education, secular or Islamic.

I had some children who were going to school and to the local Islamic school when I was in Gamba, but from the time I was moved they have stopped going to any learning institutions. First of all Dida Ade—where we ran to safety—did not have a school when we arrived [and] our situation did not allow us to think about Islamic education either. And as time went on, life became more and more difficult with the loss of my cattle…And now it is not possible to give my children an Islamic education because a parent has to pay a heifer when the child reaches certain stages in learning the Quran.

Several narrators observed that some young men, frustrated by the lack of education and offered places in schools by Christian organizations, left their faith to take up the opportunity. As with those who married Christians, Haji Abashora broke off contact: "There is my son who became a Christian. I chased him away from home."

"They don't recognize us as people…they don't recognize our rights"

Haji Abashora relied on selling firewood and charcoal for income: "The firewood is nowadays a vast distance away, so I go very early in the morning and I come back about three o'clock. I don't get much money."

My life is very different now, as a long time ago I used to move around independently. I used to drink milk. I sold my animals when there were no rains and could obtain whatever I want, but now I am forced to work for people to bring something home for the children.

Haji Abashora was another who lamented the fact that he was no longer able to make the Hajj pilgrimage:

This is one of the very important things that I would have done in the past but cannot anymore…We lost our wealth, our pride, the livestock. We lost our brotherhood, it is no longer there. All good things have been lost…We knew our land tree by tree…When I remember the days when I had a large number of steers, when I could drink milk the way I wanted, those good days when I could marry as I chose—when I think of all these things I feel downcast…

> This was all brought about by the government...When they chased us
> from our lands we also lost our livestock, and that is why we do lots of odd
> jobs that we used not to do before...This was caused by the ignorance of the
> government, that they don't recognize us as people, that they don't recognize
> our rights.

He also believed they were disadvantaged by their lack of education and it was a
cause of deep frustration that because of their changed circumstances they were
unable to properly educate the next generation. And one result of this, he said,
was that their young daughters had begun working for other Kenyan "ethnic
groups" and in his view had become vulnerable to exploitation and intermarriage. Yet the parents' dependence on their children's wages made them powerless
to protest:

> Another thing that I came to hate is that our children...have interacted with
> other ethnic groups, who have some money, and they get married to them.
> These are people who were brought here by the government from other places
> in the country: people like the Luo, the Kikuyu, the Kamba...These people
> are now taking the Orma daughters to do everything for them, for example
> wash their clothes. These are girls of 12 or 15. They grow up working for these
> "foreigners" till they reach the time for them to get married...but what can the
> parents do? The father had to let her do such jobs. The father and mother are
> waiting to take the money at the end of the month, from the work these girls
> do. Yet these are the kinds of things that destroy [the girls'] lives.

"This wouldn't have happened if [they had] asked us about our lives"

He felt that if they had received proper development support after "eviction,"
they could have made better lives for themselves. Above all, he made a plea to be
treated properly, to be consulted and listened to. Things would have been different, he said, "if they had informed us all about what they wanted and if they had
also asked us about our lives."

> If the government had discussed the problems of these pastoralists, because
> they don't know how to farm, [if they had discussed] how the standard of living
> for these people could be raised, by digging boreholes, appealing for aid from
> outside so that these people were given some animals—about ten, five or even
> three animals—so that they could shun this life of poverty—so that their lives
> could be changed—it would be good.
>
> After all, all this wouldn't have happened if, before the government
> settled these people, they had bought the land from us, and if they had

informed us all about what they wanted and if [they had] also asked us about our lives.

The fact is we would have resisted [eviction], but if they had showed us a way forward with their request, we would have agreed to what they would say. But instead they decided for themselves and evicted us from our good land where our animals didn't get diseases, where we didn't lack water, where we prospered.

But if they had dug boreholes for us [in the new location] so that our animals don't lack water and if they would have done everything to please us we would at least have made the move without hatred and we would have accepted our eviction.

A Different Perspective

[Pastoralists] just look at the pasture and water and see them as of importance to them, but...until recently land was not seen as an asset.

—Hussein Mursalle

The following accounts are from Boran herders, who had experienced two kinds of resettlement. The first was in the 1960s, when they were confined to *daaba* (literally "to stop") camps set up by the Kenyan government to restrict Boran pastoralists whom the government alleged were supportive of Somali pastoralists during the Shifta War (1963–1967).[12] After the cease-fire, the Boran were released from the camps. Hussein Mursalle's small Boran community then settled in a grazing area called Duse, near Garba Tulla, and with relief returned to herding.

Hussein Mursalle was 51 years old when he was interviewed. He recalled how he was displaced again in 1972, when "blue sapphires" were discovered in Duse and the land was taken over. He says the company that exploited the area was owned by powerful people in government. He told the story of how one old man in his community found fragments of the precious stone, and sold small amounts for food, not realizing its potential. Eventually he attracted attention from outsiders and inadvertently lost the community their grazing land: "People saw that there was money in the business... [And] so they asked to be shown the place, they put a mark on it and went to obtain a licence and he was asked to keep off." Shortly afterwards, the whole community was removed from the land.

Hussein Mursalle expressed no resentment towards the elderly man's action. This was partly because he received only small payments for his pieces of gemstone, but more importantly, it was because pasture and water had value in the eyes of the herders, not "soil." They didn't see the land itself as valuable, just what it provided.

> The Borana then did not take land as an asset and they only valued the land-based resources like water and pasture. They just look at the pasture and water and see them as of importance to them, but the soil...until recently land was not seen as an asset, so no one bothered about the land...Afterwards people opened their eyes and started to know the value of land, but at that time no one placed emphasis on the loss nor was it followed up.

When they were first forced off the pastures at Duse, some refused to move, but over time they were pushed further away as more land for mining was dug up and fenced. Eventually, they settled nearby in Garba Tulla, which has no significant pastures.

> By moving out, we had moved out of a land of water and pasture. We could not negotiate with the government, we did not know any laws about this [or anywhere] we could take our plight. We are told the people who took the land are government people—[but] it's just individuals who took the land.

"There is nothing wrong with farming"

Hussein Mursalle explained that when his community had come to Duse a decade or so earlier, after their forced confinement in a *daaba* camp, livestock numbers had fallen dangerously low. People were becoming malnourished and realized they had to supplement their diet with crops. At first Mursalle did not take to farming easily, nor the food.

> That work is nothing to joke about. It is a work of blood...If you dig for even a short distance, you cannot sleep at night due to tiredness...[but] with time we got used to it...our bodies had hardened. We even liked it; we started feeling body pains if we did not dig...
>
> We also had a problem with cooking...people did not know much about it. What disturbed us was something called beans; people did not know how to cook this thing. So they ate them raw and it gave children stomach ache and diarrhoea which became persistent. The government did not have any community education programs on cooking.

Hussein Mursalle was a teenager during their confinement. Some 30 years later, he had two wives and owned a farm, where one wife lived, and another home where they sold the produce and kept some livestock. Unlike the Orma elders, he came to terms with farming as an occupation. Some of this may be because he was much younger when he first learned to farm, and also it was a decision his community took themselves, a pragmatic response to their situation after confinement in the camps. Hussein also felt that the prejudice from some Orma and Boran towards farmers stemmed from pride as much as anything else:

> The herders...got everything they wanted from livestock and had no business with the land—that is why they said these things [against farming]. But there is nothing that makes one who farms "mad," a supernatural being. It's only that those herders had no problems that would make them take up "digging," so it was just said because of pride.
>
> It is an activity that is good because it gives us food and one does not have to sell the animals now and then to buy food and you eat what you plant—so there is nothing wrong with farming...But the herders made it custom and traditional rule that blacksmiths and farmers are inferior—so this is how they...put a distance between themselves and these other people.

With declining herds and cattle-rustling on the increase, Hussein believed the "fools" are those who don't grow their own food: "Now everybody is a farmer and whoever does not farm is a fool. Then, if someone farmed people wondered if he was mad—but now if you just follow livestock and depend only on food from the shop you are taken for a fool." Although he said he could never live without a few livestock, he saw no future in herding: "The life I want for my children is a settled life and not a nomadic one, a settled life where they can go to school and do some business."

A Different Kind of Migration

> Before, we only moved when there was a shortage of pasture but now we move in search of food. People are poor.
>
> —Girr Huka Kampe

Girr Huka Kampe, 62, also experienced time in a *daaba* camp in the early 1960s. He dated the decline of his Boran community from that confinement: "Since then our life has never been good again." Some five years after their release from the camp, the area they returned to was taken over for Meru National Park. "This is the land we lost, the land of nine rivers, which was taken from us and given to the wildlife and we—the ignorant people—got nothing, not even compensation. We lost that land like that and moved to Garba Tulla which is dry and has no pasture."

They lost most of their livestock and had to rely on famine relief: "I have a few livestock, about five. When I left that land...I had about 1,000 goats and about 700 head of cattle. I also had about 60 camels. I lost everything after we moved."

Despite loss of livestock, he maintained that they adapted their ceremonies and kept some traditions intact. "Our customs are our laws and so even if the

Boran have lost livestock they have not thrown away their laws." For example, "If in the old days a dowry was five or six heifers, today this can be reduced to as little as one and others do not pay even that, because the goodwill that existed between their grandparents is what is required and they can just marry without being asked for dowry."

But he carried a deep sense of loss:

> When I reflect back and think of that land's pasture and water and the many livestock that I had that time, I really feel sad, I feel bitter... At times I just stand on the other side of the park fence and look at the land because I still long for it...
>
> The little we have [now]—shelter over our heads and small plots—are of no significance compared to what we lost. We have a few schools. Sometimes the county council gives us bursaries to educate our children. Other times we sell firewood to pay for fees, pens, and books, so this is the kind of life we lead. To me this is no life.

The Search for Work

Having lost his cattle and access to seasonal grazing land, Girr Huka Kampe searched widely for work, but without success. "Although I have not taken my family with me, I have gone to many places. I went as far as Nairobi to look for a job." When interviewed he was growing vegetables and fruit to pay for his children's education. The need for employment was, however, constant and some men's nomadic life had continued, albeit in pursuit of paid work rather than following transhumance routes for pasture and water:

> Before, we only moved when there was a shortage of pasture but now we move in search of food. People are poor... Our life has become that of migrating, one of moving always; there are people who have a family of seven or ten who leave their families and go to Nairobi in search of a job and they get *bortha* [large sticks] and guard people's properties. Some of them get killed by thugs and robbers in the process.

Like his fellow Boran who was interviewed, he was not against farming on principle and was more measured in his discussion of the two lifestyles than the Orma elders who also feature in this chapter:

> These lifestyles, both are good, livestock is good and farming is also good for those who know how to do it well—but for us, we are not very good at it so even its goodness is not very much pronounced with us.

Given a choice he would have preferred to remain a herder:

> Because I know about livestock...they have good milk, good meat and even when sold it makes good money, but the small plot that we are farming has no benefit to us...The little sorghum that we grow has no market, the same thing with sugarcane and tomatoes...
>
> Even now my few cattle that I have, I move with them—especially during the dry season. I take my spear, axe, and a jerrican of water, and I go with the cattle and goats in search of pasture so that they survive the drought. When the dry spell is over, I bring the animals back...and come to town to check on those children who are in school, or who live in town. I sell a young bull or a goat and pay their school fees. So I am still in this life of mobility; I am not leaving the life of nomadism; neither am I staying away from towns—so I am in both.

Although Girr Huka Kampe had not completely lost his herder's identity, he was bitter about their inability to resist displacement: "Because it was the government, I could not fight."

> I feel very bitter about our removal. It's only that it's a government order and I could not defy it [that I did leave] but if it had been somebody else [ordering me], I would not have moved; I would rather have died...
>
> It was a forced thing, because that was our land, our grandfathers were born there, our great grandfathers were born there, the graves of our fathers are there, our grandfather's grave is there; our mother, our grandmother is all there—so it was force that moved us but it was not something that we liked.

The Next Generation

All the narrators in this chapter highlight the centrality of livestock to both Orma and Boran culture as well as to their livelihoods. Those who can no longer call herding their primary occupation expressed deep concern for their children, growing up in a world where the defining feature of their parents' existence had all but disappeared from their own. The story of 26-year-old Jare Mohammed Wario bore witness to the break-up of families that so many people described.

Jare was eight when his Orma family was evicted in 1981 from land that was turned into a registered game ranch on the border of Tsavo East National Park.[13] They were given no other land and had a difficult journey to Assa, where they were living when interviewed in 1999. Some of the evicted families were

Figure 4.2 Orma pastoralists watering livestock. Photo by James Pattison.

defeated by the conditions in the new location and left; Jare's family, however, stayed and dug deep wells, using the water "very economically, but still it was not enough":

> We lost many animals. I was told we had over 600 cows...but were left with only four...Four cows aren't enough for the family [to live]; that is why I ran away. I had to go out to look for a better way to survive. [I have] four brothers, and they are just like me. Some of them went to Malindi to look for a livelihood. They are watchmen.

He subsequently worked as a herdboy for nine years, and was rewarded by his employer with one animal for every year he worked. Three of these, which calved, he sent home to his family, who survived principally by making and selling charcoal. When he was not working, Jare returned to help them: "Sometime we sell it; sometimes we don't. The little we get from this business is what we use to buy food."

"Our future looks very bleak"

Jare had had no formal education or training to help him make a living, and he felt abandoned by the government. During the interview he admitted that he was prepared to kill any wildlife that threatened the livestock for which he was responsible, in part out of "revenge" for being removed from land that was subsequently given over for the exclusive use of animals rather than people. His community particularly resented not being offered jobs as park rangers; they knew the wild animals' habits well having living alongside them all their lives: "But the [ranch staff] thought that we were too inferior to them as we were illiterate."

In addition to having no formal schooling, Jare, like others featured in this chapter, regretted his inability to keep up with his Islamic learning:

> According to our religion and culture, when studying the Quran it is a must for everybody to pay a heifer after completing the course and I wasn't able to do that, so I didn't get a chance to study the Quran. After we lost our livestock my father sent me to a *madrasa* where I could learn a few things...not much but just something to perform with prayers.

He explained that the community could no longer afford to hold its traditional celebrations or build a mosque:

> During the old days, in the month of Mowlid [the celebration of the birth of the prophet Mohammed] our people used to gather, animals were slaughtered, food prepared, and we prayed hard. Now, as we haven't had animals for a long time, we can't afford [to celebrate]...
>
> There is nowhere the children can be taught...Nobody even comes together for prayer...because when we were moved and came here, nobody built a mosque. People couldn't because all the livestock died...[Before] we made a collection of animals from every family and then we sold them and built the mosque.

As previously described, one aspect of this decline in religious activity was a loss of social interaction: "Let alone other clans or extended families, close relatives do not visit one another now." Jare was also disappointed that the lack of cattle wealth meant that young men and women could not marry. But "the one [change] burning my heart most," he says, "is that our people have developed a culture that has never been seen in the Orma community, which is begging."

> The Orma community nowadays beg for maize and water...Once in a while I see chiefs and government distributing either a tin of 2 kilos or—the upper limit—two tins, to every household, which is actually not enough for the whole village. Some people have to miss out. This really burns my heart and makes me feel very bad.

Embracing the Settled Life

Some of the younger interviewees identified positive aspects of a life that was no longer dominated by livestock herding. Twenty-one-year-old Amina Bakero was fulsome in endorsing her family's new settled existence. They were forced to leave their grazing lands in Wadessa when the land was developed for an irrigation scheme. They traveled for two days and nights to Bura: "Now we have adopted town life. When we started moving, our cattle died on the way. The little that remained was sold and we decided to live in the town. My father started a shop and we never moved again."

Amina described a situation that was markedly different to that of Jare Mohammed Wario. At the time of the interview she was, unusually for women from her background, studying at Kenya Medical Training College. In contrast to most of her peers: "My time was consumed by education. If it were not for education I would also be married and bear children." Most women of her age group, she commented, were married in their teens, with two or three children, and struggling economically, while most men, she observed, had little to do and spent hours by the roadside, talking:

> After they were displaced they became demoralized—there is nothing they can do except their previous occupation—so the women end up fetching and selling water, sticks, firewood, and grass, and the men roam around the villages chatting. They go to bus stops to check on who has arrived from a journey and how many vehicles have passed by. If you make a mistake of asking them about a vehicle, they can even tell you its color!

Some of the money her father made from selling his remaining cattle paid her school fees, another unusual decision. "Boys were the only loved and educated ones. They say that boys, after they complete their studies, will be employed and assist their parents—but if they educate girls, they go to their husbands or become prostitutes."

Women's position had improved, she felt:

> [In the past] women were taken as inferiors in the home, they had no say in front of men, they were not even given the respect they deserved. They have now improved [their position], because the women are now working so they are now the same [as men]. They share decision-making...
>
> In the past men [did a lot]...digging wells, looking after animals and the whole family. [But] after losing their property [livestock] there is no proper job except charcoal burning, firewood and water-fetching, which is mostly done by women.

Measured Nostalgia

Amina remembers her life as a young girl, when she used to work the "grass for making houses, making ropes, milking goats and cows, moving with cattle—the whole of the nomadic life were the activities that I did...I fetched firewood; we held the calves when the cows were milked."

> [I remember] the drinking of milk whenever you want—but now milk is scarce and also expensive, so you cannot afford milk to drink by itself but only to put in tea. Also, the age mates used to play together. They plaited hair for one another and they danced in the traditional way, which is of course hard to find nowadays.

While she described feeling a certain nostalgia for the simplicity of the past, its social gatherings and rituals, and the periods of relaxation and celebration, she believed that her family's displacement had brought distinct advantages: "Now we are leading an urban life and a better life." For her, the greatest benefit was education: "We became civilized, educated people who understand what life is." Now they get the news from radio, television, and newspapers instead of "through messengers who told us what was said today in Bura town; at times they gave incomplete information."

She also welcomed the comfort of their new homes and she missed little about the constant moving around: "I don't miss it because it was hard—we used to move, with no water and no food, and people stayed for weeks without taking a bath, but now it is not so in our new homes."

Amina commented on how many young women were obliged to marry outside of their community, because of the practice of those with cattle shunning families making a living from farming or charcoal. In some ways she approved of the mixing with different cultures: "The tradition wanted us to remain alone Orma and Orma alone. But I see intermarriage as normal, and in fact I want it to be encouraged because we are also developing by doing so." But she was less certain about young people leaving their religion for the sake of an education. Like Jare, she knew quite a few young people who had done so and as a result had been "cursed and chased away from their homes." She laid this family break-up squarely at the door of resettlement: "Yes, loss of property [livestock] is the key to all this."

Accelerated Change

> Those of us who lost our animals have deviated from our culture, and this therefore makes us two distinct groups.
>
> —Roba Dakota

These interviews illustrate how, for some of the displaced Orma pastoralists in particular, the speed of change was extreme. Although long-standing tensions with the government and other groups have been putting the pastoralist way of life under strain for decades, the almost total loss of livestock that generally accompanied these narrators' displacement has been a massive accelerator of change. Many of those interviewed had lost virtually all their animal wealth within a year—and with that the diet, religious and cultural ritual, occupation, and status that these animals represented. Because of the taboos associated with other forms of livelihood, another "class" of Orma had developed.

These stories about what happened to those Orma and Boran in the 1980s and 1990s suggest that the loss of their animals and the social networks that sustained their way of life made them much less able to cope with the challenges of the next decades. Some have been able to shake off long-held prejudice and adapt to new circumstances and occupations; some have been supported to gain an education. But for many, the change in lifestyle they underwent as a result of displacement—and the sense of isolation and shame that often accompanied this—made them particularly vulnerable to impoverishment as a result of the recurrent drought, further conflict, and mismanagement of the region's resources that were to follow.

CHAPTER 5

"The people's place became the animals' place"

Resettlement Policies and Conservation in Botswana and Namibia

We have lost our land, the ruling of it, leadership, a generous life, culture and traditional healing systems, which was our whole lifestyle. Now our lives are dependent on the other tribes. The government stopped us from moving around, but they do not give us the power to improve the Khwe communities' life like the other tribes do, through what they are receiving from the government... We are the last, the last ones in a bad life, not like the other tribes here in Botswana.

—Maruta Diyonga

Sixty-year-old Maruta Diyonga gave this interview from his home in the small settlement of Kaputura in Botswana's Okavango Panhandle. He belonged to one of many groups of San in Botswana who had been removed from lands to which they had a long-term attachment but which had been redesignated as commercial farms, cattle ranches, and wildlife management and reserve areas. As a result of removal and exclusion from their traditional lands, they found themselves, according to Maruta, without a voice, dependent on others, living in poorly serviced settlements with neither the training to take up employment, nor the possibility of pursuing important aspects of their previous way of life.

Chumbo Maraka, from the same settlement, was 57 years old when he was interviewed in 1999; he had grown up living what he described as "the past way of life." He explained that they'd agreed to settle, as the government demanded, because they welcomed the modern services that they were led to believe would be provided: "Of course we agreed—we also need the present life." His disappointment with life following resettlement was because he felt it had left them stranded, no longer able to live as they did, but lacking the promised benefits of modern life. Both men, and the other San who describe their experiences in this chapter, indicated that they were prepared to become part of modern society, but that they wished to do so on the basis of mutual respect, equal citizenship, and opportunity. Chumbo Maraka said: "The government stopped us from moving around and said that we should live in one place only, and then they would support us in what we need in our present life... [but] it has not attended to the needs of our community for many years."

Their strong sense that they were being ignored is the more striking because the San, also known as Bushmen, are by no means an unknown or forgotten people, having a far higher profile than most of the displaced groups in this volume. But many San felt that they had gained little from the wealth of coverage by outsiders intrigued by their society. The San have been romanticized in literature, in the anthropology of the region, and to a certain extent in indigenous politics, and their aboriginal status and traditional form of existence on the margins of the African continent has often served to define them as vulnerable and in need of protection. Such paternalism, however, while it has contributed to the acceptance of important new international laws on indigenous rights and some concessions at home, has yielded few tangible benefits for Maruta Diyonga and his fellow San. The nonrealization of the political rights of the hunter-gatherer lifestyle as a legitimate land use system has its sharpest impact in the involuntary relocation that has taken place to create new game parks and reserves in south-western Africa, which is the subject of this chapter focusing on Botswana and Namibia.[1]

The interviews that inform this chapter were gathered between 1999 and 2001 by San interviewers as part of a wider political initiative by the San to better represent and pursue their interests at a time of rapid and enforced social change. Through the personal stories collected, people affected by the removals took the opportunity to express their own thoughts about development and its influence and, aware that a new generation was growing up with very different experiences, to document their traditional knowledge.[2]

The accounts represent the experience of a small group of San, some living in Namibia and the majority in Botswana. As their stories unfold, they reveal that their experience of and response to resettlement has continued to be shaped by their often negative experiences of competition for resources with other groups. These range from European settlers to different Bantu-speaking groups such as the Tswana and Herero, especially farmers and cattle ranchers seeking land and water—but also successive governments who have sought to enclose the land for tourism, environmental protection, and resource exploitation. A strong theme in the interviews is the degree to which these San narrators felt that contact with others in the settlements, in this instance particularly the Hambukushu in the Okavango, had worked to their disadvantage. They describe experiencing prejudice and bullying in the schools and finding themselves dependent on other ethnic groups for work and political representation.

Introduction and Background

It is estimated that 100,000 San, belonging to more than 13 different language groups, live in the southern African region today, the majority in Botswana and Namibia.[3] In Angola, Zimbabwe, Zambia, and South Africa, the remaining San live in small bands on the margins of mainstream society. Only in Namibia, where many San groups have been displaced by the establishment of Etosha National Park and by commercial farms and mining concessions, do a few retain any scope for practicing some of their hunter-gatherer traditions, in the Nyae Nyae Conservancy.

Settlement Policies in Botswana

In Botswana, the San's traditional livelihoods have been under almost constant threat from cattle-ranching, wildlife conservation, and mining, as well as from prejudice from society in general and from colonial powers and post-independence governments. Here, as elsewhere, the dispossession of their land has been a creeping phenomenon. As the cattle industry grew to dominate Botswana's economy, large areas of land traditionally inhabited by the San were carved up into private and communal ranches. Many San families remained on those ranches, but as laborers with no legal title to the land or other forms of security. When no longer able to work, perhaps sick or too old, they were frequently deemed to be squatters and joined other destitute families looking for employment, settling on the fringes of desert towns such as Ghanzi and Maun.

Resettlement of the San in Botswana as a policy had its roots in the immediate postcolonial period. Botswana gained independence in 1966, and in the early 1970s, the government began its Bushman Training and Settlement Project. This piloted a resettlement scheme and offered some of the San who had been pushed off the land, primarily by cattle ranchers, subsistence plots and houses on sites where they were promised basic facilities (water, clinics, and schools) as well as help with projects to generate income. In 1978 this project became the Remote Area Development Programme (RADP), aimed at all "remote area dwellers" (RADs), regardless of ethnic identity.

The Botswana government, in direct contrast to neighboring South Africa with its system of apartheid, had determined at independence to ignore ethnic and cultural differences and to treat all its citizens as one people. Its RAD Programme now included some of the Bakgalagadi, Herero, and Hambukushu peoples, who are all Bantu groups, as well as the San. The premise was that geographical isolation and inadequate access to services were the primary constraints to the development of all of Botswana's remote populations.

However, in this instance, the government's decision not to acknowledge ethnic identity meant it failed to address some deep-rooted issues. The development schemes in the settlements were based on the assumption that the San's problem was simply poverty. Yet most of those familiar with the history and development of the San would assert that their cultural difference—and prejudice and discrimination against their culture—was and is at the root of their disadvantage and poverty.[4] The other remote populations sharing the settlements, although among Botswana's poorest, still had a status higher than the San, were better educated, and tended to monopolize services and opportunities for employment. A 2003 review of the RAD Programme highlighted the particular situation of the San "who are historically disadvantaged, and who cannot easily take advantage of their entitlement...without special assistance," assistance that had not been forthcoming.

Several decades of development have seen only a few San reach the level of a university education or really prosper in mainstream society. The people are still not recognized as a separate ethnic group with specific needs, and they only have representation in the House of Chiefs or parliament through other tribes' chiefs.

Resettled in the Name of Conservation

From the late 1980s, groups of San also were forcibly removed from the Central Kalahari Game Reserve (CKGR). The CKGR—a huge tract of the Kalahari Desert—was set up in 1961 by the British colonial authorities as a wildlife reserve and to protect the land use rights of the local people. In recent decades, the recognition that the reserve, with its abundant game and untouched environment, represented a valuable resource, especially for tourism and diamond mining, led the Botswana government to begin removing people to official settlements. Legal arguments about whether the original intention of the reserve applies in a changed political environment remain inconclusive, in spite of court cases on behalf of some of the San who were moved from the CKGR. The government justified its resettlement policy on the basis that the provision of modern services—water, education, health care, housing—was not only out of place in a game reserve, but would be hugely expensive, due to the area to be covered. It also claimed that the presence of modern-day San, in growing numbers, was incompatible with conservation.

To have the benefit of water supplies, schools, clinics, and jobs, the government had long been urging the San to move to settlements; other benefits offered were pensions for the eligible and various forms of state welfare. The same process had happened to the San in and around other game reserves, such as the Moremi

Game Reserve, a few decades earlier. ‡Geru Mananyana, who was in his nineties when interviewed, was one of many who felt their way of life was sacrificed in the name of environmental conservation: "The government has only saved the world, but not the people."*

Organizations working with the San, such as the Kuru Family of Organisations, have documented many examples of discrimination and mistreatment, and of low morale in the settlements.[5] Families and once-cohesive communities have broken up as adults searched for paid employment and children attending school were forced to live away from home in hostels. Opportunities to gather *veld* foods on land around the settlements proved minimal, as the land was heavily overused. The San freedom to hunt was drastically proscribed by law, and there was little scope for earning a living beyond selling crafts to passing traders, or intermittent work for Hambukushu farmers.

Namibia

The indigenous San of Namibia have similarly long faced competition for land and water, notably from the cattle-keeping Khoi-Khoi; then from the Herero herders in the 1600s; and from white farmers, mainly Boers, in the 1800s. In 1884, the area became a German colony, known as South West Africa, and it was the German authorities who first proclaimed Etosha a national park, in 1907. In 1915, after Germany's defeat in the First World War, the League of Nations gave South Africa the mandate to administer South West Africa. The persecution of the San declined in severity as they became less of a threat to the settlers, but "they were still perceived by the authorities as people with even fewer rights and needs than other Africans."[6]

In 1950, South Africa refused a UN request to give up the territory, and the bulk of southern Namibia's viable farmland was parceled into farms owned by white settlers. It was renamed Namibia in 1968. (South Africa continued to call it South West Africa.) It was not until 1990 that Namibia gained independence. Although the new government gave a degree of recognition to the needs and status of the San, and its land policy prioritized them, a 2007 report found that it had largely failed to deliver on these promises. The San remain the most marginalized people in Nambia, and some 80 percent lack land rights.[7]

The Narrators

It is usual for the San to identify themselves by local groupings based on linguistic differences; the group in Botswana whose experiences feature in this chapter

---

*San languages are characterized by clicks that are produced by drawing the tongue sharply away from points on the roof of the mouth. Clicks are a type of consonant and are usually represented by symbols.

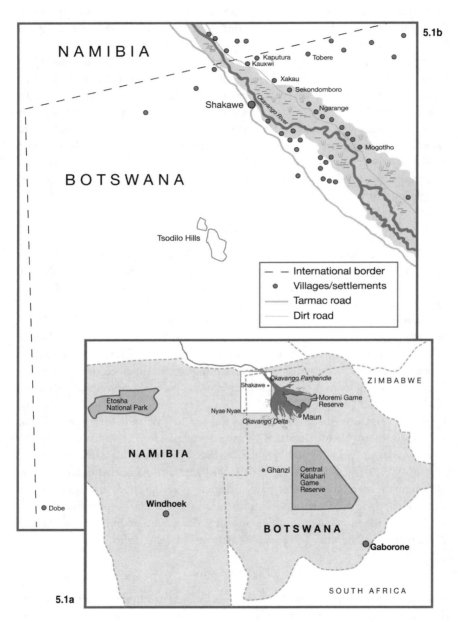

Figure 5.1 a. Botswana and Namibia, showing the game reserves and parks from which many San interviewed in this chapter were displaced. b. Detail of area where many of the San narrators in Botswana settled. Map by Julie Anson.

are the Khwe and the ||Anikhwe, living on the fringes of the "panhandle" of the Okavango Delta, a stretch of approximately 90 kilometers (56 miles) from where the river enters Botswana from Namibia before fanning out into the desert. Some narrators were displaced by the establishment of the Moremi Game Reserve while others were subject to the government's settlement policies. They were interviewed some 20 years after the first government settlements were established.[8]

This chapter also draws on interviews with the Hai||om, in Namibia, many of whose families were removed from the area that became the Etosha National Park and came to "rest" on farms, as laborers, or in squatter settlements round townships.

"We Have No Power over Our Own Lives"

The Khwe in Botswana

The present life has destroyed our lands, culture, and leadership, and our past life has been lost since we met with the other tribes... Now today we find that the Khwe communities are in trouble because we have no power over our own lives; we are just in the other tribes' hands.

—Peter Goro

Resettlement has led the San to adopt permanent rather than temporary accommodation. Traditionally the San lived in bands of 10 to 40 people, which, contrary to popular stereotype, occupied well-defined territories enjoying access to water, plant foods, game, and other resources. The San often refer to themselves as "mobile" rather than nomadic, returning as they do to specific places. The idea of fixed permanent housing however is largely alien. The Khwe, the group to whom these narrators in Botswana belong, would leave their base to go on hunting trips, and would also sometimes build temporary camps, as Ôâna Djami, aged 63, recalled:

When hunters killed a giraffe far away, not near to the camp, they had to move to that place where the giraffe was killed, but that did not mean that they had left for good. The purpose was just to eat the meat and use the skin for making clothes, shoes and bags. After these activities they moved back to the original place. The Khwe community was known as mobile, but not nomadic. Nomadic [to us] means that people have to leave their place and move for good.

Ôâna Djami remembered how they sometimes set up temporary camps when they needed better supplies of wild food and animals:

The old men had to search where and which lands had good natural features... After [a successful] search... then the old men gathered the community together and allowed them to go to the new place and make a camp there. In the assembly meeting they narrated which area had the good resources. They had collected some wild food, which they showed the community...The day after the assembly meeting everyone would leave, but would say that they were not leaving the old camp for good, but would be back again.

The activities at the new camp were that while the women gathered wild fruits, the men had to make some storage containers [for the fruits], but not all the men, only some of them—because the other men had to go out hunting. After the collection of wild food and the hunting in the new camp, they would move back to the old camp. These foods—wild fruits and animal meat, which was already dried—had to be carried back to the old camp before the community left the new camp. When the community saw that there was nothing more to carry then they would all return to the old camp.

Tanaxu Khôâkx'oxo explained that their traditional huts were made of woven grasses supported by wooden sticks and poles, and were easily transportable. After being settled in Ngarange, in the Okavango Panhandle, such traditional shelters were replaced with the Setswana style of housing, using mud or cement bricks, and iron sheeting for roofs. This was partly, he said, because the grass they traditionally used was in short supply in the resettlement location and also because they no longer followed game or searched for food and water, thus removing the need for "movable" homes:

> We used only grass...When the rain came we did not get wet, and when you woke in the morning you would see: Oh! It had rained during the night! When we wanted to go and stay somewhere else, we used to take our house with us because it was removable...
>
> Today we sleep in Setswana houses...Now there is no grass for making our traditional huts and because of the lack of rain the grass does not grow up to the required size. The elephants are too many, and they are a menace because they eat up the grass. The cattle also eat the grass. When we moved from one place to another we removed our huts, the women took the blankets and some other property and then we went where there was plenty of water and food.

Restrictions and Limitations

> The present life has fenced us in.
>
> —Peter Goro

With the government settlement program came new policies on hunting and gathering, which had a significant impact on the narrators and on their ability to support themselves. These restrictions were one of the most painful and resented manifestations of government control over the lives of the San people. Traditional land uses such as hunting and gathering were not recognized in newly introduced policies such as Botswana's National Agricultural Land Policy (1991) and the Tribal Land (amendment) Act of 1993, and access to natural resources was subsequently steadily reduced, as the implementation of these policies allowed much land to pass "into the hands of those outside the 'remote areas,' and belonging to different ethnic groups... [often] for the purposes of establishing cattle posts."[9]

Tanaxu Khôâkx'oxo was 59 years old and he, like many male narrators, recalled at length how he had learnt to hunt and trap, and the many complex rules involved, including who eats which parts of the kill. Many women recalled the array of different fruits and foods they gathered from the *veld* (the Southern African bush). The interviews reveal a striking sense of loss among the relocated San. Tanaxu Khôâkx'oxo explained how the laws prohibiting hunting forced him to settle among the Hambukushu, to work on their farms and to rely on them for food. To hunt in the new settlements, people needed permits, and many of the older generation could not read and did not understand the bureaucracy of applying for permits. They feared the wildlife officials if they were caught hunting. Similarly, many of the traditional *veld* fruits were no longer found near the settlements in the Okavango Panhandle. Xokwe Tendere, a woman of 60 from Sekondomboro village, said, "Today we are no longer using or eating any of these foods because of the government, and since our parents died, we are just mixed with the Hambukushu people. We do not have oxen for ploughing, and are just working on the farms of the Hambukushu."

Peter Goro spoke forcefully about the menial jobs they were forced to do for the other Bantu groups among whom they lived. The fact that their children were also obliged to work in this way had a detrimental effect on their education and limited their opportunities:

> We are tired of looking to someone else's hands for what we need. What we need is to operate our Khwe lives ourselves—because that would improve our lives, just as it has improved the lives of the other tribes before us. Today you find us looking after the herds of the other tribes, we stamp millet for them, we collect wood for them and we also fetch water for the Hambukushu tribe. This is our unhappy way of life...
>
> Their children do not stay home to look after their own cattle; the Khwe people have to do this. All the Hambukushu children attend school and others attend [higher education] and some are working for the government. This means that their children are learning to be wise and clever like the adults, so they can improve their life. So today they are starting to take whole families of us to look after their cattle at home.

Those who worked on the fields of the Hambukushu would often be paid with some of the produce, mainly sorghum or maize, rather than cash. The narrators depicted a troubled relationship between the Khwe and the Hambukushu. Some advantages were gained, for example in learning about cultivation, but most spoke of dominance and discrimination.

‡Geru Mananyana was in his nineties and living in Tobere. He expressed frustration with development policies that were inappropriate or not feasible without sustained support:

> They have changed our way of life and said that we should try "crop farming" on our lands, and the department would pay us an amount from the harvest yearly, and for ploughing as well. Even with the above objective of the government, the Khwe people do not know what they will plough with, because they are known as the poorest people in the world.

The difficulties for the San in taking up a settled life based on food production have been discussed elsewhere, with researchers Draper and Kranichfeld emphasizing that the San "were poorly equipped to compete with ethnic groups that were far wealthier in expertise, technology and stock ownership...Even the poorest of the Bantu had a clear economic advantage over [them]."[10] "The Report on the Review of the RAD Programme" acknowledged that "arable agriculture is unlikely to become a major source of livelihood in the remote settlements, because of low rainfall and poor soils. Where crops have been grown, they are frequently of a type that remote area communities do not consume, and there have been problems over selling the produce."[11]

Employment and Income: "Less than the word 'less'"

Although resettlement brought about a process of accelerated change and uncertainty, it would be misleading to suggest that the San were entirely unprepared for or unused to change. The San had, of course, been part of the money economy before resettlement; several narrators discussed their experience of being farm laborers and of working in the South African mines. For many, working as migrant laborers was their first exposure to paid employment and the cash economy. Several narrators, including Moyo Tcinde, perceived this to be a significant turning point for the San: "We left the past life when we had to go and work for money to buy clothes. That is when the past life was lost." Chumbo Maraka made a similar observation: "The present lifestyle started in the Khwe community with the process of its people going to work in the mines. This is how we learnt about 'artificial work,' money paid per month."

Ôâna Djami, who was settled in Ngarange, recalled his time in the mines:

> We worked for nine months, and then after finishing the work, we got pay, and with this money we bought clothes for our wives, blankets, belts, sheets...we also bought some cups. We also bought some buckets and shoes. After the nine months were finished, we came home with the gifts we had bought for our wives at home.
>
> When we arrived at our homes, our parents were so happy, because we returned home alive...Our parents then killed a goat for us, and...the following day we gave our wives the clothes that we had bought. They liked the clothes we bought for them. It was very nice. When other family members saw the clothes that your wife was wearing, they would say "He has a good job," and started asking if there was another good job, because he and his wife were still wearing [traditional] leather clothes.

Work in the mines offered excitement and reward—money, modern clothes, and implements—but ultimately it was only going to be for a limited period. The restructuring of the regional economy and the end of apartheid reduced migrant

Figure 5.2 Ôâna Djami, one of the narrators in Botswana. Photo by Alison White.

laboring opportunities in South Africa for the San and others in the region, and alternatives were not available to fill the gap. Ôâna Djami explained:

> Money at that time was important, and we used it to buy many things like blankets...[But] If you were not working in the mine, there was no way to get money in the past. The person who was working on the mine was the only one who knew money at that time, and he was the person who could count his money and say, "This is one, three, or five *pula*"[12]...That is how we lived then, and today we men are living here without work.

Tanaxu Khôâkx'oxo was also a migrant laborer in the South African mines. Several of the women narrators described how hard it was to get enough food for their families when the men went away, and when Tanaxu returned from his first contract he found his family struggling with their daily lives. He chose not to return to the mines because he felt he should remain at home to help out. However, he found himself without any real opportunities for earning a living, apart from short-term farm laboring. "When I came back from the mines I started [helping with] ploughing. Thereafter I lost my job and even now I am not working."

According to ‡Geru Mananyana, often the only income-earning opportunity for the San was construction work offered as "drought relief" and he commented,

> The amount paid in this project is less than the word "less," which means that the people are not able to buy shoes and soap. The amount may be outstanding for several months, which then means that once they receive it, it goes into accounts paying for food and clothes during that period of several months.

Moving closer to economic opportunities was one of the real "lures" or promises of resettlement, but it had not delivered. The 2003 "Report on the Review of the Remote Area Development Programme" concluded that there were "few livelihood opportunities...and resources around them are currently being depleted...Employment opportunities are scarce...since they are far from suppliers, and from markets where the produce of local enterprise can be sold. The market within the settlements is very small, consisting mainly of a small number of government workers."[13]

Natural Resources

> In the past our lives were organized by rules that we all agreed to...The most important...was the rule to take care of the environment, which was important

to our survival. Now, today, the land has gone... Our waterholes are all dry, and we can only remember some of the *veld* food that we used to eat in the past.

—Moronga Ntemang

The impact of having had their access severely restricted to the natural resources that formed a vital part of their livelihoods was more than economic. The San described losing important spiritual and cultural connections to those resources. This was a source of deep unease, which permeated the interviews. Tanaxu Khôâkx'oxo expressed some of the anxiety this caused those who grew up respecting the "rules" of their former way of life:

> If you were hunting you could find animals anywhere because you respected the law of hunting in the forest. Today none of us would be lucky—even if we could still hunt—because today's people do not respect our tradition or culture as in the past. It is not good if you do not respect your own culture, but you respect other cultures. Even for God it is not good; and if you lose respect for the culture God has given you, then God will no longer give you what you want in life.

Moyo Tcinde spoke movingly of how he learnt to hunt by following his father but as a result of the restrictions, he suggests, a certain peace of mind has been lost: "The government has taken our animals from our control, and we do not know how to get the government to give it back... these animals were given to us by God, saying, 'This is your life.' So today we do not live peacefully because our game has been taken away from our control." Unemployed yet unable to hunt, trap, or gather food as before, he added: "We do not know how to feed our children."

The anxiety associated with a loss of access to their traditional hunter-gathering lands was further heightened by the observed deterioration of the land. ‡Geru Mananyana described how farming activities had degraded the environment and depleted plant resources. *Veld* fires were described as being larger and more dangerous than before:

> In the past we kept and controlled the earth as it is, because we knew that it was our 'farm'... Our grass has gone because of the *veld* fires; we used the grass for thatching roofs and it stopped soil erosion... Wild foods have been destroyed because of the *veld* fires of today. [Ranchers and farmers] also cut down trees for fields and fences; that is how the Khwe communities' lands have disappeared today... Many lands used by the Khwe communities in the past have been made into pastures by the government of the present day.

‡Geru also pointed out that their traditional territories have been divided by national borders: "The lands which were used by the Khwe communities of

the past life, were bisected by [the border between] the countries Botswana and Namibia, and it has separated the Khwe communities' lands used in the past life."

Recurrent drought and increased demands on the land and water from growing human and cattle populations and from diamond mining have also had an effect on water supplies; narrators said that their old wells and other water sources had dried up. The scarcity of water was a factor in the decision of many to move to government settlement villages, but in so doing, and finding themselves without piped water or wells, they described becoming dependent on settled farmers. Peter Goro lived, as did several other narrators, in Tobere, in an area that at the time of interview still lacked services, including water. This caused problems with other residents living nearby who had water supplies. Moyo Tcinde settled in Ngarange, where they too were still waiting for the promised supply. As he pointed out, this had made them dependent on others: "Today we are mixed with the Hambukushu and we do not have our own wells as we had in the past. Now we have to ask for water from the Hambukushu people."

This feeling of being "cheated" into resettlement with promises of modern services and mainstream opportunities was a consistent theme in many of the interviews. Chumbo Maraka lived in Kaputura, another settlement in the Okavango Panhandle that lacked essential services: "The government has said that they would support us, if we pass our needs down to the government offices, for example with projects, transport, developments by extension services and [education]." But he was disillusioned:

> We do not have any of the good life—we do not have hospitals, clinics, shopping centers, and schools here in Kaputura village, and we do not have a water supply like the other villages, such as Kauxwi, Xakau, Shakawe...This has already been reported to the government, many years ago.

The government had seemingly ignored their complaints: "We are tired of waiting for the government to help us with our needs."

Frustration and Representation

> There is one thing...which makes me unhappy and that is that we should be allowed to speak for ourselves just as the main groups do today. I repeat that I would like the government to give us a way to speak for ourselves as the main groups do. This is what makes me unhappy, and I sleep with this unhappiness and think about it all day.
>
> —Chumbo Maraka

From the interviews given, it would appear to be the case that much of Chumbo Maraka's frustration about "the present life," and that of other narrators, had to do with a lack of political representation. The narrators voiced a strong sense of powerlessness, an inability to change their circumstances. Many narrators described how they had sent off letters and complaints to the government, which others present on their behalf, but nothing had happened. The fact that most San groups live in places that are physically isolated from centers of decision making is a contributory factor, but so was their marginal position in society: the San started with the disadvantage of being outside the mainstream political structures, lacking a voice in society.

Chumba Maraka was an unofficial leader—his role had not been formalized by the government, he explained: "Here in Kaputura village, I'm the Khwe chief of the traditional chiefdom of the past. My father lived here in Kaputura land before the independence of Botswana." The San today are represented through the existing government structures, which came into place at Botswana's independence in 1966. These represent the many different groups of people now sharing the same land, and the same settlements, with the San. But many San felt they were not truly represented by these elected chiefs because they said that the other groups, being better educated and more powerful, failed to respect the San or to advance their interests through government institutions. Peter Goro, a 59-year-old narrator, explained the problem facing the San:

> This present life is not good for the Khwe, because they do not have their own chiefs to represent them and solve their problems like the other tribes do. People of other tribes say that the Khwe are "owned" by them at present, because we have no Khwe chief like they do. They say that in the olden days their fathers tamed the Khwe communities like cattle, and we had to do the hard work.

Living on the fringes of the settlement at Tobere, in an area occupied by more prosperous Bantu-speaking Hambukushu farmers, Peter Goro described the situation. "We the Khwe are not represented, and do not have an elder or headman to support us. The present Hambukushu headman has to represent both the Khwe and the Hambukushu tribes." He was "surprised" by this:

> The government said that Tobere village would only belong to the Khwe, but now a Hambukushu man is going to be the chief. We know there are Hambukushu chiefs in Sekondomboro, Ngarange, [and] other villages, but the government gave some villages to the Khwe community only. Today we find Hambukushu tribes also living there, taking over our land and voting for their chief to rule over us on our lands.

He gave his interpretation of why such things had happened:

> The difference is that all the Bantu-speaking people were well educated. These
> people are the government of today, and we are in their hands, and we the Khwe
> people are "owned" by the Hambukushu. I do not like it, because these people
> own us like tame animals, and in the past we did not live like this.
>
> I am just a person who lived a happy life in the past with gathering of fruits
> and hunting. I was used to eating different types of food like honey...I was
> hunting but I did not destroy my wildlife...Today we find that the lands used
> by our animals are now used for crops, and the animals are fearful of open areas,
> which make them stay far away from us.
>
> This was our life from the time of our great grandparents...The ones who
> tried to break up our leadership were the Hambukushu who also tried to change
> our land and culture. That caused our families to break up or separate and we
> started accepting their rules and lifestyle. The present life has destroyed our
> lands, culture, and leadership, and our past life has been lost since we met with
> the other tribes...
>
> Now today we find that the Khwe communities are in trouble because we
> have no power over our own lives; we are just in the other tribes' hands. The
> present life has fenced us in, like a cattle kraal [enclosure], which is very dif-
> ficult. Everything that the government gives to the Khwe community only ends
> up in the hands of the other tribes. They take our support from the government
> for themselves, thus they have tamed us like animals in their villages.

The other Bantu groups had an advantage over the San, he stressed, because they
"are all educated and qualified in the skill of reading and writing." He talked
about how the San "understood" their way of life in the past and how knowledge
was handed down from generation to generation, but the rapid changes of the
last decades had brought about "a new lesson of life for us we do not know or
understand." Without representation, he saw little chance of improving their
situation:

> The government should enable us to have a Khwe chief to improve our society
> as the other tribes do. If we had a member of parliament for the Khwe he would
> act with the government to support the needs of the Khwe tribe...This is the
> only key to the future.

He summed up his position:

> We are tired of living with the other tribes, because they represent us in govern-
> ment. Because they think that we are not well educated, they share the govern-
> ment benefits they receive for us amongst themselves, and we receive nothing.
> We also want to do things for ourselves like the other tribes do.

A Gradual Process (Namibia)

The people's place became the animal's place, and the Hai‖om had to get out.
—Kadison Komob

So far this chapter has focused on the Khwe living in the Okavango Panhandle. Kadison Komob lives in Namibia, a member of the Hai‖om group of San who formerly lived in the territory now claimed by the Etosha National Park. At the time of his interview, he was working in a garage for the Ministry of Environment and Tourism, at Okaukuejo, one of the camps within Etosha. His story was one of gradual change and dispossession:

> Life in the past was difficult sometimes, but the people were traveling freely, and they could walk where they wanted to. In this present life, you cannot move freely, everything is prohibited and you also cannot eat the food that you saw then...there were a lot of things that were very good [about the past], but sometimes there was also hunger...There were some men who were too lazy to work with the bow and arrow, and just slept in bed, waiting for the neighbors to give him some food. Those things were also there.

He explained that his people had had some contact with tourists there even before he was born. He described how the San used to be taken in trucks to perform dances for them:

> The Germans brought them with trucks to Okaukuejo, and there they had to do the traditional dances. They danced and performed traditional games, and when they had finished, they were taken back. Okay, that was good when we were staying like that, but later we heard that the Hai‖om people must get out of that place, and that it would be proclaimed a game park.[14]

Kadison Komob depicted a gradual process whereby their traditional way of life was restricted, until eventually "the people's place became the animal's place, and the Hai‖om had to get out." In childhood, he said, he learned the different skills and rules of hunting and tracking from his grandfather, as well as how to make clothes and other items out of animal skin. But as the number of tourists grew, rules started being imposed about which animals could be killed:

> During that time they started saying that the big animals should not be killed such as giraffe...Then later we heard that they said that the goats should be removed from the game park and be killed. They took the goats [we kept] out of the game park, and we remained with only our dogs and bows and arrows.
> They took our things out and the [South Africans] were coming in. When the whites became more numerous in the Game Park, they said that we

should...not suffer from hunger [and] they started shooting animals for us, and gave us the meat as well as sugar and tobacco...We were even given clothes, but we did not know what plan they had in mind for us...They told the men to work by making a road with axes, and they started from Namutoni, and then via Okaukuejo to Outjo.[15]

The implication was that by culling the wildlife and providing the San with meat, park staff were removing any justification for them to hunt. Next, he said, their hunting dogs were killed by "the whites" and the Hai‖om finally left the area and were taken to surrounding Boer farms; later their bows and arrows were confiscated by the police. He also described what seems to have been a policy designed to bring disunity among the relocated population and undermine any possibility of resistance:

They were the police officers. They were the ones who divided the people. For example: if we were two neighbors, those two people were given to one different farmer [respectively]. So we were divided and divided.

He ended his description of this process by saying:

We think of lots of things, because they took the land from us while we saw it, and you cannot really forget if someone has taken your property while you were looking at them; that is really difficult. That is why we feel the pain, because it was our forefathers' land. It does not matter if you are not aware of the land, but we knew that it was our land. They took the land and we do not have access to it, and also we have no benefit from that land. They don't even give us another piece of land outside or even inside these empty places.[16]

Nowadays we want to wear European clothes, and we have forgotten about our own clothes...[But] we did not really lose our culture and tradition...People still know a few things...how to gather [foods] and how to make a bow and arrow. We still have a few women here who go and gather at Ombika. We are only afraid because you cannot just walk around [the land] as before, and that is a big problem.

Kadison Komob described work as being scarce; he thought most jobs went to the Ovambo, the largest ethnic group in Namibia: "Today it is difficult, because there is no work for our people, only for the Ovambo." He described the hurt that prejudice against the San caused him:

I cannot really talk about having a good time, because we do not have any peace. Whenever I sleep or am working, and if someone tells me something bad about myself, then my heart is unhappy. I feel as if I am being discriminated against, and I do not have good times in my life.

He explained that he couldn't say that he was "hindered" in his current life, but that the thought of what had been lost saddened him:

> There is nothing that hinders me, but if I look at the old people, and remember how they walked around, looking for wild food, then I think of how the old people must have thought and felt [when they were displaced], and even I am very unhappy about how they feel, those who were used to the bush. Those are my special feelings, and I don't have rest in my heart.

Negotiating Past and Present

While the dispossession of their land, in both Botswana and Namibia, has been a gradual process, resettlement accelerated the pace and content of change for the San, because the shift from being mobile to being settled entailed such a fundamental modification of lifestyle and introduced new risks and uncertainties. As the accounts of mining and farm laboring revealed, these communities had already undergone considerable change and had ever-increasing contact with mainstream society and the modern world. And while there were some laws driving change, such as those proscribing their freedom to hunt, or prohibiting them from following their tradition of burying their dead uncoffined, the interviews suggested that social pressure was another force for change. Older narrators often expressed dismay at the degree to which the younger generation was influenced by the customs of outsiders.

Katjire Seloka, a 75-year-old male, was one of many who regretted that young people no longer respected some of their traditions: "Now you cannot tell other people about the past because they will say you like the past things or you are prehistoric; they want the modern things, so there is no help." The costs were material and psychological. Tanaxu Khôâkx'oxo, for example, says his people felt burdened by expenses involved in the "mainstream" marriage customs they were following: "In the past [when] we married...we did not have to give the parents thousands [of *pula*] as today. We are lost today, because people are marrying giving rings but in the past we did not use rings, we just married each other." And several narrators drew attention to the rise in antisocial behavior that has accompanied the dilution of their traditional way of life. They felt people had lost their self-respect, which for some had led to problems with alcohol, and also to conflict between generations.

Some of the younger people interviewed acknowledged this trend away from tradition, and indicated that one factor was a growing lack of confidence to carry on doing things the San way because some of their traditions had been stigmatized as "primitive." Their experiences at school had tended to reinforce this. Peter Goro agreed that the fact that children who attended school usually stayed in hostels far from home for most of the year, living with other groups who have little knowledge of or respect for San custom, was a key factor:

> Because the young people attend school very far from our village, they have adapted to the other tribes' behavior in the schools, and have also learnt their culture, languages, and the relationships between the different tribes, as well as their lifestyle. They do not understand their own parents' past...I think the change in relationships [between young and old] in the Khwe communities is because we have forgotten our past.

The interviews reveal that some customs and traditional practices were continued and had been adapted to different contexts. Traditional healers and medicine, for example, were in demand in some of the new settlements. Nxisae Nxao, a young woman from the Ju|'hoansi San group, living in Dobe, a relatively remote settlement on the border with Namibia, explained:

> My people are not really living near to the hospital or the clinic. That's why they like the plant roots, because they are near them, and it is what they have been using in the old days...They don't like to go to the hospital or the clinics because most of them say: "When you go to the hospital you are going to die." That is what they believe—because most of the people go there when they are really sick, and they just die, because they have not gone to the clinic when their sickness was new.

Nxisae Nxao herself expressed a preference for modern medicine in certain circumstances: "There are some [traditional remedies] which can make you feel better, but there are some which can take a long time, so I prefer to go to the hospital. Sometimes I will use the plants and also the medicine from the hospital." It appeared from her testimony that this was one area where others respected the San ways: "Especially the Baherero and the Batswana, they like to use both systems. Some of them go to the hospital first, and when they don't feel better they go to the San people and ask for some plant roots." But later in this chapter another young woman, Victoria Geingos, described a different experience. She was living in a much more urban environment, and found that people in the towns were "laughing" at the practices of San traditional doctors.

Nxisae Nxao described *dikgaba,* a form of sickness or misfortune associated with ill will or punishment, which could be experienced by those pining for family members from whom they are separated. The fact that San children attending school had to live away from home for most of the year, plus the need for adults to search far and wide for work, lead to much separation within families, which was often mentioned with sadness and regret by the narrators. It seemed that it was usually the traditional healer who would identify that separation was the cause of ill health and that to be reunited with a distant family member may be the cure:

> This sickness called *dikgaba* happens like this. If I haven't gone to see my parents for a long time, maybe a year, they may talk about me a lot and worry about me, and this will cause me to catch the sickness called *dikgaba*... When you are suffering from *dikgaba* maybe you will have a headache, or maybe your body will just be thin. And when you try to go to the hospital they give you medicine but you don't recover, and when you go to the traditional healer he will sing the songs and realize that the person is suffering from *dikgaba*...
>
> Sometimes the traditional healer will notice you while you are just sitting round the fire, and he will be singing and afterwards he will say, "This person is suffering from such and such, and this person is suffering from *dikgaba* caused by her mother who is in such a place."
>
> To be healed from that sickness, the person who has caused it should come and touch the sick person, or lay his or her hands on the sick person, and use a plant that is also called *dikgaba*... If she cannot come herself then someone who is related to her can do it for her.

She added: "This disease is only caused by someone who is related to you—it cannot be caused by someone who is not related, even if they worry about you. And they must be elderly people, not just small children."

Nxisae Nxao was in her twenties and like several other narrators of her age demonstrated the perspective of younger people who were making some headway in negotiating past and present. For people such as Nxisae, this did not involve letting go of all the past, but finding elements within her community's history and traditions that she could retain and take pride in.

Education

> At school, even inside the classes, the students were laughing at us.
>
> —Victoria Geingos

Education was a constant theme in these accounts, but more often in a negative context. Among every other group of displaced people who feature in this book, there was near universal agreement that education was the one clear benefit of resettlement. However, the San accounts revealed a much more ambiguous attitude. Although they wanted to be educated, to close the gap between themselves and other Bantu groups, schooling had proved a double-edged sword with many believing it had hastened the erosion of their language and identity, and undermined self-esteem.

Peter Goro argued that the lack of mother-tongue education was at the heart of the problem:

> We also need school development in our villages, and to teach the Khwe language to both San and non-San, which we think would be helpful to us. Because then we could all read and write the Khwe language. We would like the other tribe to learn our language at school, which may stop them doing the things they are doing to us today. It is not fair that we have to learn their language, but they do not learn ours. We can speak their languages very fluently but they do not learn ours. They don't want to learn our language because they say they cannot speak "the language of slaves."
>
> We are living on Khwe land and therefore all of them should also learn the Khwe language. The only languages which should be taught here are English, Setswana, and Khwe. This will allow our new generation to live in peace in the future. We are very unhappy that our language is not taught at school. We would like our language to be made known at schools, then we would understand the present life better as well as one another, and then the new generations will have a better life. This is the only way to make our present life better.

Peter's views on the importance of learning San languages at school and how it could do much to foster individual and community esteem is echoed in many of the interviews. Their accounts suggested that one major reason why resettlement proved such a socially and culturally impoverishing experience for many San was the expectation that they would join mainstream society exclusively on its terms. Integration meant adopting the language and lifestyle of the Batswana and witnessing the steady erosion of the San's own languages and culture. Nowhere was this trend more evident than in education.

Attendance at boarding schools separated children and parents for long periods and in many cases, the narrators asserted, alienated children even further from older generations and from their culture. Interviewees recalled living with and being taught alongside other groups, who looked down upon them. In Botswana, the schools they attended taught in Setswana, almost exclusively by teachers who did not speak a San language. Some were unable to pronounce the children's names correctly because of the complicated "clicks," and so simply gave them new, easy to pronounce names. A similar situation prevailed in Namibia. The interviews were full of people's uncomfortable experience of school.

One of the most powerful stories came from 22-year-old Victoria Geingos of Namibia, whose experience ultimately inspired her to fight back against discrimination and prejudice. She began: "I am Victoria Geingos and I would like to tell my life story as a Hai‖om daughter growing up. The reason for this is to keep the historical background for our children, so that in the future they can know in which footsteps they would like to tread."

She related some of her educational history and how she was encouraged to work hard and try for university as part of a government initiative to support the San. But when she first went to school, she was humiliated: laughed at by other children for her language and also for her hair.[17] She describes the dawning realization that their language was not "official":

> The first day, arriving at the school, the children were laughing at us, the Hai||om children, because they found our language very funny. They even counted our hair, counting one, two, three, every day, laughing at us. These schools were mixed so there was nothing you could do to change that. We went to school with Hereros, Ovambos, and different ethnic groups. But at last we decided that we must also learn the other languages and then we realized that our language is not an official language, but only the language spoken by the people who stay in the bush.

There was some attempt in her school to teach about the San way of life, but it was done in such an atmosphere that she felt it served to reinforce stigma rather than dilute it:

> At school, even inside the classes, the students were laughing at us when there were lessons taught about the Hai||om people, or the San people, for instance how they hunted in the past, what was used for hunting, that our people were nomads, not staying at one place and moving around the different places which they liked. About these things the other students were always laughing at us.

To go to school meant boarding from January to June, followed by a brief holiday, and then returning in July to board again until December. Victoria Geingos's parents were displaced from the Etosha National Park and found work on farms where and when they could. Victoria spent most of her time with her grandmother, who also worked on a farm and she described the disruption boarding caused family life:

> Our parents were moving from one farm to another, and we did not even know where to go to find them at times, when we had to go home for a holiday. We were transported by big trucks from the school to the farms. Then, when you arrived at the particular farm for the June holidays you would find that your parents were not there, and as a child you would have to look around and then start to cry.

Neighbors would come to the rescue, she said, but ultimately this kind of separation caused some parents and children to give up schooling.

So this was really a big problem for us at holiday times, and for our parents, because they were moving around from one farm to another, and this caused them to decide not to send their children back to school again...The parents also thought that if the children attended school and had completed Grade 7, they had completed their schooling...Their views were that once a young child could read and write, they did not think that it was necessary for them to continue with the school.

Girls in particular, she said, gave up when young and chose instead to have children at an early age.

Having to move for work between farms caused her parents other difficulties:

Moving from one farm to another caused our parents to lose their property because some of the white farmers were very strict. There was one of them who had said, "You have to move from my farm—now—and I don't want to see you." Our parents only had donkey carts, and then they would have to put their blankets and children on the donkey cart. This meant that you could not load up your goats and everything. So if the owner said "You have to go now," then the people had to leave their animals and everything on the farm, like their shanties [temporary homes], et cetera. The only thing was to go with the donkey cart, loading only your blankets, children, and wife, and in this way our parents lost a lot, a lot.

She added that some farmers communicated with each other and "blackballed" certain people: "they spread bad rumors." Without jobs, those San had little choice but to drift to the towns, where problems of alcoholism often began. Young people also moved to the towns, sometimes for education. Victoria described a gradual process of deculturation:

We, the young people, after we finished our primary school Grade 7, we also decided to move to town, sometimes to attend our secondary school, like me. After primary school, I decided that I should to go Khorixas to attend the secondary school there.

Once I had returned to this school, I did not think it was necessary for me to go back to the farms to look after my grandparents and other relatives. I decided to stay in town, because I am now big enough, and people are laughing at those...who are staying on the farms. So, I said that there was no need to move back to the farms.

In this way, one does not recognize you are losing your culture, tradition, language and everything, until it is too late. Now I can say that maybe it was better for us in the past, [when we used] to move around from one place to another.

[Then] they were moving around freely in one place, in the Etosha Game Park. This land was theirs, and they moved freely from one place to another... they were only using trees and grass to make their huts. But nowadays, you have to buy these shanties [to live in] and there is no land left on which you can move freely.

As the process accelerates, she explained, traditional methods do not just lose significance, they may also be the subject of scorn. In this instance, her experience was in direct contrast to that of Nxisae Nxao:

Even... our traditional doctors who were practicing their beliefs on the farms would not do this in the towns nowadays, although they are free to do it. Some are shy to do this, and nowadays some people do not believe in the traditional doctors anymore. If you do these things in the town, the people pretend that they don't know anything about it, and they look on it as "funny."

Even if they [came from] the place where the traditional doctors are practicing their knowledge, if they saw this clapping of hands and... dancing and so on, these are the things which the people in the towns are laughing at. They do not take it seriously. But on the farms it was better, and each and every person... would not be laughing at these people because this was our belief. I believe in the traditional healer, because my father was one, and I saw how they practiced on the farms.

Victoria's experience led her to fight for a better approach to San history and development and she became involved in various community-based initiatives with support from the Working Group of Indigenous Minorities in Southern Africa (WIMSA).[18]

I decided to encourage the young people of our community that they should not leave behind their traditions and everything that our parents and forefathers had. They should not throw these things away, but they should let these things work in today's life, because we have already lost such a lot in the past. When I hear about how our forefathers lost their land, culture, and tradition, then I, as the Hai||om daughter become very unhappy. This is why I had decided to fight for my people and my community.

The Power of Prejudice

Victoria's story had a positive ending, but many young San failed to complete school because of the kind of discrimination and loneliness that she described. And those who did complete often found it a mixed blessing, with job expectations unmatched by reality. These accounts strongly suggest that education needs to be accompanied by other forms of support, otherwise pupils leave with no confidence or marketable skills. Gerson #Neibeb, a 24-year-old Hai‖om, learned to hunt from his grandfather and at first said this was why he left school early: "When I was at school, I was thinking of what I would be doing if I was on the farm. I would either be shooting birds with a *kettie* [catapult], or be out hunting with the men. That is what I would be thinking of."

Later he admitted that the real reason was his family's poverty:

[It was] decided that I should stay away because money was a problem...It was a problem, because you had to go to school with shoes. It was also compulsory to wear school trousers, shirt, and socks. If you did not wear these clothes you were beaten...

The people [Hai‖om] did not tell of their difficulties because they were very shy and could not say the things that they were thinking of. So that is why the people did not go to the teachers [to explain why they were wrongly dressed]...That was the cause for my leaving school...

Many Hai‖om children were having this problem. Some did not even go up to Grade 4 like me, but only stayed to Grade 1 because it was so difficult. The other ethnic groups [such as the Ovambo and Herero] were already standing on their rights, and were not having these difficulties. As you see nowadays, they were already on top and we were at the back.

These San interviews highlight that what should be a benefit of resettlement can too easily become a humiliating and divisive experience that ultimately does little for those involved.[19] As Gerson said, even at school he already felt he was "at the back" and other ethnic groups "were already on top." And almost all narrators felt that the school language policy in particular had perpetuated their people's feelings of inferiority and low self-esteem. Time and again, they asked for mother-tongue teaching, for learning to include their own history and traditions, and for books and radio programs in San languages. One response within the Kuru Family of Organisations has been the establishment of the Bokamoso program, a preschool teacher training program for community caregivers and teachers. It aims to foster a familiar linguistic and cultural environment to prepare San children for school, and to support the development of education that does not compromise cultural identity.

Ultimately, these interviews suggest that when displaced people are already on the margins of mainstream society, battling discrimination and virtually excluded from the political process, resettlement policies have to take this particular dimension into account, or they will almost certainly fail. Addressing poverty alone is not the answer when prejudice plays such a powerful role.

CHAPTER 6

"Our fields have gone, our lifestyle has changed"
Coal Mining in India

Earlier we were farmers and potters...masters in our own professions, now we are like slaves working for others. We earn money by any means we can, just to survive...since we had to leave our traditional jobs...We used to work with our own hands as and when we liked but now we have to obey [our employers]. Anytime they ask us to come for duty, if it is day or night—we have to obey...[Central Coalfields] has not only destroyed our forest, and environment, and culture, but our identity is being lost.

—Sadhan Prajapati

Interviewed in 2001, some 15 years after Central Coalfields Limited (CCL) began to take over the agricultural land used by his community, Sadhan Prajapati described the enormous changes that mining had brought to the villagers of Benti, where he grew up, and the surrounding areas. The Damodar Valley, where Benti lies, is in Jharkhand state and contains huge reserves of coal, and the land and homes of many communities have been lost to the vast open-pit mines and heavy infrastructure of CCL.

The considerable tracts of land acquired by the mining company, a local subsidiary of the state-owned Coal India Limited (CIL), resulted in the fragmented exploitation of the environment, which directly displaced some residents from their homes and left others in place, but with severely restricted access or no access to the natural resources that formerly provided the basis of their livelihoods. Rather than being surrounded by forests and fields, many residents of this part of the Damodar Valley found themselves living adjacent to the Piparwar and Ashoka open-pit mines of the North Karanpura coalfields, trapped in an industrial landscape of mechanical excavation on an enormous scale. Sadhan described the impact on his environment: "Coal dust and smoke pollutes the environment. The sound of vehicles and machinery penetrates the eardrums...the ground water level has fallen, the wells are drying up and the streams have disappeared." It was, he said, impossible for the majority of the residents to continue farming.

Some of the displaced were resettled in concrete houses grouped together in cramped "resettlement colonies." Other households and communities, such as Sadhan's, did not fall into the category of the officially displaced, but nevertheless lost access to their agricultural land and common resources. The interviews in this chapter were gathered, from both kinds of affected groups, in 2001 and 2002.[1] Almost all describe being affected by noise, air pollution, and water pollution. Proper laboring jobs in the mines were scarce, forcing people to adopt marginal and often dangerous strategies to survive. For many, the only options for earning income revolved around mining: occasional laboring jobs loading and unloading coal or illegal scavenging.[2] "Sadness is creeping into our lives," said Sadhan. "The essence of life diminished when CCL came."

One aspect of resettlement that these accounts illustrate is how the nature of the development that is causing displacement can have an impact on people's ability to respond. Open-pit coal mining does not necessarily involve the exploitation of an area of land all at once; it expands steadily, taking over some parts while affecting others. Displacement was piecemeal and gradual, and the pockets of affected communities found it hard to unite, or even to recognize in time the magnitude of what was happening.

Recognizing the scale of the problem is difficult from several perspectives. Mining-induced displacement figures are "neither comprehensive or reliable because of the project-to-project nature of displacement... [and] the discrepancy between official records and claims made by those living in the affected areas is pronounced in Jharkhand."[3]

Introduction and Background

Constituted in 2000, Jharkhand is the newest Indian state, created from what was formerly southern Bihar. The name means "the land of forests" and it is India's richest state in terms of mineral resources, but one of the poorest in terms of per capita income. Over 40 percent of the population live below the poverty line, a rate that is significantly higher than the national average.[4] While rapid industrialization is widespread across India, and other mineral-rich states are supporting the fast expansion of the mining sector, Jharkhand has been described as "unique in its continued existence as a resource-periphery for India's centre and in its complicated 'ethno-national frame' which arises from the large tribal population that was also the raison d'etre for its creation."[5]

Of Jharkhand's 26 million population, some 28 percent are *adivasi* (*adi:* "original"; *vasi:* "inhabitant"), the collective name used for the many tribal peoples of India. *Adivasis* are not a homogeneous group—they vary greatly in ethnicity and culture, with over 200 groups who speak over one hundred languages—but the vast majority are at the lowest point of almost every socioeconomic indicator in India.[6]

In the coal belt of Jharkhand, it is the tribal or *adivasi* population, especially of Santhals and Oraons, that has been particularly affected by the industry's rapid expansion since the 1980s. These are people whose livelihoods have been largely dependent on land and forest resources.[7] For them, the environmental damage and loss of land and common property resources has had severe economic consequences. The forest was crucial to their survival, providing water, fuel wood, fodder, wild fruit, and medicinal herbs.

Coal India Limited (CIL) is the largest coal-producing company in the world. Its mines contribute approximately 85 percent of the country's coal production, much of this being in the tribal belt of what was southern Bihar.[8] With 29 percent of India's coal reserves, Jharkhand contains the highest number of collieries in India. Since the 1980s, the industry has been shifting from underground to highly mechanized open-pit mining, which uses large amounts of land, mostly forest and agricultural land.

Not surprisingly, the impact in the region has been massive: environmentally, economically, and socially. Not only are fields lost to mining infrastructure, subsidence, and waste dumps, but there is also often a reduction in the productivity of remaining land as a result of disturbances in the availability of underground water. Fires and emissions from the mines and coking ovens cause air pollution, and various effluents pollute local water sources, affecting the health of people and livestock.

Compensation

When populations lose land and other assets as a result of acquisitions for a development purpose, it is set down in the policies of most companies, parastatals, and also in state and national resettlement and rehabilitation laws in India, that losses should be compensated for and the means for rehabilitation provided. Companies and state authorities are encouraged to provide land-for-land compensation, as this is thought to offer the best opportunity for displaced communities to reestablish their livelihoods. However, in most cases alternative land of an equal size and comparable quality is rarely made accessible to the displaced in India; compensation is predominantly in cash, with some requirement to provide either employment in the project or additional training to enable the displaced to build new livelihoods in the resettlement locations. There is considerable literature on the flaws in these approaches, and the problems associated with asset valuation and cash compensation are discussed throughout this volume.[9]

The Piparwar and Ashoka mines began operating in the mid-1980s, when Coal India (CIL) had no rehabilitation policy. The company's first Rehabilitation and Resettlement Policy appeared in 1994 and was revised several times, most recently in 2008, to bring it in line with India's National Rehabilitation and Resettlement Policy. Coal India's policy has been criticized as being inadequate and poorly implemented. In 2001, for example, the Chottanagpur Adivasi Seva Samiti (Service Committee of Chottanagpur Adivasi; CASS) wrote to the World Bank, drawing their attention to poor practice by local subsidiary CCL at East Parej, West Bokaro coalfields, another open-pit mine that displaced some narrators who feature in this chapter, and one financed by the World Bank. The World Bank's Inspection Panel (IP) agreed to take up the case, and its 2002 report listed over 30 violations of World Bank Guidelines.[10] A document published by the international human rights organization FIAN at the end of 2006 concluded that "on many crucial points" the IP's recommendations had still not been properly implemented.[11]

In the case of the Jharkhand villagers who lost land, housing, and/or access to natural resources as a result of the mine development, land-for-land compensation was not provided and instead, displaced communities reported being paid cash compensation for lost fixed assets, such as houses and fruit trees, where they could show legal title over the land. Common property resources, such as the forests, streams, and wildlife, were not deemed "owned assets" or proof of ownership could not be provided, and there was no compensation for these communally owned and managed resources. A few displacees were able to join relatives living elsewhere who had some surplus land, but the majority experienced a dramatic decline in their resource base. Many forms of forest produce, including herbal medicines, fuelwood, and the flowers and fruit of the *mahua* tree, *Bassia latifolia,* were used by the local population, and some were important sources of livelihood. For the *adivasi,* their loss proved to be a major deprivation.

Coal India's policies at the time when many of these narrators were being displaced in the mid-1980s had included a commitment to employ one member of each affected household, but there is evidence to suggest that fewer than half the families were offered jobs by the company.[12] One reason for this was that in order to be considered for employment, an individual should have had at least three acres of land prior to being displaced. Those with secondary education were eligible for a job if they owned at least two acres, but very few *adivasi* had attended school. Moreover, many *adivasi* did not hold title deeds to land known as *gair majurwa* ("deedless land"), which included the fields, pastures, and ponds they had used for decades but for which ownership was not recognized. Further complications were that some families did not have sufficient acres to qualify for jobs for all the potential adult earners in the family, leaving many without work but no longer able to pursue farming or forest-based livelihoods. More recently, as mechanization in the mines has increased, even fewer jobs have been available and CCL's emphasis has shifted from "jobs for land" to monetary compensation alone.[13]

With few exceptions, women were not offered employment by CCL and it was widely believed that there was an "unwritten rule" to reserve jobs for men. This was compounded by the fact that when *adivasis* did register land, it was required to be in the name of the male head of household. As *adivasi* women did not own the land, they were not eligible for the jobs. Cash compensation was also usually paid to men, and later research showed that women often had little information about the sums and even less control over its expenditure.[14] In addition, the "jobs for land" policy had a number of small-print conditions that precluded many of the displaced from qualifying, whether male or female. A high proportion of the new employment opportunities were taken by more educated outsiders.

The interviews reveal that this influx of outsiders employed by CCL added to growing social tensions. For example, CCL staff was housed in colonies with many facilities, including health and education services provided by the company. Anjlus Bek was a 46-year-old whose village of Malmohra was destroyed by Piparwar mine. He moved to Kalyanpur, one of the new sites built near Benti. He commented: "CCL officials are enjoying all facilities like schools and colleges provided by CCL...From CCL we only got electricity, but we did not get water, hospitals, schools, and toilet facilities et cetera. The electricity is also uncertain most of the time, due to the transformers burning out or supply lines breaking."

The disparity of income created by employment in the coal industry generated new inequalities within the project-affected population as well, increasing the marginalization of those who had been resettled but who had not been given employment, and of those who had not been displaced but whose livelihoods were affected by the deterioration of their environment. These people found themselves less well-off than the displaced who had secured CCL jobs, and ill-feeling developed, reported narrators. The "jobs for land" policy had other destabilizing effects: narrators quoted later in this chapter described how dynamics and relationships within families changed.

Given the degree of upheaval to traditional livelihoods that mining had brought in its wake, it is not surprising that these narrators were preoccupied with the ways their lives were changing: work and occupation, relationship with the land, women's roles and associated status, and family dynamics, as well as language and customs. Many also expressed concern about a more fundamental breaking down of community ties and bonds. Some of this seems to predate actual relocation, and to stem in part from the negotiation process.

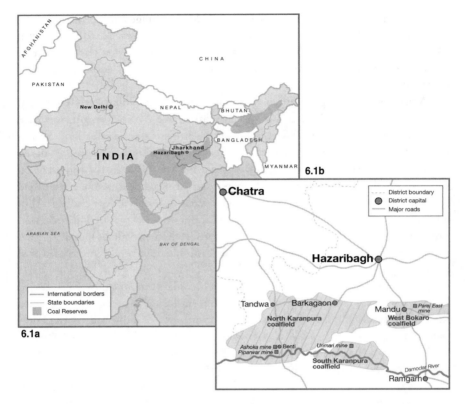

Figure 6.1 a. Map of India, showing Jharkhand state. b. Detail of area around Hazaribagh, showing coal fields. Maps by Julie Anson.

"Our Identity Is Being Lost"

> Displacement is like cancer. It completely twists and breaks the structure of society.
>
> —Devilal Hembrom

A common thread in these narrators' stories of negotiations over compensation is the uneasy sense they had that because of their lack of information, education, and organization, they were taken advantage of. Time and again, men and women described muddle and confusion as CCL declared an interest in specific areas of land, and laid out their policies relating to compensation—often using a local leader, a *neta,* as the link between the company and the community.

Although the basic rehabilitation package seemed straightforward, accounts suggested that negotiations were often characterized by uncertainty. The fact that many Santhali and other *adivasi* groups had been living in the locations identified for mining expansion for several generations but could not provide written evidence of ownership placed them at a severe disadvantage in negotiations with the mining company and their lawyers. Another issue, according to those interviewed, was that asset valuation did not take account of land quality: some felt more fertile land should have been valued higher than less productive land. But CCL was interested in the coal beneath the land, not the soil above.

The iniquities brought about by the qualifying criteria for employment linked to land ownership have already been discussed. Anjlus Bek, for example, described having nine acres of land, but his five children were too young to work, so as the only working adult, he only got one job, even though his land entitled him to more. Some people in that situation, such as Tetri Kisku, a mother of five, were told to claim the jobs later, when their children were old enough to work, but when Tetri Kisku did this, she was told there were no more jobs. Anjlus was upset that his community agreed to the conditions offered: "We feel that the CCL has bought our lands as if they were buying vegetables...we feel that we were cheated."

Many narrators implied that the negotiations with CCL were divisive and weakened the bonds that traditionally led communities to resolve issues collectively rather than individually. The loss of land and the struggle for compensation pitted people against one another and militated against cooperation both between and within families, as brothers found themselves in competition with one other over compensation money, land, and employment. Communities were described as sliding into confused and unhappy groupings, with people struggling to argue their individual cases and feeling any sense of unity slipping away.

It is common practice in resettlement operations for authorities to identify community leaders through whom negotiations take place. CCL worked mainly through the *neta* or village heads, who were frequently placed in an invidious position and were vulnerable to accusations of favoring some families or individuals over others, and of corruption. Bigan Ganjhu, aged 62, like Anjlus Bek, was displaced from Malmohura village by the Pipawar mine. He described how the actions of their *neta* spread confusion and fear, rather than supporting the people. "There was a lot of wrongdoing. He used to keep all information from us." Misunderstandings about the criteria for jobs and compensation developed and in the uncertainty villagers "became divided...because no one was helping anyone out in any way. And because we didn't have much information, the village headman was successful in scaring us. Just to fill in the employment forms, he took [money] from us. So many people had to sell their wives' jewellery just to meet his demands...Now he doesn't live in these parts."

Anjlus Bek explained that the villagers felt isolated and alone when they had to make decisions, as they knew so little about the arrangements or the possibility of challenging them:

> Due to lack of knowledge and information, we did not know on what basis CCL gave the compensation. The papers were made in CCL and we were made

to sign them and they prepared the cheques and gave them to us...About six months before we were given the compensation, we were given notice, but we were not told how the compensation was being prepared. If we had been able to make enquiries we would not have been cheated like this. We did not make any protest and took the compensation easily.

CCL did everything according to its own wishes...CCL was threatening us and people thought that they would send bulldozers to break down our houses. Although this did not happen, out of fear of losing those jobs which were on offer, people started worrying—how they would take care of their children?

The land was going and jobs would also go [unless we agreed], so we thought to take whatever we were offered, fearing that we would not get any help from anyone else.

Sadhan Prajapati, whose words open this chapter, and who lost his agricultural land to Piparwar mine, also felt that CCL exploited weaknesses in the communities: "We demanded just compensation for everybody and to be paid all at one time. All of us agreed to this, but the CCL authority divided us by giving different rates to different persons...There was corruption while informing people. To some they offered 500 rupees [approximately US$40 at 1985 rates], some 1,500 rupees and some 5,000 rupees, and to some 9,000 rupees per acre."

In particular, he felt that CCL took advantage of the villagers' lack of numeracy and familiarity with money: "The interest was also added on, to lure people. Thus the unity of the people was broken up by the promises of employment, title deeds, and even money." There were other "tricks," he added:

There were a few [farmers] who had 20 to 23 acres of land, and these were drunkards and illiterates. CCL officials took them into their office and got their thumb impressions on the agreement. They handed them cheques instead of cash and for lesser amounts. In this way CCL took away large amounts of land with lesser compensation.

Manbahal Karmali, 50, originally from the village of Marangdaha, was resettled in a new site at Chiryatand built near Benti for those whose villages were destroyed by the expansion of Piparwar mine.

We were easy touches for the *sahibs* [CCL officials]. When they came they said that in [another village], they had given jobs to 75 young men and would do the same for us. We were perplexed. We felt that there might be 50 youths here altogether. How could we make use of the extra 25 jobs? Then we thought we will get our relatives to get the jobs. The *sahibs* said that whether anyone had land or not, they would still get a job.

Promises of this kind led to confusion and tension among the affected villagers. In particular, those who owned larger tracts of lands began to feel aggrieved about the idea that everyone would get jobs, regardless of the size of their landholding.

> Jitan Oraon had 27 acres of land and only two sons. The Muslims and the Rajputs also had more land. Jitan Oraon said, "Manbahal has only three acres but he has four sons. All four sons will get a job? I have 27 acres but only two sons, so we will get only two jobs? This is not fair. Jobs should be given according to the land we are giving [to CCL]." Many others also agreed.
>
> So—CCL did say that they would give a job to everyone regardless of land acquired: it was our own in-fighting and people's self-interest that did not allow this to happen.
>
> Ultimately we felt defeated...Everybody was self-interested. We were fighting amongst ourselves. Those who had six acres of land and two sons: both of them got jobs. But I had six acres of land and four sons eligible for jobs. So we kept on demanding but did not get jobs, and meanwhile those who had two sons gave their consent...Yes, we in the village had infighting.
>
> My soul was saddened. I had educated my son by "cutting my stomach" [living a poor life] and now due to lack of land he didn't get a job, and those who were illiterate and had more land got jobs so easily.

A few people said that CCL offered everyone jobs when they first approached communities but then changed their policy. It is not clear whether this was a misunderstanding on the villagers' part, or one created by the middlemen in order to expedite the villagers' agreement, but there is research that suggests that corruption did mar the process in Jharkhand.[15] Whatever the reality, these extracts show how mounting confusion over the terms of compensation contributed to the undermining of a common front.

Resistance

The interviews reveal that despite the intracommunity and intrafamily divisions that were a consequence of the compensation policy and its negotiation, some communities were able to come together to oppose some of the actions taken by CCL. However, as the mines and related infrastructure extended through the districts of Hazaribagh and Chatra, the fractured nature of their progress resulted in relatively isolated islands of affected people experiencing losses at different times. This reduced the numbers of people who could have come together with a common cause to demand fairer treatment from the companies and local officials who oversaw the development.

One such attempt to resist encroachment was led by Ramprasad Ganjhu, 45, the leader of Barisimar village, which was close to Pipawar mine:

> When our lands at Barisimar started to be taken away, we took up sticks and fought back. We were fighting for our basic needs because if our land is taken, how will we survive? CCL had given us a year's notice for land acquisition...
>
> The people of our five *tolas* [localities], Vishrampur, Jehlitand, Barkitand, Dakra, and Barisimar, sat together to discuss how we were to make our living if CCL took our land away. We thought that if only one job is provided, how will we look after our whole family? Because all our land will go.
>
> We decided not to give the land...So we were to unite so that no one could operate machines on our land—because unity has power.

But the call for unity was unsuccessful, as uncertainty grew and people's determination to act wavered: "We did not take any decisions, and nobody knew on what basis they would get jobs."

> Then there was a second meeting with the *sahibs* [CCL officials]; they told us to bring all the papers to do with our land. They decided that we would get jobs in lieu of our land. At the time, we neither had enough information, nor were we organized enough, so we just agreed to the rate of compensation offered—one job for every three acres of land. It was too low.

Some of the details in his story revealed how individual cases are often not straightforward, suggesting a need for support and some flexibility in the implementation of compensation policy:

> My father was one of two brothers. My father had approximately three acres of land and my older uncle had six or seven...Anyway, for our three acres we could get only one job. The elder uncle didn't get a job because he is a drunkard. So his [allocated] job was just wasted. I told my brother to arrange for his son to get the job instead. He kept saying he will do something, but died without arranging anything concrete.

Organized opposition to the land seizures came to an end, and when the heavy machinery moved into the area, they left their homes:

> CCL didn't actually evict us [from Barisimar], but when we were given compensation for the land, we no longer had the right to live there. The machines and trucks created dust and then CCL began to dump soil in front of our house. We had no choice but to move. And we villagers weren't organized enough to tell them that "we will not move from here until you give us an alternative place."

Everyone was scattered. If we had been united we could have done an *andolan* [protest].

Following their departure, Ramprasad's family built a temporary hut on fields and stayed there for six months: "People went here and there; some went to their in-laws. We felt helpless. We had nobody to support us and we were scattered. There was just so much pain in our hearts." Eventually they moved to some forest land, hoping, he said, that CCL would help them settle there permanently. When no help was forthcoming, "We started to clear the forest ourselves, and prepare the land. But then the Forest Department started harassing us. So we went to the CCL office [and they] told the Forest Department to allow us to settle."

Later they were joined by other scattered families. At the time of the interview in 2001, he explained that they continued to fight for better facilities from CCL, including employment:

Here there is no agriculture. We have to sit idle...There is no scope for employment in CCL...Outsiders have come here as contractors and are taking everything...If we had been organized we could have launched a movement for employment. If I go to the CCL office by myself, they say, "Don't you have any other villagers to accompany you? Do only you have a problem?"

There is no consensus among us. We should have raised our voices together saying that we are local people: we should get priority in jobs. We can even work on the roads. All this has happened because we don't know how to express ourselves and are illiterate.

Women Take Action

Although most of the women interviewed said that they were excluded from discussions about compensation and new locations with CCL officials, some women were active in resisting the takeover of land and campaigning for improved compensation. One of the most striking examples is the story of 35-year-old Balo Devi, who was evicted from her home in Khijur, near Benti.

Married at a young age, uneducated, and with children to support, Balo Devi gained the respect of the community through her physical courage and leadership of protests against the company: "If the menfolk fought, then CCL would beat them, chase them away. Because I am a woman nobody could dare touch me." Indeed, she proved to be such an effective leader that, she reflected, people wondered what she would have achieved with even a smattering of education:

When CCL began its mining here, at first they went from village to village measuring land. They did not consult anyone. They got all the *baniyas* [merchant class] under their influence and gave them jobs, as they are the business-minded ones. Then when they started working on our land, I spoke to the village women. I talked them into understanding that they should do something for their land. I organized everyone to have a women's rally one day. We also decided that we would take our sickles and any other "weapons" we could lay our hands on.

First we went to Piparwar mine, near Benti. There we saw three trucks hauling and packing coal. We created a big ruckus. But there was nobody official there to talk to, so we all returned home. In the meantime some men had prepared plans of their own. They slipped into the mine that night [and] set fire to the three trucks and ran off. All three vehicles were burnt to ashes.

"We felt fear in our hearts"

When we had our rally I felt very satisfied and proud...I am just an illiterate woman, but that day I was leading the entire rally. That day there was a large number of women with me. That day there was a lot of anger in our hearts. Whom did the CCL ask for permission, and on what basis did it start working on our land? But when we returned home and came to know about the burning of the trucks we felt fear in our hearts...I began to worry that the blame would fall on us...

My in-laws also started saying that now that I had become a *neta* [leader] I would lead [them] to their downfall. Then I told myself that it wasn't us who burnt the trucks, so we will tackle things as they come. They could only hit us, they couldn't take our lives. If they insulted us, we would hear them out. Still, members of my husband's family and even people in neighboring settlements started saying that "if you are too much of a leader, it is you who will be blamed." So I started feeling scared.

"Women have to fight with their common sense"

The women were not blamed for the burnt-out trucks and following that incident CCL left the area alone for three years. Balo Devi's courage was recognized:

Slowly people started making me their leader. Even today, if there is a rally, they always put me in front. All the men said, "You should lead us. You're not scared of anyone and you can answer back."

When men fight, they are beaten up and CCL chase them away. The authorities can get into physical fights with the men, but they dare not lay a hand on us women. They have to respect us and they know that if they as much as grab us by the hand, there will be a heavy price to pay.

People think women are weak, but we can reach great heights. Women have to fight with their common sense. If one or two women come together, they will be able to speak up. If they stay united and help each other out, then definitely things will be done. There is a big difference between one woman saying something and ten women saying the same thing. Now all the women of the village congratulate me for what I did.

"I told them no one could intimidate me"

CCL eventually resumed operations around their communities, and Balo Devi took up a different battle.

When, after three years, CCL resumed work, they got everyone to fill up an employment form. One of my brothers-in-law, who can read and write a little, got my husband's name removed and put in his own. So while everyone got a job, my husband was left out. Then a local official told me how my husband's name had been removed. He assured me that the matter would be rectified, but nothing happened for three years. Then we were told to vacate our house. We were told there was a lot of danger due to blasting for the mines and that it might collapse. I told them until we got the right compensation and job we would not leave the house.

Only I know how those three years [of resistance] went by. My in-laws even started creating problems with food, and gave us only two plates of rice daily for the four of us—at a time when I had just given birth...

When we were facing starvation, my husband started work at a brick kiln. He told me, "You stay at home. But if a CCL truck comes on our land, you must stop it, even if your life is in danger." After that, if someone turned up to do some drilling or any other work, I would chase them away with a spear. They became very scared. They said, "Don't blame us. It's CCL that sent us here." I used to respond, "Go and call your CCL bosses then! I'll fight with them! Why should I fight with you?"

"What's the point of living?"

Sometimes CCL would say it is not our land, and sometimes that it was "deed-less land." We just wouldn't leave the house, whether they were blasting in the mines or trying to level the building. I told them that I wasn't going to go anywhere...I took the children and sat down at the blasting site. I thought to myself, "I'm going to die of hunger at home. If I die here at the hands of CCL, at least they won't like it. They don't give us jobs, there's no farming left, so what's the point of living?"

A truck driver told me, "There's such a lot of equipment here to do the blasting. By stopping our work, you're destroying everything. Will you take responsibility for all the wasted labor and dynamite?"

"Are you taking responsibility for our lives?" I retorted. "You take responsibility for our lives, then I'll take responsibility for your explosives." I could have killed him.

Then CCL sent a guard to my house. They also sent the police. They bribed my in-laws and told them to make me understand. But no matter who came, I just picked up the sickle and chased them out. I told them that no one could intimidate me...

When CCL saw that I was willing to campaign all by myself, they tried to reach an agreement under which my husband would be given a job after six months. I [refused]...After three months they came up with the condition that we vacate our house. Again I said not until we were given the job. For three more months I stayed put.

Resistance Crumbles

At first my relatives were with me. Then they too moved to the resettlement site at Tilya Tongri. The elders started chiding me for having pretensions to leadership, even though I was illiterate: "If she had learnt just one letter of the alphabet, God knows what she would have done!" Even my husband asked me if I had gone mad—and he moved our belongings. I said, "I won't allow my children's lives to go to waste. If we don't get a job, nothing will work out." I used to stay in that house all day by myself, but I never felt scared...

They offered my husband a guard's job for the time being, and later a permanent job. I said if he takes a guard's job, if something gets stolen they will throw him out! CCL people might do some stealing themselves and put the blame on my husband. Then what would we do? "Guard duty is not acceptable." Then they understood that this was a very smart woman. They agreed to give us a job from the very next day. The local official finally had to admit, "You are a very brave woman." My husband got a job because of my boldness.

Balo Devi's story reveals how difficult it was to sustain resistance. CCL did suspend their takeover of that area for a while, but in the end the villagers were displaced. Balo Devi took a leading role in challenging CCL, but her supporters gradually wavered and weakened, and her lasting success was on an individual rather than a community level: to get her husband a job.

From Self-Sufficiency to Wage Labor

Look at the people who have been displaced and you realise what a crime it is. They have nothing. They are totally dependent on whatever jobs they have been given.

—Devilal Hembrom

Although some men, and a few women, acknowledged that they used to take work outside their communities in lean times, or when the agricultural burden was at its least demanding, most narrators still lived a largely localized and self-sufficient life before the encroachment of the mines. But with the loss of their land this changed. From formerly using the forest and the land for food and materials for sale, barter and consumption, raising livestock, and supplementing this with crafts such as pottery, they found they had no option but to compete for employment in the local economy.

Those who had not qualified for a company job, or those families who for some reason lost that job (for example, through the death of the breadwinner) were the worst-hit. Anjlus Bek expressed concern about those who did not qualify for employment:

Life was wasted for those who did not have three acres of land: they were displaced and yet they did not get jobs. When they were displaced they got very little compensation because of which these people are left nowhere...they are living a life worse than an animal's. Their land has been taken over forever and it won't be returned to them and they have got scattered. Due to the mines their identity as human beings as well as their land was lost forever.

He said some of the displaced migrated on a more or less permanent basis: "People have to move out to distant places like Kolkata to earn their livelihood." Many others, such as Manju Devi and her husband, were forced into the illegal mining and selling of coal.

Manju Devi was 40 when interviewed in 2001, and lived close to Parej East mine in the West Bokaro coalfield:

The mines started after my children were born. In the beginning their spread was not so much but now the mines have expanded right up to [where I live]...What benefits have we got? We have lost our land. Only two people [in the family], Suman's husband and Nanki's husband, got jobs. My husband and the husband of my elder sister-in-law did not...

We face a lot of difficulty and find it hard to make both ends meet. We cannot get enough coal to cook...[My husband] works sometimes in the colony and at other times he sells coal...What else can he do?

She admits that the coal they sell is stolen; the police take a hefty cut:

We steal the coal from the mines. Three to four people are required. The coal is dug up and then hauled over to a few places. Then it is kept [there for a few days], put in sacks and brought over the boundary wall. Later it is burnt to make coke and then put into sacks which are put by the roadside to be sold. All this is hard work.

After all this...the police take away a couple of sacks. We tell them, "You have jobs and you earn enough, but we are poor people." They just don't listen to us, and sometimes even prevent us from taking [any] sacks. Why would we do this if we had jobs and were earning enough? With great effort we sell 10 to 12 sacks of coke in one to two weeks and from that small amount all our expenditure on food, clothes, school fees, et cetera has to be met.

Many of the affected villagers had little or no education, or experience of skilled work, and they were poorly equipped to take up new opportunities, as Sadhan Prajapati pointed out:

Those who learnt a new trade, only they came out unscathed. Those who could not adjust [to the loss of their traditional livelihood] became unemployed and desperate. Without knowledge of any new trade and capital, it is very difficult to survive.

Sadhan had been a potter, making earthenware pots and roof tiles to supplement what he harvested from the land. Having lost access to the land and its resources, he became a shopkeeper. He is one of many who commented how poor education reduced the job prospects of the displaced: "Our village people make up only 25 percent of the employed. Those from outside are also in better posts; we are the laboring class so we also get less money."

Increasing Divisions

CCL has done good for some and the rest are unemployed and have nothing.
—Phulmani Soren

Sadhan Prajapati argued that the divide between those who received CCL jobs and those who did not (the majority) had created new tensions:

After coming of the mines, those who got employment earn much more and have become proud...When we were doing agriculture alone...people helped each other...Whatever one earned, the other earned nearly the same.

But this had changed:

[Today] here are fights between the village people...because those who have got jobs in CCL do not think much of the people who did not get employment and are still carrying on with agriculture. People don't understand each others' problems.

Some people in employment can afford to keep a few cattle, he said, but these "are being let loose...[and] destroy the crops of poor people dependent on agriculture."

Phulmani Soren, a 30-year-old widow, expressed the view that CCL's coming had not been all bad. She was determined to educate her children now that schools were within reach. Nevertheless, she agreed that the "jobs for land" policy has caused division, especially within families between those who qualified for jobs, and those who for various reasons ended up without work:

> In my thinking those who have got jobs in CCL are doing well. But those who do not have land, for them CCL has done nothing. [Also, in some cases] the authorities have taken the land of the whole family and have given a job to just some of them, thus other family members are out of jobs. [Say there] are three brothers...but CCL has given only one job. What will the other two do?

"The joint family system has perished"

The loss of common land and resources, the dependency on wage labor, and the nature of the new housing and resettlement sites or colonies created fault lines in communities and large extended families. Family units became smaller. Some narrators, such as 70-year-old Somar Soren, felt CCL actively followed a "divide and rule" policy:

> It is CCL policy not to resettle everyone in the same place. The management always tries to create friction between us. This is the real reason they try to divide us—so that we can't get together and make demands.

In his interview, Sadhan Prajapati did not accuse CCL of deliberately dividing communities and upsetting family dynamics, but he did see it as an inevitable result of the policies pursued:

> CCL takes over the father's land and gives a job to the son. The son becomes the earner and the rest of the family turns into "consumers" [dependents]. Earlier, the father used to earn, feed the children, guide them, and maintain control over them. By staying on his own land, the father used to make the decisions. Now, by getting jobs, the son has become the *maalik* [head].
>
> Now the father has to obey everything that the son says and does. And that is how the self-centered disputes break out in families...The main reason for these changes in society is the policies of CCL.

Sadhan was one of many who deeply regretted such changes in family relationships. Bhaju Ganjhu gave the example of a family with four sons, only one of whom was employed by CCL:

> Earlier all four of them were working the same land and everyone used to get his share of the living it produced. [But if] CCL has given employment to only

one of them, the others have no employment and they are suffering. That is why there are a lot of quarrels and fighting…The cooperation that kept the family together is gone and families are scattering, moving away from each other. The joint family system has perished.

"Now I have to obey his every command"

Waged labor had other impacts within families. Balo Devi, the woman who campaigned to secure a job for her husband, found her achievement was double-edged. Although they were better off with her husband in employment, family dynamics shifted:

> Earlier my husband and I worked together. We lived by hard work. We all had the same rights. Now, my husband says sometimes that he "produces" and I just "consume."
>
> Earlier, if he ever asked me to massage his legs, I would say, "If you are tired, so am I." But these days in winter he will only bathe in hot water, and after his bath, he wants an oil massage. Now I have to obey his every command—after all, it is his earnings that are feeding the house. Even if he slaps me, I will have to bear that.

Balo Devi was adamant that CCL's intrusion in their lives had disadvantaged women: "The coming of CCL has increased the harassment and exploitation of women. They didn't give women jobs and they have made them sit idle." For all her determined and successful campaigning on behalf of her community and her husband, Balo Devi said her life had lost its color:

> We don't feel happy in our hearts. For a year I have not gone anywhere or socialized with anyone. Now we are idle and bored, as there is no farming. Life has turned a dull yellow from a brilliant green. Earlier we women used to work on the field and at home. Now there's nothing to do other than to wait for our husbands to return home.

"Now All the Women Are Sitting Idle"

Balo Devi lamented the negative changes resettlement had brought about for women and this observation was repeated by other interviewees. Women in Santhali and other *adivasi* societies perform key tasks in the fields and forests as well as in the home, including being responsible for the paintings on the mud walls of their homes, a tradition that creates a link back to the prehistoric rock art for which the area is famous.[16] The small concrete houses provided for displacees allow for no such artistic expression, and many other roles have diminished or disappeared.

Phulmani Soren, 30, was interviewed in the courtyard of her small house, 50 meters (about 54 yards) from the dumping grounds of Urimari open-pit mine, in the South Karanpura coalfield. It was noted during the interview that the roof and walls of her neighbor's home had been badly damaged by rocks and debris from the blasting and Phulmani's own home bore cracks in the walls for the same reason.

Phulmani's husband managed to secure a job with CCL in exchange for their land, but sadly he died very suddenly:

> The very next day [after the last rites] I went to CCL to give me a job, but they informed me that it will take four to five years [to sort out]. I told them that my husband attended the office right up to the Friday. Only on Saturday he was absent because he died. And here I am on Monday, so why can't I get the job? But they didn't listen to me.

When interviewed Phulmani was farming their remaining land, and she took paid work whenever she could: "I earn 40 rupees per day [approximately US$0.89 at 2000 rates] for loading the truck [with coal]." She was still trying to get his job, but "I have no money to bribe." Sometimes, she said, "We go hungry—our lives hang by a thread."

Although the overwhelming majority of jobs with CCL went to men, the interviews suggested that in exceptional cases women were able to benefit from these opportunities. For example, 80-year-old Bhaju Ganjhu from Benti, who owned three acres of land and so was eligible for one of the positions, told how he was too old to work for CCL and had no sons. However, his married daughter agreed, in an arrangement negotiated with the *panchayat* (village council), to look after her parents and younger sister financially in exchange for getting the job.

It was more typical that women had little choice but to resort to piece-work loading coal or selling what they could scavenge. Phulmani described the extremely harsh conditions in which she worked and lived, which contrasted so starkly with the environment prior to the expansion of the mines:

> I was happy where I was brought up; there was beauty. Here I see only dust, coal, and coal fires, and the trucks' noise. In my house there was no noise, no dust. Everywhere you looked there was greenery...all types of vegetables.
>
> We got fruits, yams, tubers, bamboo shoots, mushrooms [from the forest]. And we used to get *kachnar, jarhul,* and *palas* flowers, for [use in] worship and to decorate our house and place in our hair. We used to get wood from the forest and also sell it in the market. With the money we used to buy grain...So in this way the forest used to give us both greens and grains. Without our forest, our existence is nothing.

She related the deterioration in her environment to the changes in women's lives:

> We women used to work in the paddy fields and the forest...We were all employed on our land...raising crops like rice, *dhal* [pulses], and other food grains. We used to eat our noon meal in the field and return only at dusk, so there was work for everyone, for the whole season...People in the house distilled liquor and sold that too. That is how we were raised...Now all the women are sitting idle and doing nothing.
>
> We used to cook food and take it to the fields where the men were working. We used to weed and plant seedlings...When the planting was done, we went to get other things to eat such as roots and bamboo shoots from the forest...Now we women go to fetch water, and after this we don't have anything to do.

As there was no future in working the land, Phulmani was determined to put her four children through school. "The children would blame me for not educating them, and giving them enough knowledge so that they can take care of themselves," she said, but she also wanted to educate them in "their tradition and their ways... [and] show them that our ancestors were wise men who dwelt in harmony with nature. Natural resources were the only source of life and livelihood."

Devcharan Munda, a 45-year-old father of six, had been resettled for some five years when he was interviewed in 2001. He also recognized the extent to which women's worlds had narrowed and recalled how closely everyone had previously worked together:

> [In the past] men and women worked together in the fields. Women helped in the field by removing shrubs and bushes and clearing weeds...At harvest time also we got together and helped each other. The bullocks were taken to plough the fields and to transplant paddy. Plenty of food and *mahua* drink...was kept. The drink had a cooling effect and removed all tiredness. The food and drink were offered to all who came to help; no money was given.

He noted how, after their displacement from the land, women were confined to their homes. He voiced a concern that if women were to go out for work, then they were vulnerable to being molested and insulted by men from outside their communities: "They are not used to working as laborers." However, rather than concerns about their safety, women expressed unhappiness about their enforced "idleness": "Since we have lost all the land there is no agriculture at all. We don't feel good. We are not lazy but we have nothing to cultivate, so we sit idle," Tetri Kisku said.

Punia Devi, 60, spoke for many when she described how women's sphere of activity had been reduced.

> Before CCL came here, women worked in the fields. They also worked at home. They used to cut the grass in the fields. They would do all the work. There was no mechanized grinding then. All the threshing of the grains and grinding of pulses used to be done at home by hand. In those days, you could farm for seven to eight months.
>
> As long as there was farming, it was good for women. They would sow seeds and share the produce. You would be engaged in harvesting and threshing pulses and rice. It would keep your mind occupied. Twice a year, we would pick *mahua* flowers. But the mines have finished farming.

She recalled gathering wood, yams, tubers, and *datun* (toothbrush sticks) from the forest and helped raise and sell poultry and livestock:

> When we had visitors, we could cook a chicken. [And we] sold them in the village market to earn some money. We used to sell goats in the market, and if necessary, sometimes we used to eat one at home. If we had extra cows or bullocks we used to sell them and earn some money.

But in the new resettlement colony, she explained, there was insufficient space to keep livestock, and poultry became sickly and died young:

> Now women just sit idly. All that they do is light the stove, clean the utensils...They go to gather firewood. They bring coal, cook food, and feed. This is what they do. When there is no work, what else is there to do?

Unlike Devcharan Munda, Punia recalls that before resettlement some women in the villages did take outside work, particularly when the domestic and agricultural load was lighter: "We used to go out to work...We usually worked locally but also went out if required [for] contract work. We used to go to the Rai mines to cut coal." Despite some male concerns about women working outside, it is clear from the interviews that many of the women competed for casual laboring jobs in and around the mines and coal depots.

Education Is a Benefit

Tetri Kisku was one of the interviewees who spoke of the advantages that came with the mines. Her village turned down offers to relocate them in residential "quarters" in a purpose-built site, preferring more space, and she was interviewed in the home she had built in a small hamlet close to Urimari mine, South

Karanpura coalfield: "We said that we can't live in these quarters so give us money instead...The quarters were not according to our choice. We, who live in villages, don't like such small houses...We had cows, buffaloes, and goats. It is not possible to keep cattle in the quarters."

As a result, CCL provided them with compensation, but offered no help with relocation. Some villagers, including Tetri's family, then moved to the other side of the mine, and built their homes on land that they had previously used for cultivation. She recalled the way her extended family used to live:

> We had sufficient produce to run the house. My father's brothers were many, so they divided the harvest. Even then it was still enough for six months...Oh, we felt happy living then. There were no problems of food. But we did have problems of cash. And because of that, we had difficulty buying clothes and other things.
>
> [To get cash] we produced vegetables and sold them in the market. And then there was *lac* [resinous pigment, used in dyes and varnish] from the trees, which we worked for, tapping it and selling it. Some sold it for cash; some exchanged it for salt which they stored for the rainy season.

Tetri was 17 and married when CCL began operating in the area:

> They told the villagers that they were starting the coal mines here and that they were acquiring land. They surveyed and measured the land, then checked everyone's ancestral land deeds, then divided the land among the descendants...Three people got jobs for the land my husband's extended family had. One went to the grandson of the oldest *sasur* [literally, father-in-law, meaning her father-in-law's oldest brother], one to my husband, and one to my younger *sasur* [younger brother of her father-in-law].
>
> CCL said that whoever's land has been acquired would get a job in CCL and compensation—that we won't be poor any more, and we will no longer have money problems. Those days men and women were uneducated. There were few literate people. There was a government school at Jarjara. It was far away and so nobody went there. As it is, the tribal people are a superstitious and fearful lot. A few did go to school but those who didn't know any better didn't go...
>
> My *sasur* [father-in-law] was the one who gave his thumb impression [as a signature]. So he did everything. He knew we had a money-crunch. At that time we were very happy with what we got. Now we have come to know the value of the land. We got only three jobs. But we gave 16 acres of land, not nine acres. We don't know what happened with the rest of the land. Did my *sasur* arrange for some other people to also get jobs? We don't know. He has been dead for the past five, six years...

The management told us that first you take the three jobs and later on claim the others. We thought, well, the other boys are young still. When they grow old enough to work, we'll claim the jobs that were due to them. [When they were older] we demanded the jobs but the management said that the matter is finished and you won't get any more jobs now. What the agreement was between my father-in-law and CCL, we don't know...What will my children do?

Like many narrators, Tetri felt their lack of education put them at a major disadvantage in the negotiations over compensation. And although she believed "we could have been more prosperous doing agricultural work," she identified one positive outcome of CCL's presence:

We got the opportunity to educate our children...I feel that my parents did wrong in not letting me be educated. My husband is a little educated. I don't want my sons and daughters to be like me. I ask myself that why should we *adivasi* not be educated and thus progress?

At the time of the interview all five of her children were in school, and her husband's "little" education had helped him improve his prospects. Tetri was evenhanded in her assessment of the situation. She criticized the local leaders, who had conducted negotiations on the villagers' behalf, for quarreling among themselves and for not always being open and honest: "Now the people are realizing that a lot has been lost. People say [the leader] is the one who has created the confusion in the land acquisitions for his own advantage. He was the one who used to talk to the officials." However, as time moved on she observed that the leaders were representing the interests of the workers in the established collieries, and that "in some ways they are good":

As far as departmental promotion is concerned they are good. They go and talk to the General Manager and demand promotion and increment for those people who are good workers but who are being overlooked for some reason...Yes, they have done some good for the workers. Now my husband has become a fitter, earlier he was just a mechanic.

Of course, you have to be a good worker. If you are, they go to the management and make a report in your favor. The management then sends you for training and there is a rise in the salary. My husband has received training. He now has juniors under him whom he trains.

However, a 2010 report found that most local people from the 14 villages displaced by Urimari mine were working as casual laborers, as was Tetri, loading and unloading coal trucks in the nearby depot, which she said CCL set up in response to their demands for local employment. Many were under 20 years old, and there was a high proportion of *adivasi* girls and young mothers with infants.[17] Work at the dump was irregular and tough. "But we have to work [there] otherwise how else to earn a living?" asked Tetri, who was determined to keep her children in school. A machine for loading coal was introduced, increasing people's anxiety: "The job that ten people used to do is done by one machine. Yes, we protested, but the leaders chose not to hear. Both men and women protested and blocked the road. Then the Block Development Officer came and said the machines are for loading coal dust only, and for lumps of coal, it will be the people who will continue doing the work."

"We have an opportunity to mix"

Tetri, determined not to become a prisoner in her home, had embraced the opportunity to learn Hindi. "Yes, definitely, the language we use to speak has changed. We talk a lot in Hindi now, though still not too well." Although she was concerned about the loss of tribal languages, the increased use of Hindi brought some advantages:

> Now we have an opportunity to mix with other communities. We go out and talk. There's a girl whose father died and she actually got a job in the Office in his place. But she needed a transfer which they wouldn't give. So we women marched to Ghutwa in protest. They had to transfer her. We felt better [for doing this]. This way we can help other women and stop them from being oppressed and exploited.

For Tetri, resettlement meant that her community had access to electricity, water, and education and, through the gradual mastery of Hindi, new social opportunities and the potential to improve their circumstances by speaking directly with company officials. However, the loss of land and a growing dependency on uncertain wage labor had created new vulnerabilities:

> Earlier we grew our food. Now we have to buy everything. How can we earn money? Prices have increased, and they will increase even more. Now we can give money to our children, but if we die what will the children do? There is no guarantee of jobs.

"Our society has been broken"

> We worship nature but when nature itself does not survive, how can there be any prayers? The biggest harm that the colliery has done is that we losing our own identity.
>
> —Somar Soren

In spite of her increased confidence about being a part of mainstream Indian society, Tetri had wider concerns about more fundamental threats to tribal culture and religious beliefs and practices as their assimilation deepened.

> We are *adivasis* but nowadays we are also counted amongst the Hindus. So in the colliery area we also do the same as others and worship at the temples. Before, we never went to the temples. Now I see *adivasis* have even constructed temples everywhere...My ancestors did not do this...This is because of the coming of the colliery.

Many narrators, for example, commented that their festivals were declining in popularity. Sadhan Prajapati believed they were losing their significance, and simply becoming occasions for demoralized young men to behave badly, citing the abuse of alcohol in particular: "I don't feel like going to celebrate the Karma festival, since most people get drunk on that day. Gradually we are forgetting our festivals, the significance...some people don't even remember the day for this festival."

Punia Devi agreed that the celebration of festivals is declining in intensity, but she didn't attribute this solely to a loss of cultural pride and identity. For those who work, she pointed out, the nature of their new lives has had an impact:

Figure 6.2 Sadhan Prajapati, one of the narrators. Photo by Justin Imam.

"Previously we were living off the land and could afford time to celebrate festivals. Now people have to go for work to earn and cannot devote much time to celebrate festivals." Not only are they constrained by the demands and timetables of paid work, she observed, they are "very tired" by their labor.

Sadhan Prajapati drew attention to a further negative trend, stemming from the adoption of mainstream practices: the expectation that parents were expected to provide dowry to the groom's family.

> It was not like that in those days. The dowry was given to the bride and the groom did not get anything except clothes...I feel that respect for daughters has gone down. The girl's parents have to bow down to the wishes of the groom's family... Earlier, a girl's father used to be proud of his daughter, but now he is really worried... one who lives on his labor alone finds dowry a big burden.

It is hard to know at what pace these changes would have occurred without resettlement. Certainly life was anyway transforming for many tribal populations as the fast-growing Indian economy, the encroachment of state authority into rural lives, and new information and communication technologies imposed on traditional lifestyles. However, what can be observed from these interviews is that resettlement dramatically accelerated that process, while also removing some of the props that might have cushioned people's adaptation to these increasingly powerful influences. More importantly, the process of resettlement—the protracted, divisive negotiations—significantly weakened them, so that they were demoralized and anxious at precisely the point they were required to face the challenges of new livelihoods and environments.

Certainly, a constant regret of these narrators is a strong perception that their societies were fracturing and weakening. In addition to the loss of trust in their leaders that Tetri and many others describe during the negotiation period, there were other important changes to traditional practices. Many narrators spoke approvingly of how disputes between individuals and families used to be resolved within the community. This system remains, Tetri said, but has weakened: "If somebody doesn't want to obey the community then he goes to the *thaana* [police station]. This never happened earlier. Our sense of community is gone since the coming of the mines. It will go even more in the future generations."

Ramprasad Ganjhu, 45, also regretted the changes to traditional structures that previously held the community together:

> Earlier, there was unity...If there was a fight, we all sat together and discussed it, and the various parties were made to understand each other and the problem was solved. If there was much trouble then the *panchayat* [village council] sat and everyone collected at one place...In this way, problems were discussed among ourselves only...

But young people don't want to sit in the *akhara* [community meeting place] and discuss their problems... Boys are attracted towards the bright lights [of the city] and no longer have any interest in the old customs... Tribal dancing is slowly ending. The Karma festival is seldom celebrated. All of this causes me deep pain in the heart.

Earlier in the chapter we heard Ramprasad's story of the unsuccessful stand against CCL taken by his village and four other villages. Since then, Ramprasad said, his community had lost its way, and he felt the psychological toll was visible: "Our fields have gone, our lifestyle has changed and our society has been broken... These days everywhere you go you hear the same thing—someone has drunk himself to death, someone has TB [tuberculosis], or someone has lost their mind. Those whom we brought up in our own laps, they look older than us. Everyone is jobless and they are ruining themselves with drink. In our village two or three have died."

Despite such demoralization, he felt it was not too late to fight back: "The land that has gone is not going to return. But one thing we have to do is to be united... Misunderstandings between ourselves give others the opportunity to put pressure on us... If we show unity, then we can scare CCL... If we stand together, then we can gain a lot."

CHAPTER 7

"The wisdom of living in this place will be lost"
Mohale Dam, Lesotho, before Resettlement

It is a sad state [of affairs] to leave behind fields—our fathers' fields—because we had hoped that our children would also use them. We are very concerned about how our children will live without access to the fields...We need help from anywhere, because we never thought that some day we would move out of this place—but because we are nothing, the planners planned and we are not part of the planning.

—Lipholo Bosielo

These are the reflections of Lipholo Bosielo as he contemplated leaving his village in the foothills of Lesotho's Maluti Mountains, prior to the construction of the Mohale Dam. He had been born in and had raised his family in Molika-liko, a mountain valley, which was to be inundated by the dam's reservoir. He was interviewed in late 1997, when he was 67, some six months before the Lesotho government initiated the resettlement plan. As a young man, recently married, he had left Molika-liko each year to take contract work in the South African mines, as did many men of his generation. Working conditions were tough and he contracted an infection in his legs that forced him to give up mining and continued to cause him great pain. Since the 1960s he had supported his family by farming, basket-making, mending shoes, and transporting cattle and goods to markets for others. His wife brewed beer and made brooms.

This chapter draws on interviews with Lipholo and others in Molika-liko, who took the opportunity to describe their current way of life, as well as their hopes and fears for the future.[1] His experiences and those of others reveal important insights into the complex ways in which the prospect and then the inevitability of relocation have profound impacts on the lives of communities and individuals. These are impacts that carry through the displacement, relocation and resettlement process but, as the interviews reveal, they are insufficiently acknowledged and understood by development planners. The accounts drawn on in this chapter cast a light on the negotiation process that takes place between affected populations and state authorities in land acquisition and resettlement. It reveals a distance of understanding between officials and local populations made worse by bureaucratic language and minimal accountability. The following chapter takes the story on, and looks at what happened to the people of Molika-liko after they were moved.

Introduction and Background

The kingdom of Lesotho is entirely surrounded by South Africa, and it is the only country in the world with all its territory more than 1,000 meters (3,588 feet) above sea level. It has little cultivable land and few mineral resources. However, its mountains form the region's most important watershed. In 1986 the government of Lesotho signed a treaty with South Africa to implement the Lesotho Highlands Water Project (LHWP), one of Africa's largest and most complex engineering schemes. The LHWP was designed to divert water from Lesotho's primary river, the Senqu (Orange) River, via a series of tunnels and five dams, to South Africa's industrial heartland. In return, Lesotho was to receive royalties from the sale of water and to gain hydroelectric power for domestic consumption. The 1986 treaty was followed by a series of feasibility studies and the massive construction task was divided into several phases.

Under Phase 1A the 185-meter-high (607-foot-high) Katse Dam, the mainstay of the scheme, was built. According to the LHWP about 372 households, approximately 2,300 people, were affected by the construction of the dam and related infrastructure, such as roads and powerlines.[2] Some 1,800 hectares of arable land and 3,000 hectares of grazing land were also lost. Lipholo Bosielo and his neighbors were resettled at the end of the 1990s under Phase 1B of the multiyear, billion-dollar project, to make way for the second major dam, Mohale Dam, and associated infrastructure. As well as the displaced, others were affected and were compensated for partial loss of land, and loss of other assets or access. The LWHP states some 390 households, approximately 1,700 individuals, were affected, but as with Katse, other estimates are higher.[3]

In addition, Molika-liko was a particularly fertile river valley. Thayer Scudder noted, "The rich alluvial soils lost to the Mohale reservoir were literally some of the most fertile land in Lesotho" and LHWP's 1997 Environmental

Impact Assessment for Phase 1B estimated that around 3,000 people relied on food grown in the area now in the inundation zone.[4] Given Lesotho's lack of cultivable land—FAO estimates it to be just 6.9 percent of the total land area—loss of any cropland can affect local food security. The governments of Lesotho and South Africa are negotiating terms for the construction of further dams at Mashai, Tsoeliki, and Ntoahae.

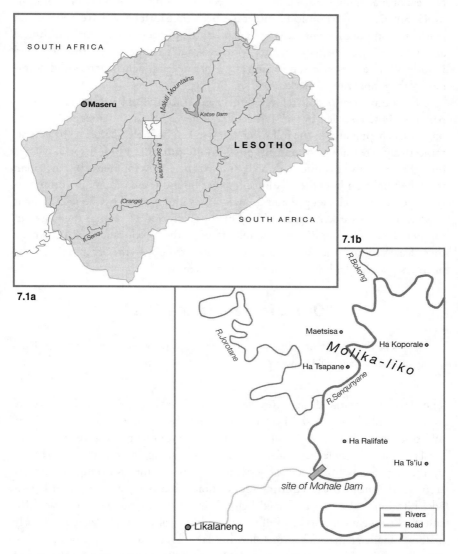

Figure 7.1   a. Map of Lesotho, showing area affected by the construction of Mohale Dam and reservoir. b. Detail of Molika-liko valley, near Mohale Dam construction site. Maps by Julie Anson.

The background to the LHWP is one of extremes: one of the world's largest and most costly engineering projects sited in the most impoverished region of one of the globe's poorest nations. The treaty that sets out the agreement was signed between South Africa's apartheid government and Lesotho's military regime during a period in which relations between the two countries were strained and neither government was characterized by transparency. The strengths of the management team lay in boring tunnels and building dams, not in the complex process of managing land acquisition or reconstructing livelihoods and communities. Since then the political context has been transformed, as have policies and guidelines on resettlement, yet the legacies of the project's focus on the technical and engineering challenges remain.[5] Moreover, such a huge project overwhelmed Lesotho's human resources, dwarfing any other development schemes and dominating the employment market.

The number of people relocated in Phase 1B of the LHWP was small compared to those resettled by the Tarbela Dam; nevertheless, the interviews drawn on in this chapter and in the following one—taken before and after resettlement, respectively—reveal important insights into the processes of local social change brought about by this internationally funded mega-development. In particular, they shed light on how the relationships that bound these mountain communities together were challenged and in many cases undermined by the resettlement process, in turn weakening the ability of those affected to rebuild their lives in the new location. The disempowering effect of the development, which made them feel as though they were nothing, features strongly in the testimonies: "The planners planned and we are not part of the planning."

"Our Life Here Is the Soil"

> The things that are going to be lost are many, [above all] the wisdom of living in this place will be lost.
>
> —Sebili Tau

The interviews featured here provide a compelling description of the everyday lives of people living in the Lesotho Highlands before the construction of the hydro schemes that so drastically altered the environment, social relations, and local economy. They reveal a life that was far from static, but one that was shaped by the regional political economy, which saw many men working as migrant laborers in South Africa, remitting money home, but being absent for long periods. Life for those who remained behind, in particular the women, was difficult as they were expected to fulfill those additional tasks that were previously in the domain of the men. But following lay-offs in the South African mines, opportunities for work declined after 1990. By 2000, many migrant laborers had returned home for good.

Those workers who rejoined Lipholo in the villages of Molika-liko came back to a way of life that had changed little for generations. Agriculture and livestock formed the mainstay of the villagers' existence, though most of them supplemented this with a variety of income-generating activities. The isolation and relative fertility of their sheltered mountain valley, far from police and other authorities, had allowed cannabis cultivation to replace migrant labor as the main source of income. It proved an effective strategy, and many narrators explained how the income made them feel "wealthy" and in a position to pay their children's school fees.

As well as selling cannabis, surplus crops, and animal products such as wool and mohair, people bartered or earned money from small-scale commercial ventures. They harvested medicinal plants and, like Lipholo and his wife, brewed beer and made mats, hats, ropes, and brooms from local grasses.

Farming marginal lands such as these mountain valleys, however fertile they were relative to the rest of Lesotho, required skill and accumulated knowledge of the agroecology. Mountain farms, partly because of the steep slopes, are characterized by a diversity of climatic conditions and thus of natural and cultivated plant life. One field may present the farmer with several different microclimates. The residents of Molika-liko were proud of their knowledge, but they were all too aware that such skills are localized and might not readily transfer to different environments. For Sebeli Tau, the greatest loss resulting from resettlement would be that of "the wisdom of living in this place." The examples he gave included knowing the most favorable times and places to cultivate crops or gather wild foods and medicinal plants, and where to shelter livestock, find the first spring pastures, and collect raw materials for building, carving, or weaving.

Sebili, a former worker in the South African mines, was 46 years old when interviewed, and he spoke with pride and affection of Molika-liko:

> You see this valley is beautiful. Even you, when you arrive, you see that this land is a special mountainous area. You know, we even plant sorghum here. It succeeds quite well. It is warm.
>
> It is really a [sheltered] valley. Even the frost takes some time to arrive here. The snow falls but it usually snows on the high-lying area. Even when it comes down here, [it does not stay] because there is a lot of water. There are reedy areas. Snow is a thing that is afraid of water. It goes away quickly.
>
> [Neighboring villages] understand each other well. We support each other well. I can easily leave from here to go and plough in partnership (sharecrop) over there. It is a thing that is well supported. Well, even when they have rustled animals we still talk to one another...Sometimes it happens that there are little quarrels...but there's no fighting and spilling of blood.
>
> I like it here a lot...The people of [surrounding villages] buy food from here...If you were to go into the houses of people who have planted, you will

find, right there at my home, you will find bales—maybe four—still there, in
storage—from this same year's maize harvest... I have one field of my own, but
I usually plough in partnerships. Right here with the old people, or here, with
people who do not have cattle. Or those who are needy in the hands like the
handicapped.

The narrators spoke frequently about successfully functioning informal institutions within and across the villages that made "ploughing in partnership"
possible. The field's owner supplied the land, and the sharecropper provided
seed as well as the labor and cattle for ploughing. The harvest was split equally
between owner and sharecropper, who in many cases had lived alongside each
other for decades. People often sharecropped with the elderly or infirm, who
lacked the strength to work their own land, and so the arrangement was mutu-
ally beneficial.

Sebili described the productivity of the land and livestock:

> Seedlings are still grown in the village here. They are going to be planted there
> in the fields. You will find that maize has been planted. Cabbage has been
> sown on the lower side. Now, things like wheat, you can see for yourself also
> as you are walking by the fields here... Maize is especially liked because it is
> the [staple] food.
>
> The things that are going to be lost [when we resettle] are many... Things
> like [wild] vegetables which we are now used to, and we know their places,
> where they grow... As to a certain medicine, when I want it I know where to
> find it. Or when I plant a vegetable here, how do I plant it, in what month?
> I know what time to look for them and when they will germinate and sprout,
> and so on.
>
> It is true that there is not a lot of grass here, but the cattle here are used
> to it... Our cows grow old here and they have seven calves. [Usually] it is dif-
> ficult for a cow to have seven calves. A cow usually ends up [in the course of
> its lifetime] with four calves but ours here have seven. Now our grass is not
> tough... you know even in winter, once it feels a little rain it immediately starts
> growing again; now our cattle are used to this *mokuru* and this *lesuoane* [variet-
> ies of grass]—even in winter the pasture does not dry up.

Sebili acknowledged, however, changing climatic conditions and a growing pressure on their natural resources. Rainfall was described as less predictable: "This
land was very good for crops but now it is... changing and is causing us hunger
during these times of drought." Some of the wildlife was disappearing, and it was
a struggle to persuade others to conserve stocks:

> Animals that were always here were springboks, steenbok, bucks, and
> hares... They are of benefit to us [so] we once protected them a lot, so that they

should not be killed...Springboks I no longer see. Now these steenboks and these bucks, they are the ones that we protect a lot so that they should not be shot at. A lot of people have bought guns from the government. They should leave them alone...and the hares. Now sometimes they try and set dogs on them but we are still trying to show them the mistake of doing so.

"The field I trust"

For most of the narrators, land was not only their prime asset, it was an integral part of their lives and identity. As Motseki Motseki said: "Our life here is the soil, we live by agriculture." Many spoke with pride about how their intimate knowledge of the landscape, in all its variety and changeability, ensured the survival of their families, farms, and livestock. Fields were described as having a nurturing quality, almost as though they were members of the family. Motseki Motseki said of the land he inherited: "These fields...truly they are able to bring up the grandchildren and great-grandchildren of their owners," and Thabang Makatsela captured the essence of what would be lost with the dam's construction:

My memories of this place [would be] firstly, my father's big field down the valley which was a source of food for the whole family throughout my childhood. All my brothers and sisters knew we all survived because of that field. This is to say we grew up feeding on that field...This field has also been of great importance to my family as a whole, in the sense that my son and I consume food from this field. It is so big that it allows us to grow different crops on it at the same time.

'Manthatisi Motšoane, a mother of six, saw the relationship between the farmer and land as one of "trust," a certainty that she could rely on one particular field to keep her family fed. As part of the preparation for resettlement she was instructed not to plant that field, as she would have left the area by harvest time. "We have just been stopped from ploughing our best field that manages to feed the whole family...It is within the area that will be covered by the water. [That is] the field I trust. There are others I don't trust that much. They do not give me enough crops."

The ban on cultivation was one of several initiatives from the Lesotho Highlands Development Authority (LHDA) that led to confusion. The authorities first announced a date for the removal from Molika-liko to take place, but then missed the deadline and failed to provide food aid to compensate affected farmers for the forfeited harvest.[6] This change of plan fueled the villagers' growing lack of confidence in the authorities to deliver what they promised.

Unlike most of these narrators, 'Manthatisi Motšoane was from Ha Koporale, a village that was going to be affected by the dam construction, but would not ultimately be inundated by the reservoir. At the time of the interview, she was hoping to relocate somewhere not far from her present home, and she did not therefore have quite the same fear of the unknown that troubled so many others. She was also keen to point out that there had been some gains from the project, not least because it had brought the first signs of development to the area by building bridges and an access road to the dam site. One son, who previously lived higher up the mountain in the cattle posts, herding livestock for a living, now had a job with the project, bringing much-needed income into the household.[7] She commented:

> We have long been asking for a road. Even our husbands, while they were work-ing in the mines, they wanted so much to join hands and build a bridge, but all in vain. LHDA has come to our rescue...If I go to Maseru now, I return the same day. In the past...I had to go [the night before] to a village nearer to the road, then in the morning wait for a bus. When I reached Maseru, I did my business and then I had to ask for accommodation in somebody's house and to spend the night there so that I could wake up early in the morning to queue for a bus coming back home...
>
> This big river is the Senqunyane...It gave us problems because when it was flowing high, we were unable to go to the other side, because there was no bridge. Sometimes we had to cross it the previous day and spend a night on the other side if [someone was] sick or someone had died whose body had to come home...To me [that river] was just a troublemaker. Well, these days the problems are over because of the bridges.

"Our sons are employed"

She continued her commentary:

> [My husband] is doing nothing now. We are helped by our son who left school at standard five. He got piecework with LHDA, though people were not happy about that. They objected to him being employed when he is unmarried. They said he was too young to work...The chief, together with his committee, complained that the boy was never on the list of those who sought jobs. It is true I didn't give them his name to be listed because he was then at the cattle post, but when he came home he found that his companions were working with LHDA. He also went to queue for employment and he was lucky...
>
> There may be some problems here and there, like in any other things in life. But generally our lives have changed [because of the project]. Though our husbands are no longer working in the mines, our sons are employed by the project—they are helping us. Our children manage to buy clothes for them-selves, which we could not afford if they were still looking after animals like

my son was. If it were not for this project, my son would be looking after somebody's livestock to earn money. He is now helping his father who is unemployed...People [like my husband] who are affected by the project are usually promised jobs, but it is just a promise that is never kept...

Many people are hungry and therefore need work. So I don't mind when people are employed. The only thing that does not satisfy me is that most of these people come from outside our area. Our people here are just watching them work and they do nothing. We are told that these people are "experts," they know this and that. It is not fair...After the chief of the place complained to the officials of the project about the employment of the outsiders, [more] local people got employment...

Coming to my opinion about moving, I can just say I have accepted it...We have learned from people who have been moved already. They are given money, which is called compensation. This money covers many things like houses, fields, *kraals* [livestock enclosures], gardens, and others...I personally don't like [what has happened], but what else can one do? It has come to our lives; we simply have to accept it.

Motseki Motseki, 45, was less sanguine about his future prospects. He compared the power of the land to support his family through generations against the short-lived benefits of cash compensation: "These children of mine—are they going to bring up their children with [that compensation]? Money that just goes out and there being nothing to come back?" Money, unlike land, is a finite resource; it enables people to engage in the market but is described as being spent "without returns." Motseki's experience of "the lowlands," by which he meant anywhere below Molika-liko, was that it was a place where everything must be bought and so "the only thing that matters is money."

The life of the lowlands requires a person to be working. Both the father and the mother have to work to avoid hunger...[Here] whether you work or you do not work, you are still able to get [food and other necessities] from this agriculture of ours. Now where there is no agriculture...the only thing that matters there is money...you go and buy paraffin there [for the primus stove]...Now here, it is ten times better because...here people still collect wood, plant in the fields. We do not buy food in tins or in those packets...

Our life here is the soil, we live by agriculture. We cultivate the fields, we plant maize, we plant wheat, we plant beans, peas, cannabis, *harese* [barley]. We are already eating the *lehoetla* [autumn harvest] of peas. By the third month we will be harvesting wheat and by the fifth month we will thresh it...Immediately it is harvested they start brewing things like ginger beer...they cook wheat bread, things like that. Now...we have already started harvesting the new cannabis...which means now we already have money...

> We plant crops to eat—but even these we sell, too, and we make a little money, like that. You will find that sometimes we harvest four bales or five, depending on the size of field... Maybe someone from the lowlands... comes with a bag of sorghum. You exchange with him this one of wheat. Or maybe you take this wheat down and you are going to sell it in the lowlands.

Although Motseki and the other farmers were prepared to engage with the market, they chose to do so on their terms; the concern was that relocation would bind them into the monetized economy and the new social relations it demanded. He also expressed some doubts about one of the reasons given for leaving the land:

> The chief, when he speaks, he says the land is used up and there are no longer any places [to farm]... One year we sow maize, in the other field it would be wheat, another [year]... we change them... If you now plant only one thing in the field for up to three or four years, it no longer comes out well... On occasions, when it is said that [the crops] have not done well, truly I still come out with maybe four bags from that one field... [We manage] very well... My children... have already been to those high schools...
>
> Most places we go to, you will find that these people who harvest a lot... would have used manure or animal dung or whatever. But here at the place of Molika-liko there is not even one person who plants with manure or fertilizer or anything like that. The crops here grow high; they are up to here [gestures]. And ever since we started the practice of sowing in lines our harvest grows in a wonderful way, whereas in years of old we were people who just sowed by hand [broadcasting]... We collect seed for ourselves when we sow these fields of ours—we do not buy it.
>
> Drought [is] the only thing that bothers us, nothing else. Snow, when it is there, it does not destroy anything... Sometimes it falls while we are harvesting but then it does not do that much harm. The damage might just be to the animals. They might die when they are still up the mountains there, but not in large numbers even then... Here at Molika-liko, here snow does not last even two days. This place, it is as if it were not a place of the mountains... The warmth that is here, again it is not like that of the mountain area. Our animals succeed better than those from many places because it is warm. It is like the lowlands here, yet it is in the mountains. The soil does not even need to be improved.

There is evidence confirming his view that the Molika-liko valley featured especially fertile soils, and that it generated a food surplus that was bought by neighboring communities.[8] Motseki further described the land's livestock potential:

In summer like this, the animals have left and they have gone up to the plateaux there. And then it would be that we suspend [grazing] here...and now this grass which is at home will grow again...it becomes plentiful...The small part of [the herds] that has remained—those cows that have just calved—will be given an area big enough for them...

Who looks after the animals? [It could be] a person who has no children, who is still a boy...It has always been the case from the beginning that we lived by hiring other people's children and, even as it is right now, I still just live by them, the children of other people. I would have a herder for cattle; I would have a herder for sheep; each and every year...When the year ends—one, I pay him with a cow. One wants sheep—I take out 12 sheep—the other one wants money, I take out money that is equivalent to those sheep...

Ach, there is nothing that we do, truly, except for our caring [for the soil]...Life here is much better than in the lowlands...When [an elderly person] does not have relatives and then, let us say, he or she does not have fields—they are still able to plant for themselves. Sometimes they do not have animals but they will talk to a person who does and they will plant in halves [sharecrop]...The elderly of here do not need much money...

We are not persecuted by those police pick-up vans; the police do not bother us [about cannabis]. When you hear me so insistent on this matter about the life of the lowlands...that the people there live on this flour that is "put under the armpit" [prepacked and carried in paper packets]...[it is because] now, here, we live a very good life.

Motseki spoke of the investment he had made in constructing a cement house, which was intended to provide a home for his children:

I have made expenses here, [making] this expensive building, because I did not think even one day I might find myself emigrating from this place of my home. I took it as my home area, where even these children of mine will also grow up...I actually never felt, even on a single day, that I would find myself not being inside Molika-liko. I shall miss too many things.

In contrast to the way Motseki had actively looked after his family by working the land and livestock, along with various income-generating activities, he felt he had had no voice in the decision making around resettlement: "But today, it is with misfortune [that] we are befallen by this thing, which has already been decided and us as people, we do not have power."

He was also worried about how they would be received by the new communities. Those who were likely to play host to the resettlers from Molika-liko knew that compensation had been paid and there were rumors that thieves were intending to target the new arrivals: "At those places we have chosen, we have already heard it being said that we are like 'cheques'...[and] the thieves will be trying to get that compensation money...That is a saying, which we hear is coming from these places where we are going."

Different World Views

> The [LHDA] tell us that they will compensate us...They say that, on the matter of our fields, an acre will be so much. Now, an acre—we do not know [what it is]...because we have not been shown it. Now these are not things that we can trust because we have not been shown how much an acre is.
>
> —'Malibuseng Mosotho

As well as being concerned about exchanging the long-term reliability of land for the more finite resource of money, narrators expressed anxiety about the terms of their compensation. While their financial skills and experience varied, even the most astute had some difficulty understanding the compensation arrangements, not least because they changed several times. A significant number reported that they had tried to understand the complicated arithmetic of the different compensation packages but had failed: one man said it was just a complicated morass of numbers, like a deliberately puzzling game they played to trick each other called *morabaraba*.

The country's lack of cultivable land meant that that people's preferred option, to be compensated by "soil for soil," was rarely possible. Compensation packages were complicated but in brief, the resettled were to get individual recompense for fields and other material assets, and community compensation for loss of access to shared natural resources. People could elect to receive some of their annual compensation in grain rather than in cash. There was also a one-off "disturbance allowance" (payable over the first three years), and there were to be income-generating projects and training.

One of the first sources of concern was the method of asset valuation employed, in particular the way the LHWP staff measured the resettled's fields. For the villagers, time, dates, and measurements are expressed in different ways than those of the LHWP staff. The past, for example, may be expressed in terms of memorable events, not specific years. Tlali Mokhatla described himself as born during the time of "Germany," meaning the First World War. His "grandmothers," he explained, moved up the valley and settled in Ha Tsapane "during the time of the dust," meaning the severe drought of the 1930s that was preceded by a massive dust storm. He recollected how as a boy he had herded livestock in the mountains but had had no education, which he regretted: "I see it that it has a benefit, you help your children and your parents live. At that time I did not think anything [of it]."

He believed his lack of education disadvantaged him in the negotiations and he confessed that he found the terms of compensation almost impossible to understand. His testimony revealed that he was distressed at the prospect of leaving, agreeing with Motseki that agriculture was as productive as ever in the late 1990s, prior to their relocation: "There is no change."

> The only change is because when we are being removed, agriculture we are not going to find. Now we see that we are being killed, we are being butchered...[The LHDA] affects us by taking our lives away from us. Fields are our lives. They are taking them away so that we cannot plant them...
>
> [People of the lowlands] are going to hire us; we are going to cut wood for them. Benefits [for us] are not there. Even just a small one, it does not exist...We are being lied to, and being told that we will get amazing wealth of bags and bags of money. I am saying there is not even one person who has got a cent!

Tlali Mokhatla frequently returned to the fact that the authorities had promised compensation, but how it was to be worked out remained a mystery to him:

> Even though I forget the amount, we are [going to be] compensated. These same houses that you see, these same vegetable gardens are being taped [measured]; they keep saying that we shall be compensated. These trees we have planted, they are many: "You will be compensated, old man." But I do not know how I shall be compensated for the big trees that I am already using. The trees which are still young shoots, they say it is 3 rand [approximately US$0.48 at 1999 rates]; the big ones they say they have not been told the price. They are promising us but now we no longer know where we stand.

He suspected that those with education were treated more favorably by LHWP staff, and he resented being told by his village chief that when he relocated he could only bring a few livestock because of the lack of grazing:

> We see that the chiefs are now turning in the direction of the Highlands Water [Project] and the government, [saying] that we should not have animals...We are not pulling in a similar direction...
>
> Me, I chose for myself that I want money for those fields...I will then eat from it, because there will be no longer a place where I would be going [to farm]; I would not ploughing, I would not be doing anything. I would just be sending a child to bring me flour wrapped in paper so that I can eat.

The difference in perception and expression of time and measurement between LHWP staff and the older villagers in particular, allied to the complexity of the compensation arrangements, undermined the villagers' confidence in the resettlement arrangements. Tsatsi Motseki, who was in his seventies and lived in Maetsisa, articulated his fears that those losing their land and being forced to relocate away from the dam site were somehow being cheated. They were not familiar with units of measurement such as hectare and acre. For many of the villagers, the productivity of a field—how many bags of maize it yields, for example—is a far more accurate measure of its worth than its size, especially in a mountainous area where steep terrain can mean one field contains a variety of soil and temperature conditions and productivity is closely allied to the farmers' knowledge and inputs.

Tsatsi Motseki's description of the way the value of the land was being assessed revealed a clash between modern standardized forms of measurement and traditional approaches, a clash that left the villagers feeling that their own values and ways of understanding the world were being ignored. He observed that LHWP officials measured with the longer strides of "a European," so when he argued that his land equated to a higher number of strides, they said it equaled fewer strides and therefore was of less value:

> You know we are going to be cheated cruelly here. Cruel cheating. It is here we are in misfortune...they were in fact stepping [measuring] in a European way, like this. They were not stepping like a black person; but [like a European] who makes a long stride, who does like this [*he takes a big stride*] and then they say that this field is this many hectares.

It is not hard to see how such misunderstandings would compound feelings of distrust and undermine the relationship between the LHWP staff and the villagers. Further problems occurred when they were shown architects' drawings of the new housing, which employed a visual language with which they were not familiar. Misunderstandings multiplied. Thabang Makatsela, who talked so eloquently about how his memories of Molika-liko would be dominated by his father's field, gave an example of how further failures of communication increased the suspicion that the LHDA did not have their interests at heart:

> Even our houses and kraals were measured and we were around when they were being measured. But we were not told their measurements. It is to the LHDA's advantage to build small houses for us because we are not aware of the size of our houses, even though they are saying they want to build us bigger houses...
>
> My family had two rondavels and my brother had a house...This house was roofless and they told me to roof it so that it could be included in the compensation package. Then my problem is that I fail to understand the reason behind forcing us to roof those roofless houses, because we are leaving this place. So one begins to wonder and ask questions like: who is going to live in those houses? This implies that LHDA does not care about us because it wants us to spend more money on the property that we are leaving behind, and yet we still do not know how we are going to survive in the resettlement areas.

He had lost faith in LHDA's ability to keep its promises: "I know all of LHDA's promises and I have heard them from LHDA employees themselves and LHDA contractors." As time went by tension started to build up due to changes:

> When we asked them about these changes, they told us that initially promises were made by other contractors and now there are new contractors.
>
> We were promised a lot of things such as farming centers where we will be trained in vocational skills, including commercial livestock farming, poultry farming, and they even told us that those interested in keeping goats that produce five litres of milk would be helped. It was the first time that I learnt of a goat that can produce five litres of milk and I was so shocked!
>
> Now all these promises are no longer mentioned. Now the talk of the day is that "you are leaving," next year in February. No more promises.

Breaking the Threads

A key concern expressed by many narrators was how they would maintain their support systems, the formal and informal institutions and associations they had established in the valley, once they were scattered in different locations. Some systems were already under strain, giving them a foretaste of what might lie ahead. Institutions comprise complex sets of rules and require trust, time, and participation for them to be effective, including redress when the rules are broken. Many narrators described how friends and relatives in Molika-liko supported each other through periods of hardship, sometimes with cash but more often in kind. Repayment for food or cash at a crucial moment might be through an offer of labor at harvest or when ploughing or weeding was needed, or when seeds had germinated, or when livestock had produced offspring. But some of these methods of repayment were already becoming obsolete. They had been forbidden to continue cultivating their fields, on the basis that they would be relocated before the crops could be harvested, and some herders had already sold off much of their livestock because resettlement required people to reduce the number of their animals, at which point prices inevitably began to drop.

The elderly or infirm are particularly vulnerable to the breaking of these threads between neighbors. 'Maseipati Moqhali from Ha Tsapane was in her eighties at the time of the interviews. She did not know the exact year of her birth but recalled that when Lesotho's Paramount Chief Letsie II died, which was in 1913, she was a young woman. She wondered what would happen once those they depended upon for occasional assistance are scattered in different locations:

> We are dispersing like the young ones of a bird, others here; others there!... We do not know, now that we are going to live in other people's villages, who do

not know us, we do not know them. We are separating from our friends, these ones who were looking after us saying, "Grandmother, take some porridge"...It is cruelty.

As well as payment in kind for services rendered, Molika-liko residents had organized themselves into self-help associations, primarily to help one another with funeral costs. These burial societies, *Limpate sheleng* (literally, bury-me-shilling), were a key feature in the villagers' social landscape. Members made monthly contributions to a common fund that was used to assist people in cases of bereavement, but could be an occasional source of credit for other requirements. Virtually nobody borrowed from formal banking institutions because they lacked access to them and were unlikely to be seen as viable customers.[9]

But once they are scattered among strangers, asked 'Maseipati Moqhali, how will they know when someone is dead?

As for us, I feel that we are perplexed now that it seems that we are dispersing. And yet we had formed this society of "bury-me-I-bury-you," as to now, what shall we do? Because now, one is here! And the others are there!...People are saying "Hela, people will write to one another, people will listen to their radios [to hear news of a death]." Is it a thing that will happen?

It was not only the old who feared the pulling apart of the bonds between families and neighbors. 'Malibuseng Mosotho, a mother of six children in her early thirties, was interviewed in her home village of Ha Tsapane. She expressed her concerns about the dispersal of the community:

We live together well with [other villages in this area], we still help one another. They always come to help us with hoeing. A person would leave her home area and come and help me hoe...Well, when I harvest I would also see as to what I can give her. I am still expecting [such help] can happen, but now I no longer have trust...I am going to people whom I do not know, whom I am not used to. Now, I do not know how we shall behave to one another...

She went on to describe the fragmented way in which relocation decisions were made:

One said, "As for us we are going there." Two said, "As for us we are going there." Now you hear it was now a thing which was confused, and we are no longer going together. Some are remaining in the mountains; others are going somewhere else.

She was one of many who appeared to be uncomfortable at the way families were consulted about their relocation choices in their own homes, rather than in the traditional group meeting, the *pitso*. Lipholo Bosielo, whose words opened this chapter and who eventually relocated to Ha Nkhema (see Figure 8.1b), also expressed concern about the way people were encouraged to make decisions on an individual basis:

> I think it would have been better for the project to have marked a single area for resettling this village. In this way, only people who had a different view could be allowed to go elsewhere. But the project only told us as individuals to make our individual choices...
>
> We have already made our choice [of location] as the project asked us to. We are going in different directions and each one has hope that wherever he would go, he would get relatives to help him in time of need.

Some suspected that the consultation process and the subsequent scattering of families was a deliberate strategy on the part of the authorities to preempt united resistance. Whether this was true or not, by the late 1990s the LHDA had a credibility problem: the villagers were well aware of the problems, delays, and broken promises experienced by those displaced by the Katse Dam.[10] In addition, LHWP staff had changed some of the original arrangements they had outlined to the villagers of Molika-liko. Some of these, such as the increase in 1997 of the compensation period from 15 to 50 years, were positive responses to the criticisms leveled at the earlier arrangements for the people affected by Katse. Other changes, for example to compensation for communal assets, which required villages to develop "business plans," added complications and generated more

Figure 7.2 Lipholo Bosielo, one of the narrators in the Molika-liko valley. Photo by Kitty Warnock.

misunderstandings.[11] People had become wary and suspicious. And, not surprisingly, many of them were scared. They were about to leave behind everything that was known and familiar and they were haunted by the feeling that they were letting down past and future generations.

"Even the dead are going to rise against us"

The elderly Tlali Mokhatla was one of many who spoke about how leaving their land also meant abandoning the graves of the generations that preceded them. He feared that their ancestors would condemn them:

> [What I shall miss] is the graves which I see that we are going to be separated from and leave behind. Even the dead are going to rise against us and say "Are you going to leave us here, so we could be submerged by water?" They should come with us... [or they] will kill me, because they would be saying that I left them to drown in that water.

The LHDA was aware of this sensitive issue, and it offered money to exhume the graves and perform reburial ceremonies in the new locations. As the next chapter reveals, this turned out to be one of the promises that it fulfilled to almost universal satisfaction, despite this being a process fraught with difficulty with, for example, some people unsure where the oldest graves were.

It wasn't just past generations that the resettled felt they were letting down. Many parents felt the compensation money could not last long, once they had to pay for everything, and so they felt they were betraying the next generation as well, since they could no longer leave them land and the means to feed themselves. Leronti Moubane Chala, a father in his forties explained:

> Now that money does not satisfy me. It is true. Well, I will accept it, but as for my children, as for them... they have been cheated... They will work [if they can], but if they are not going to get work, there will be problems. They have been destroyed because that compensation is little. The children of my children will be born when the money is already finished. Even these children of mine, when they grow up... it will be already be finished... Some of them will not find education, judging by the amount of money that must be paid to schools.

Vulnerability

> We are going to live in other people's villages, who do not know us, we do not know them. We are separating from our friends, these one who were looking after us... It is cruelty.
>
> —'Maseipati Moqhali

Much of the vulnerability that people express has to do with the uncertainties that lie ahead. Some of this is practical: how can they be compensated for their most important but illegal cash crop, for example? In Molika-liko the farmers were able to grow and sell cannabis with little interference from the police. Makibinyane Mosotho explained: "Selling cannabis is illegal and I know that, but I have no choice. I have to feed my family and pay my children's school fees. When I sell cannabis it is not like I am intruding or invading somebody's property. It is not theft or murder; it is strictly business and I intend to continue it until I die." Thabang Makatsela, who was so disillusioned by the changing promises of LHDA, was similarly clear about its importance:

> Our main source of income is cannabis. People always come here to buy it from us, and it helps us a lot because with it we are able to pay our children's school fees and maintain our families...Even during Christmas our children are able to have new clothes, such that an outsider may even think we are employed. Maize and other crops cannot match the amount of money we get from cannabis. I even prefer to sell cannabis than to work in the mines because I get a lot of money from it. I know for sure that if I can sell two bags of cannabis I will be able to pay school fees for my kids and still have something left for maintaining the family. [But] let me tell you this: cannabis is illegal and people are afraid of being caught.

Both men knew that cultivating cannabis on the same scale was highly unlikely in the more populated and more heavily policed areas to which they were being relocated.

A more serious cause of vulnerability among those waiting for resettlement was the knowledge that they would be living without their familiar networks of friends and relatives, which gave them some protection from the difficulties of making a living. "We will not have an easy life," said Mokete Mohaieane of Ha Ralifate:

> The life of the town is heavy. If you do not have money you have no means of eating. You live by going to work—when it rains, whether it is cold, whether it is hot, you will go to work. If you do not go to work you do not have the means to eat. Here at home [in the mountains] the means are many. I use soil. I sow seed. There will germinate vegetables, maize, potatoes, pumpkin...I eat and become full.
>
> My feelings here on being made to emigrate [are that] there is nothing we can do because...[the authorities have] spoken, and in fact we cannot do anything because the country is the King's[12]...It is true [the South Africans] had asked for water, and even we could not do anything to this water because it comes and it passes, going down there without us stopping it to use it. Now,

there they have found a benefit that they should stop the water and go and work with it.

Now that they are making us emigrate [from] here, and are taking us to those places...we cannot have an easy life...like the one here, where we still are. No, never. I have chickens here, right now, outside here. If you were to look at these chickens of mine, you would find that they are having an easy life, because I have planted trees—there, they have gone into the forest. Even the hawk does not find their chicks. Now where we are going, it is just a plain unsheltered place.

He has kept his chickens safe from predators; he fears no such protection will exist for his poultry—or his family—in their new surroundings. Lipholo Bosielo expressed similar concerns:

The host people will not receive us kindly, saying that we are big-headed because we have much money that the Project gave us...In this village we have always been helping one another. But resettling in different locations...we would be foreigners in a foreign land.

"And then it will be that I am that man who just sits"

When the villagers had engaged with the regional and global economy as migrant workers, and in the local economy through both legal and illegal (cannabis) trade, this engagement was viewed as being largely under their control. In addition, the villagers were engaged in a complex system of exchange and barter with only occasional injections of cash. Mohlominyane Motseki, the headman of the community of Maetsisa, voiced the scepticism of many about the value of banks: "Banks? Here 'you catch a grasshopper straight to the mouth' [you lead a hand-to-mouth existence]." When you had any cash, he explained, you spent it right away:

You are going to buy food, you clothe yourself from it, you clothe the children from it. We do not [have enough money] to take any to the bank, except when, perhaps, with these fields of ours—which we hear they are going to compensate us for—maybe it is at that time a person can be able to take money to the bank.

Thus many narrators, unused to having sums large enough to keep as savings, tended to regard money as a finite resource that must keep being replenished, rather than a potentially productive resource capable of generating a secure future. The experience of being laid off from the South African mines had touched the lives of most of the families who were scheduled to be resettled, and the uncertainties of wage labor and the fear and humiliation of unemployment haunted many of the narrators.

Tokiso Moqhali from Ha Tsapane, with five children to care for, voiced this concern about future uncertainties, based in part on his own recent experience. Moqhali had taught himself to repair radios and shear sheep, and to build and roof houses as well as farm: "I ended school at standard three...My parents could not afford [to keep me there]. And it was then that I lived by working for other people. I lived by being hired. I was herding. They gave me a cow per year...After I married I stopped herding and then I became a person who is struggling on my own."

He had spent three years working in the capital, Maseru, trying to make a living and coming home on weekends when he could afford the fare. "I was struggling to find ways of putting food in my stomach...I used to carry sacks of flour on my head. I found that life there [was hard]!" In the end, he decided that working in the city was like "playing," by which he meant it was like doing something worthless. The money he earned was swallowed up in the extra costs: "Because I am paying rent, and I also have to buy groceries [for myself in Maseru]. I am also buying groceries this side [for my wife and children]." It was there he learnt about radio repairs, by observing others:

> I watched while people were repairing them. I kept hearing that "When it's like this, it's like this; when it's like this, it's like this...When the integrated circuit is burnt, it is like this; when the volume has gone down, it is like this"—and that's the way I kept learning those things, by just keeping on watching while they were doing repairs.

Like other interviewees, he was concerned about how their burial society would continue, saying that thinking about it, "our heads have stopped," unable to work it out.

He also described "the tricks" he used to survive in Molika-liko, which he feared would no longer be possible in the new location. Before, he explained, he could borrow an animal for ploughing or for transport, make some money, and over time manage to get himself some animals of his own:

> I would try tricks. Maybe when this seed of mine had germinated and I would have planted it, then I would have the means of food production and I would be able to sell it. Then maybe I will be able to buy some two sheep from someone who arrives in Molika-liko and is hungry. Maybe he would give me two sheep or even three [for the food] and then I would be able to go and look for a donkey to buy from people who pass through selling them. If he wants some sheep for the donkey, then I give him those sheep.

With a donkey he can transport goods for others, and in return they will pay him, or lend him cattle when he needs to plough. All of these possibilities, he fears, will be lost once they are resettled. Instead, the man who used to lend him livestock will refuse, saying "his own animals are getting finished and I should take time to get some of my own. But how can I do that there when I will not have the means anymore?"

In one way, 36-year-old Tokiso was better prepared for relocation than some, because he had more than "the wisdom of this place," the detailed knowledge of the local environment. He had other skills, such as radio repairing and roofing. But it is the farming he will miss most, he said, and it is lack of occupation and purpose that he most dreads. Clearly proud of his ability to provide for his young family, he expressed his fears about the pernicious effect of forced idleness:

> The important things that I will not forget [when I am resettled] are finding work when I was still living here at home, especially the fact that I can do things for myself with these hands of mine...I build and I also roof houses...
>
> [When I am resettled] I will remain thinking about ploughing, because when I am in another place there will be nowhere where I will plough. Now, at that time it will happen that I will have folded my arms and I would be asking myself as to who will help me? Who will at least give me some food? And then it will happen that nobody will help me. And then it will be that I am that man who just sits: I do not work...I am just sitting. And then it will happen that I will change and will end up stealing, as a result of thinking too hard about this agriculture of my home area here. That agriculture is the thing that will remain here in this heart of mine.

"Like a Rock on My Heart"

One of the strongest impressions that these people's stories leave is how powerful their attachment to the land is. They and their children spent most of their time out in the surrounding environment. Their interviews are steeped with descriptions of the fields and hills around them, and contain little on their actual houses or possessions. It was their attachment to the wider environment that was at the heart of their concept of home, not the geographically defined spaces of the family huts and compound.

Tokiso's grandmother is the elderly 'Maseipati Moqhali, who talked with trepidation about how they were being separated "like the young ones of a bird." She lived with his family and they were moving together. To her, the idea of being forced to relocate and losing her home to the reservoir was so unimaginable that she saw it as a disaster of an almost biblical nature: "We have been befallen by the great flood."

Here where I have built is a place where I have lived well...I was ploughing, I was eating and getting full in the stomach. I was planting each and every single crop in the fields. I was getting wild vegetables that have been created by God on the ground and I was being full in the stomach. I was living comfortably in this land where we are being removed from...Each and every crop, we plant each and every crop—peas, beans, wheat, maize...pumpkins, potatoes, every single thing...We cut grass, we weave, we help ourselves.

Without the means to "help ourselves" or the networks that support the elderly, she feared resettlement will reduce her to begging. "This place where I am going, what am I going to eat? Who will give me a field?" Memories of her life in Molika-liko will weigh heavily on her heart, she said:

I feel that the beat of my heart will be in the direction of this place where my life was. It will remain as a rock on my heart when I think of the place that I am being removed from. There was nothing that used to torment me. I was living with joy and peace. Now I am going to be a *molopitsi* [beggar] in other people's villages.

The next chapter reveals something of how Tokiso, 'Maseipati Moqhali and others fared in their new settlements.

CHAPTER 8

"I do not have the cleverness for here"
Mohale Dam, Lesotho, after Displacement

These people have never written letters to the project, asking to be resettled. You are resettled whether you like it or not... [so] when someone is resettled, he should be given everything that is his; no one should be a stumbling block [to this], saying that we will spoil our things. Is it your property [compensation] then?...They say it is because we are careless with the use of money. But we are not the same...Why should the good ones suffer because of a few who do not do well? This is what troubles me in spirit.

—'Matsapane Tsapane

Prior to resettlement, 'Matsapane Tsapane, 56, had taken over from her husband the position of village head of Ha Tsapane, a small community in the foothills of Lesotho's Maluti Mountains. Their highland village was one of several in the valley of Molika-liko that were relocated prior to construction of the Mohale Dam. Her husband, Lebeko, was confused and distressed at the thought of resettlement and had relied on his wife to handle the compensation arrangements.

Both she and Lebeko were interviewed prior to resettlement. As head of her community 'Matsapane had closer contact with the Lesotho Highlands Development Authority (LHDA) than most villagers had. She noted that some of the changes in the LHDA's policies and their failure to keep promises made at that time not only caused immense frustration among the villagers but also placed community representatives, of which she was one, in awkward positions. Community leaders felt in some ways coopted by the authorities and were held responsible by the resettled for events and consequences that were beyond their control. She felt particularly aggrieved because, as she commented, nobody volunteered for resettlement—they had no choice but to accept it—and, despite the impression sometimes given by the authorities, the compensation was theirs by right, not by request. After relocation, she and others became frustrated by their lack of control over the disbursement of compensation funds, and she was fearful that the LHDA might not honor all their promises: "I am the same person as when I was at Ha Tsapane [but] I am troubled in spirit because of resettlement. Because in truth I do not know, now that we have been resettled, whether we will get our rights, all of them."

This chapter draws on follow-up interviews gathered in 2001 and 2002 with the communities featured in the previous chapter; they were done three to four years after resettlement. These interviews are with some of the same people, such as 'Matsapane Tsapane, however other people's stories have also been included. They cover a range of responses and situations. Some outcomes match the narrators' predictions; others do not. In particular, they demonstrate the variations in resettlement experience, even within a relatively small and ostensibly homogeneous group such as the Molika-liko villagers. As 'Matsapane Tsapane points out: "We are not the same." Those differences were further exposed through the resettlement process.

From the jigsaw of individual accounts, one overall impression emerges: the majority of the resettled felt disempowered as a consequence of being displaced by the new dam and its infrastructure. These families took great pride in their intimate knowledge of the mountain valleys and their skill at coaxing plants to grow and animals to thrive there. Their ability to exploit a marginal environment had no direct application or value in their new locations, where there is little or no cultivable land; also, the lack of training opportunities meant that most had not acquired new skills. The relatively high levels of self-reliance they once enjoyed had for many been replaced by a relationship with the LHDA, and with the Lesotho state more broadly, that fostered dependency, rather than supporting individual initiative.

Some of the displaced expressed a strong wish to wrest back a degree of agency by having more of their compensation in a lump sum, rather than in annual payments, thus enabling them, for example, to set up a small business. They felt that such requests were resisted by LHDA rather than encouraged, and that they generated confusing demands for paperwork and business plans. With aspects of the compensation arrangements remaining a source of frustration, many feared they were not properly equipped to survive in their new environment; as one man reflected, they may not have "the cleverness for here." Although these experiences provide only a snapshot of the situation, their perspectives on these issues are revealing. In particular, they suggest that well-meaning attempts to shield the resettled from bad investments have added to people's feelings of powerlessness.

Motseki Motseki, 45, had been interviewed before relocation. He had explained that he had a good life in Molika-liko, living from his crops, livestock, a variety of waged and unwaged activities, and from some savings from his mining days. Following relocation, however, many of the opportunities he employed to make a living had been lost, and he too felt that in the new place he lacked the relevant "tricks" to survive. He talked movingly about the uncertain future he faced: "I left a place I was familiar with, the place whose tricks I know when I want to live...Here I am asking myself questions as to how I will survive after the compensation money finishes, especially now I live in a land like this one, when money is only spent—without returns."

Introduction and Background

Although they represent the views of only a small group of the resettled, these experiences as revealed through the interviews do suggest that various characteristics that shaped the Lesotho Highlands Water Project (LHWP) from the beginning continued to cast a shadow on the resettlement process. As explained in the previous chapter, the hydro schemes were first agreed in 1986, when both the South African and Lesotho governments were highly repressive regimes. It was conceived as an engineering challenge, not a social one. Construction, not its consequences, was the focus of attention. Transparency, accountability, and participation were alien concepts to those governments; although the political context has changed significantly, several observers argue that this set the tone for the way the LHWP was managed.[1]

In addition, the focus of LHDA's plans for relocation and compensation placed the emphasis on restoring rather than improving livelihoods. This meant the policy was merely to compensate for loss, in cash or kind, engendering a strong sense of injustice among the villagers that they were making sacrifices for a project that was designed to bring improvement for the country as a whole, but which delivered no substantive positive changes in their lives. In most cases, because of a lack of good quality replacement land, the LHDA could not offer "soil for soil" compensation—with the result that many families were left depending on annual handouts of grain and cash. Failures and delays in the implementation of any thoroughgoing "development" component of the relocation packages meant the achievement of sustainable livelihoods was always going to be difficult for the resettled. The psychological impact of the enforced dependency that resulted came through strongly in these accounts.

A recent evaluation has shown that the community development and resettlement aspects of Phase 1 of the LHWP were poorly executed and that staff on the ground were neither given political support and nor were they sufficiently equipped to cope with the challenges facing the resettled villagers.[2] While their

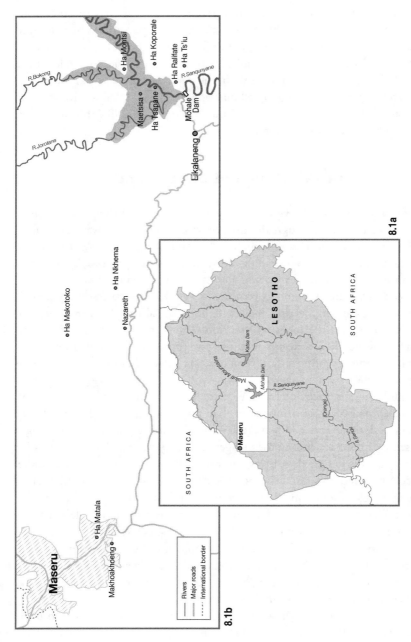

Figure 8.1 a. Map of Lesotho, after the construction of Mohale Dam. b. Detail of highlighted area in national map, showing original villages of Molika-liko valley and those to which the displaced later moved. Gray tone indicates land submerged by Mohale Dam reservoir. Hatched area indicates the built-up area of the capital, Maseru. Maps by Julie Anson.

job was never going to be easy, given the strains and stresses under which most of the resettled were operating, relationships between the affected villagers and LHWP staff seem to have deteriorated significantly since relocation. This also suggests that the project has never put the same emphasis on, or resources toward, the delicate and highly skilled task of managing change and rebuilding communities that it has on building infrastructure.

The Loss of an Everlasting Inheritance

> We wanted LHDA to compensate us with soil for soil because we are Basotho [the people of Lesotho]—we know the importance of soil in people's life . . . Fields are an everlasting inheritance. They are passed on, from one generation to the other . . . [Now] we do not have fields.
>
> —'Matokelo Motseki

Three men and three women were interviewed before and after resettlement. In addition to Motseki Motseki and 'Matsapane Tsapane,'Maseipati Moqhali was also interviewed, a woman in her eighties. In the previous chapter she described her trepidation about the move and her fears about no longer having a supportive community around her. Her grandson, Tokiso Moqhali, also features in both chapters.

Tokiso was 36 at the time of the first interviews, proud of his ability to fend for himself and support his young family, supplementing farming with building jobs and his self-taught ability to repair radios. He was anxious about the loss of independence that he feared displacement would bring. After resettlement and in contrast to his grandmother, who found she had adapted to her new life more easily than expected, Tokiso voiced despair about the lack of work to replace farming and his various income-generating activities: "We were brought here and now we are left . . . We are in great poverty. We do not benefit from the [LHWP] because we are not employed there now and never were employed."

'Malibuseng Mosotho, 36, a hard-working mother of six when she was interviewed prior to resettlement, had described her working days in Ha Tsapane: "There are many, the tasks I perform: I go and collect wood, I plaster the house with mud, I cook, I cut the grass that forms the roofs of these houses . . . Being a woman is difficult. It is a hard life." She had feared the loss of the social networks binding the different villages together, which also lightened their workload: "We live well together. We still help one another . . . A person would leave her home and come and help me hoe like that; well, when I harvest, I would also see as to what I can give her." Once she had been relocated and was living among "people who I do not know," she said, "I do not know how we shall act towards one another."

'Malibuseng's husband, Makibinyane Mosotho, and her 17-year-old daughter 'Mathabang were also interviewed in their new location of Nazareth (see Figure 8.1b, which shows some of the new sites where people settled; these were often built on the edge of existing villages). Their combined accounts revealed how the struggle to find productive ways to use their compensation money to secure a future had created tensions within the family.

Khethisa Leteka, when interviewed before relocation, had described how he had developed a knowledge of local plants and herbs during his many years spent in the mountains as a herd boy. He became a traditional healer, treating his community for ailments of both mind and body. Many of the plants he used had disappeared from the lowlands, but still grew in Molika-liko. For this reason, he took care to harvest them sustainably.

> [The plant] does not get finished up when we dig it out. When we find that here there are six or three growing together, I take one and I go to look for another elsewhere. The one that I notice to be rather too exposed while it is yet too young, I return its roots into the soil so that it may thrive once again.

Demand for Khethisa's herbalist skills had all but disappeared since he was relocated to Ha Makotoko.

This chapter also contains material from some people not previously interviewed, in particular three women whose accounts helped to build up a fuller picture of the different ways resettlement can affect people.[3] One is Motseki Motseki's wife 'Matokelo, who was 42 when interviewed. She gave the LHDA credit for fulfilling various promises, and she would seem to have integrated well into her new community. However, she too felt that no amount of financial compensation could replace the land they had lost in Ha Tsapane: "Fields are an everlasting inheritance. They are passed on, from one generation to the other." In the past, she grew food and gathered fuelwood, wild vegetables, herbs, and medicinal plants. In their new home in Ha Makotoko, she explained, everything had to be bought: "Life is difficult. Everything is money. Nowadays we are forced to scratch our heads thinking about what is going to be eaten in the household in the evening."

Makuena Mohlomi, 35, who had also lived in Ha Tsapane, had played a role in "convincing" its residents to accept relocation and the terms offered, which she felt were in their best interests. But with resettlement she had become disenchanted, feeling compromised as a result of the role she had taken within her community. Finally, 'Matsoiliti Mohajane, aged 38, was one of several who expressed frustration at the lack of agency that the LHDA allowed the resettled in using their compensation; she resented the implication that she was not able to manage the money herself or make her own plans for the future.

All these different accounts shed light on the wider implications of the loss of their primary material assets, which were land, livestock, and the diverse economic activities these supported. People spoke of how these losses affected their social capital—the networks and relationships that facilitated coordination and cooperation for mutual benefit. The lack of skills training or employment to replace their old occupations further demoralized the narrators and left them fearful for the future.

Loss of Land: "We Have Run Out of Wisdom and Means"

One of the strongest themes to emerge from the interviews was how loss of land had so many implications beyond the economic. The previous chapter contained accounts that showed the extent to which farming marginal land, as these mountain farmers did, required detailed knowledge of the environment that could only be accrued and shared over time. Narrators were well aware that such experience would not have much currency in their new locations, where conditions would be different and their ability to farm and herd was anyway greatly reduced, if it still existed. The environment yielded more than food. Motseki Motseki was one of many who emphasized the significance of natural remedies to treat minor ailments:

> As a people there [in Molika-liko], we knew where to find medicine for particular ailments, we knew where to find medicines for stomach disturbances, for aching head, in truth we would just dig them and cure the children's coughs like that...
>
> Some of these plants are here [in our new location], but we do not know where the majority of them grow. When you want them you will probably have to ask for assistance from one of the residents here, who will go with you. But in Molika-liko we knew where everything grew, and when a person became sick or a child had the runs, we would readily find them.

Motseki's comment reveals how an activity that was once part of the villagers' everyday lives—the equivalent of reaching for an aspirin—has become something they could only do with the assistance of others.

Makuena Mohlomi moved to the most urban of the new locations, Ha Matala, on the fringes of the capital, Maseru. While she acknowledged the much-improved access to health centers for more serious problems, she was now required to purchase remedies for even the most minor ailments: "At Molika-liko we just went to the other side of the hill and collected plants like the fever bush [*Dicoma anomala,* used to treat coughs, fevers, et cetera] and milk bush [*Xysmalobium undulatum,* used to treat headaches, colic, indigestion, et cetera] to cure our kids and ourselves."

For a traditional healer such as Khethisa Leteka, 49, loss of access to this natural resource had a more significant impact, since he also lost status and a key role in the community: "Since I got here...I have no clients at all and

I have stopped practicing! In truth, we have run out of wisdom and means totally, because that manner in which we brought in income beforehand, here we don't get the opportunity at all."

In his first interview, Khethisa talked with great pride of his careful harvesting of the plants he used to treat the villagers, who paid him in kind more often than cash, but his knowledge could also bring income when necessary:

> When one realizes that one is going to be faced with some food shortage, one way [to deal with this] is just to proceed to those trees over there, dig out six of those spiral aloe plants [used to treat barrenness], and then go to the lowlands. I go to sell them, and return home, having purchased some food for the children.

This source of income had disappeared, and his skills no longer appeared marketable. At first Khethisa thought the lack of demand for his services was because people didn't know him in the new location, but despite his living there for more than three years, the situation had not improved: "I was new here and people here did not know me but even now that they know me, I really don't see anything happening." The lack of interest may reflect the more urban nature of his new home and neighbors, but even if his curative skills were to be valued again, he admits that "there are many [plants] which are not available here."

When Khethisa Leteka was resettled from Maetsisa, a village submerged by the reservoir, his group named their new location Bothoba-pelo, meaning "heart-comforting," because they hoped that being there would calm their hearts: "When a village arrives in a place, it has to have a name and [we called it] Bothoba-pelo, because indeed we realized that we were people on whom pain had been inflicted." Far from being comforted in their new site, which is part of Ha Makotoko village, he explains, they "are very much bothered by hunger" and by delayed compensation payments. He was forced to sell all his animals and at the time of the interview could not afford to educate two of his five school-age children.

Sharecropping with Strangers

Motseki Motseki was one of the respondents who had described his fields almost as though they were members of the family, nourishing the land through hard times as well as good. He believed his grandfather's fields had the capacity to sustain at least the next two generations, but with resettlement this vital continuity had been broken. Speaking about their new life he said, "We are surviving in truth, but the life that that we lived...was far better than here. Because we still had what was our own, our fields, not hiring them like this."

To grow food in the new locations the resettled villagers were required to hire fields, where they could afford to, or find someone willing to let them sharecrop. As described in the previous chapter, sharecropping was quite widely practiced in Molika-liko, often by people who lived alongside each other for decades and for whom the reciprocity of the arrangement had been proven over time. But the resettled farmers, in the absence of familiarity and without established relations of trust, had to persuade members of the host communities to enter into a sharing agreement with risks to both parties. As a result, they were often working the land under arrangements of some tension. In addition, they were required to spend money on seed, fertilizer, and insecticide, which was rarely necessary in Molika-liko.[4] Motseki's wife 'Matokelo explains:

> I personally have met people who only contribute by allowing me to grow the crops in their fields. They make the seeds, ploughing, fertilizers, and everything that helps in good growing of crops to be my responsibility. And I have to see to it that any people who are working in the fields are fed. Yet they want equal shares; no one gets more, irrespective of the costs you incurred as a non-land owner. It is tough, but there is nothing we can do. The costs are still better compared to the cost of buying everything. The most painful thing with this sharecropping is that you cannot be sure that you will engage in it with one person for quite some time. Even if your toil has yielded a good harvest, it is not a guarantee that you will be in sharecropping with the same field owner next time.

Makibinyane Mosotho, 'Malibuseng's husband, described a similar experience: "It is not easy because the owner of the field will promise [to sharecrop with] you but when the time comes to go to the fields, you will hear him say he has already found someone else and you find that you are unable to plough that year."

"A god with a moist nose"

Most of these highland farmers had also kept livestock. Sheep and goats provided milk as well as income-generating wool and mohair; cattle provided milk, meat, hide and assisted with ploughing; horses were used for transport; and donkeys served to carry goods. They were an important form of wealth, which could be sold for cash at times of need. Livestock also had a sociocultural role, and the exchange or gifts of animals formed part of certain traditional ceremonies. 'Matokelo Motseki recalled that: "Animals, especially cattle, are a person's life. The Basotho were not wrong when saying *Khomo ke Molimo O nko e metsi* [a cow is a god with a moist nose]"; meaning, a cow makes life easy because people use one in so many different ways.

Many have tried to keep some animals since resettlement, especially cattle, hiring young boys to look after them higher up the mountains. Those who brought their livestock with them found many died, as the limited pasture in the new locations could not support them. Lack of livestock has had far-reaching effects, and combined with lost access to wild vegetables and herbs, has had an impact on the villagers' diets, as 'Malibuseng Mosotho pointed out: "How couldn't it change? At Molika-liko we were wealthy. We had cows, which we milked... But here the wild vegetables are scarce, our livestock is up there and we are not able to rely on its milk. Here everything is money."

In fact, many of the narrators complained about the monotony of their diets, saying they had become people who eat their staple food of *papa* (maize porridge) with just salt rather than the wild herbs, vegetables, and relishes of the past. Makuena Mohlomi recalls:

> There was never a time when the household would eat *papa* only seasoned with salt, unless we felt we had had enough of the wild vegetables. However, I see many households [now] eating *papa* with salt because cabbage costs money. The freedom that we had at Molika-liko to go and collect wild vegetables was left behind there.

It is clear that the attachment of the resettled to their animals was far more than simply economic. Motseki Motseki said: "What comes as a first concern and that which worries my spirit, is my animals." He tried bringing them down from the mountain pastures to his new location of Ha Makotoko, which now also contained the relocated graves of earlier generations, but the experiment was a failure:

> In this past year I brought down the cattle, it was only that they should come to know the [new] place, and perhaps for the ancestors to see them. But I drove them back hastily, not even looking back... They were becoming lean. They were frightened. They are not used to the grasses of this place.

The way Motseki described how he wanted them "to come to know" the new location and for "the ancestors to see them" suggested a need to bring together some of the most important parts of his life—his forefathers and his livestock—that had been wrenched apart by resettlement. His description of the cattle's distress seemed almost a way of expressing his own sadness and sense of dislocation.

Lost Diversity

As described in the previous chapter, farming and herding were not the only activities in Molika-liko. While cannabis production had become the main source of income generation, most people had a range of skills and occupations, which is important in a mountain environment where over-reliance on one crop or activity is risky. For example, many people used strong local grasses to weave hats, brooms, mats, and baskets for sale; others tanned animal hides, roofed houses, or transported goods and livestock for others.

The interviews suggested that in their new locations the range of potential activities had been drastically reduced, and a 2006 report that brought together research data on the outcomes of the LHWP confirmed this: "A total of 440 different sources of income for 214 households before resettlement were reported. This figure dropped to 202 after resettlement, indicating a loss of 54 percent."[5] By the time the interviews were conducted in 2001 and 2002, waged labor had become the most significant source of income for the relocated households, but paid work was unreliable, and to the inhabitants of Molika-liko this meant they were uncomfortably dependent upon others.

In addition, although growing cannabis was "not perceived to be an altogether illicit activity," as one report put it, it was officially illegal and the loss of income—estimated to be 60 percent of their arable crop revenue—was not compensated for.[6] Even though the resettled continued to grow a small amount of cannabis around their new homesteads, they had lost the custom of the South African traders, who had regularly visited their isolated mountain homes.

'Malibuseng Mosotho explained: "Cannabis...helped us to be self-sufficient. Now we are not able to plant it because this place is easily accessed by policemen you know! Cannabis had replaced the ploughing of wheat. It earned us a lot of money." She seemed worn down by the difficulty of getting some recompense. "We have been writing many letters asking for compensation for marijuana but I don't think they will ever listen to us. We are now tired of writing."

No longer able to practice their diversified mountain economy, the resettled had become more vulnerable to debt, undermining their traditional willingness to support each other through difficult times. 'Matokelo Motseki explained:

> Here, if a person comes to borrow some money from you, you first wonder how and when will that person repay you, yet this did not happen at Molika-liko... [But] there are no jobs here and we do not have fields in which we can work...
>
> We used to grow, harvest, and sell cannabis all year round. I used to have money at Molika-liko. But now, when I say please lend money to me, I mean it.

"Money...was not a must"

Many narrators described how friends and relatives in Molika-liko supported each other through periods of hardship, sometimes with cash but more often in kind. Repayment for food or cash at a critical moment would have been through an offer of labor, or with some seeds when they had germinated, or with young livestock when their animals had reproduced. Makuena Mohlomi explained how they used to pay traditional healers like Khethisa: "Sometimes we paid them with food after we have harvested. It is true that we sometimes used money, but it was not a must. Other times we would let the healer plough their fields [with our cattle] for a year in payment... [But here] everything is money, there are no fields."

Given that much of the villagers' previous access to credit in cash or kind was based on relationships of trust, and had nothing to do with formal lending institutions, the declining ability to operate that way was always likely to have some affect on social cohesion. Indeed, some key threads in the fabric of their society—the bonds of reciprocity and trust—had been weakened. However sympathetic they may be to each other's situation, they were no longer in a position to offer support.

"Bury me; bury you"

As well as payment in kind for services or assistance, Molika-liko residents had, as explained in Chapter 7, organized themselves into self-help associations, primarily to help one another with funeral expenses and other costs. Concern over how these burial societies would survive was widespread among those facing resettlement. The interviews suggest that some societies continued to operate but without the same level of effectiveness. Relatives were generally relocated together, but not necessarily in the same location as their old neighbors and fellow society members. In addition, because pressure on cash flow was most critical when the annual compensation payments were delayed, everyone experienced difficulties at a similar time.

Most importantly, people no longer had the range of options to pay back loans. The old relationships of trust and mutual support were strained, and people admitted that a reluctance to lend money had developed because of the knowledge that the borrower would probably struggle to repay. This would cause embarrassment and might further strain relations within and between families. As 'Matokelo says: "You first wonder how and when will that person repay you."

Although the institution of burial societies was regarded as desirable, in practice several broke down after relocation. 'Matokelo Motseki explained why her society had closed down: "We are scattered [so] we found it difficult to continue. It was terminated because we were aware that it would not be easy for members to know about a death and it would mean that contributions would not be given at the same time."

The loss of burial societies was felt particularly sharply as the expenses involved in holding funerals after displacement far exceeded the costs in Molika-liko. In the mountains, burials took place within two to three days of death. In the lowlands, relatives of the deceased have to pay to keep the body in a mortuary until the funeral, which must take place on Saturdays so that those with jobs can attend.[7] Makuena Mohlomi was relocated to Ha Matala, a new site built alongside the existing community of Makhoakhoeng on the edge of Maseru, the capital city. Their burial society also failed to survive relocation "because of the fact that we are now separated":

> When we arrived here we advised and encouraged people to join these big burial societies like MKM [a commercial company] or to take life cover policies from insurance companies. They were willing, but the problem is that people don't have money to pay for those things monthly. Many people don't have monthly income.

"Lack of stability has fastened our hands and minds, as well as our hearts"

Although the LHDA had successfully relocated the graves of the villagers' ancestors to the new resettlement sites, it was important for the displaced communities to have new cemeteries as well, for all subsequent bereavements. Indeed, as Makuena Mohlomi explained: "We heard from LHDA people that there is a site for a cemetery here in Ha Matala and it's among the most important things that convinced us to give up our land to come to settle here." But once they had moved, they learned that there was in fact no new cemetery on site. To their distress, they were then refused permission to use the neighboring graveyard, which belonged to the people of Makhoakhoeng. "We realized this when one person passed away, because we had no place to bury her. When we realized that the people of Makhoakhoeng would not allow us to bury her in their graveyard, we went to municipal authorities to beg for a site for our own." They were refused:

> We were told to go and bury that corpse either at Lithoteng or Lepereng. We tried to tell them that those places are too far away for our people [to reach by walking], but no one seemed to be interested in what we were saying. We were complaining not because we want to be treated in a special way, but because these people here cannot afford to hire vehicles to carry their corpses to those places. And if they cannot afford to hire vans to carry corpses, will they [be able] to hire vehicles to carry people who have attended the funeral to go to the graveyards? I don't think so.

This story is borne out by Kanono Thabane, a resident of the "host" community of Makhoakhoeng, who attributed most of the tension between the resettled and the residents to poor communication by the LHDA, saying they failed to consult or prepare the host community adequately. There was a belief among the residents that the new site had been built on land that originally belonged to Makhoakhoeng, for which they had not been properly recompensed. While some of their demands from the LHDA for recompense had been met, others had not; as a result, the Makhoakhoeng residents' sense of grievance had hardened and had soured relations between the two groups. The conflict was intensified and further complicated by the involvement of two politicians.[8]

This story illustrates some of the messy realities and unexpected outcomes of forced displacement, which may be hard to plan for or predict, but which, if not addressed, can cause lasting distress. At the time of Makuena's interview, the tensions between the two communities remained unresolved and rumors were circulating that the resettled were to be moved again:

> You know what, we even tried to threaten LHDA, saying that we want to go back to Molika-liko if we cannot be given a site nearby for a graveyard, but we still failed. I think the rumors that we are going to be removed from here emerged from what we said to LHDA. We thought by so saying, LHDA would pressurize the municipal office to offer us a place for graveyard. However, it seems that we gave those people who like to spread rumor a "headline."

She said they were not making any investments in the new site or their homes because of the uncertainty about whether they will stay; it was as though they had become frozen, unable to move on with their lives:

> We are confused due to the rumors about our re-displacement. We are not able to do anything [to our homes] because we don't know what is going to happen after one has made some improvements. It is as though the lack of stability has fastened our hands and minds, as well as our hearts.

From Self-Reliance to Dependence

The narrators paint a picture of quite rapid change as a result of their resettlement. Although they did not move to radically different social and physical landscapes, they had moved into a more monetized world. In Molika-liko, they had hired out their labor occasionally as an adjunct to their core activity of farming, but it was land that ensured their subsistence and a good measure of independence, as well as generating a modest cash income. It is recognized that people have a tendency to comfort themselves by selecting the best of the past at times of grief and loss, and the villagers' emphasis on the productivity of their mountain valley might seem to be part of this tradition, but, as the previous chapter showed, other documentation confirmed that their assessment of the land's fertility was based in reality.

In some respects the changes they underwent as a result of resettlement—integration into a monetized economy, coming to terms with the realities of a market economy, and a gradual detachment from the land and the wider natural environment—were already reshaping their lives in Molika-liko. But with the move to the lowlands, the pace of change was accelerated and was imposed on the resettled in a manner that took away their ability to control the process.

One of the more difficult aspects of resettlement for the narrators was turning their compensation payments into sources of sustainable income. 'Malibuseng Mosotho's experience illustrated some of the dilemmas for the displaced, and for the LHDA. When interviewed in her new home in Nazareth, she revealed her underlying worries about the family's survival following resettlement. No longer able to farm, her husband had bought a car with their savings, aiming to set up a taxi business, but mechanical problems had kept it in the repair shop: "I don't even know if it will come back because we don't have the money."

'Malibuseng was worried that this would prove to be a misguided investment, costing rather than generating cash: "It is consuming our pockets." She made it clear that her husband's purchase was against her better judgment, and expressed frustration that LHDA red tape prevented her from carrying out her own investment plan for the money she hoped to receive for the last of their three fields:

> I have requested that compensation [for that field] should come in one bulk payment but nothing seems to be happening. At some stage it was as if it was going to happen and the papers were taken by [an LHWP official] and his colleagues saying they were going to photocopy them, but all of a sudden everything about that went silent and now I am not even sure that I will get that compensation the way I want it. We are still receiving compensation for the other two fields annually.
>
> I wanted to bank the money [for the third field] myself. They refused, saying they will give me that money provided I have something solid that I am going to do with that money ... something that will generate [more] money for me ... I then decided to build *ma-lines* [basic, low-rent urban housing, built in rows] for people to rent. They asked me to find a site on which I would build those *ma-lines*. Unfortunately the owner ended up selling that site because I did not have [access to] the cash to buy it.

She felt that the relationship with LHWP staff had become strained:

> We have been working well with these people but since we were brought here, it seems they are turning their backs on us and on the agreements we made with them. We don't know what to do. We are just left puzzled.
>
> When we go to the office there asking about the compensation that we asked to get in a one-off payment, we are asked how we will turn [our business] promises into reality ... Yet we were promised that we would have water taps in

our sites, but that seems not to be happening. That is why I am saying it seems those people are withdrawing the promises they have made.

Power Relationships

> Our grievances—we no longer write them down, because it's repetition of the same things and nothing has been done to attend to them.
>
> —'Matsoiliti Mohajane

A picture emerged from these interviews of continuing confusion and frustration caused by delays and changes in LHDA policies. In 2006, a report confirmed that some of the displaced had yet to receive the disturbance allowance and said that arrangements for the disbursement of the individual and communal compensation had been altered. In addition, annual compensation payouts were often delayed by six months, leaving the villagers incurring mounting debt as they struggled to cope with food shortages and school fees.[9]

'Matsapane Tsapane, the woman who as village head had dealt with LHDA more closely than many others, explains some of the problems:

> The project keeps changing. They turn against their promises, because they had said…we would get all our rights, but in the middle of things you are asked questions…when you ask for your full compensation, they say you should produce a business plan, yet your compensation is not a business plan!

'Matsapane goes on to describe how the LHDA justified the new requirement of the production of a business plan before it would release compensation money:

> They say it is because we are careless with the use of money. But we are not the same. Some people *ba jela noyana naheng* [literally, "they eat a bird far from home"; meaning they do not take care of their families]. They do not take their money home…Why should the good ones suffer because of a few who do not do well? This is what troubles me in spirit.

At the root of 'Matsapane's frustration was a sense that the resettled were not being treated as responsible adults. They had lost control over their assets through no fault of their own, yet were not allowed to make their own decisions on how to use the cash that had replaced them. Their ability to act as individuals was also eroded: as 'Matsapane pointed out, the resettled were being seen as a homogeneous group who could not be trusted to be financially responsible.

Several narrators acknowledged that LHDA staff held back payments and disbursed them in stages in order to protect the families of those who lacked financial responsibility. But these interviews signaled evident tension between imposing a sensible policy across the board and alienating those who felt patronized by such treatment. Tailoring compensation packages to individuals would be labor-intensive, but the current approach of tightening controls so much that there is no room to maneuver can stifle people's initiative. Some loosening of the rules and flexibility in their interpretation and application might begin to restore people's dignity and foster creativity.

One of the real stumbling blocks for those wanting lump-sum payments, though, was the requirement to produce a business plan. This was not something with which the former residents of Molika-liko were familiar. Lack of support to produce the plans and poor evaluation processes led to protracted delays and even more frustration.[10] Another factor was that these villagers were not the first communities to be resettled; those displaced by the Katse Dam who took lump-sum payments had benefited from being "early investors." A 2009 study noted that "markets are small and quickly saturated and so the success rate [of those who received lump sums later] has been low."[11]

Another illustration of how hard it was proving for the resettled to take charge of events and become independent of the LHWP came from 38-year-old 'Matsoiliti Mohajane, who was moved with her husband and three children from Ha Ralifate to Ha Ts'iu.

> We are begging that the money should be given to us [in a lump sum], so that we can plan and use it for our benefit. It does not mean that when the money is used up we will go back to the authorities to say [help us because] the money is finished.
>
> As for now...supposing I have a deceased relative, the Project will not help me bury them, even though I know I still have a certain amount of money left with them. I know how much because it is written in the forms that I have. Now we are truly urging the Project authorities to give us this money so that we can deposit it into our own bank books...so that we can part with the Project, since it no longer does things as we were promised.

She also expressed dissatisfaction, as did others, with the arrangements over interest payments, which seem not to have been clearly explained: "Our money should not be kept at the Project...who is going to get the interest? We want the money to come to us so that it will benefit us and our children."[12]

'Matsoiliti explained that she needed the money to establish a new livelihood. Only one man from her community had been given work by the LHWP and no women had been given jobs. Training programs had been promised, but implementation was poor. 'Matsoiliti was one of the few who had received training—in poultry production—about which she was enthusiastic, but she had been unable to use it because of lack of funds:

> My greatest wish was to keep chickens...so that I could sell some eggs and also meat...however I am not able to do that now because the project authorities are still keeping our field's compensation. This money should be given to us, because as for me, I really want to start a project that will benefit my household in the future. I want to do this now that I am still well and I am still able to work with my hands.

"They are no longer those friends of ours"

Many narrators indicated that the attitude of LHWP staff had added to tensions, and that relationships deteriorated quite early on in the process. Published reports from the time also indicate that the LHWP struggles to recruit and maintain well-qualified and motivated staff. LHWP offices were often sited some considerable distance from the communities, and they worked in a manner that was remote and exclusive.[13] 'Masoiliti Mohajane commented:

> We are beginning to get tired of writing down our complaints because nothing is being done...[and] when we appear at the office [and] ask to see someone, they tell you that they are not here—yet they are still around the office. They are no longer those friends of ours with whom we used to have a comfortable and satisfying conversation. They had softened our hearts; we never thought that by now they will be quite different people from those we used to know...we are wondering as to what is it that we did wrong to deserve this kind of treatment? We are even thinking that if it was possible we would go back to our original home.

However well drafted, resettlement guidelines and policies are only as good as their implementation. As resettlement specialist Chris de Wet notes, by the time policy frameworks have been adjusted to different contexts and conditions and are being interpreted at the community level, "resettlement policy effectively becomes what the resettlement officer on the ground makes of it." This difficult task is made harder by the fact that those charged with service delivery "are often poorly paid, seriously understaffed and thus under tremendous work pressure and poorly motivated—as well as having considerable discretion as to how they go about their job."[14]

"It is through my tongue that these people ended up here"

It was not only relationships between the resettled and LHDA staff that became strained. Some of the resettled found themselves in difficult positions within their own communities.

Makuena Mohlomi was employed by the LHDA prior to resettlement to, in her words, "convince" her local community to accept the terms of relocation. With mounting problems in the new site of Ha Matala, Mohlomi felt she was being held responsible by the rest of the group. She shared their disillusionment and in some ways understood why she was so resented for the role she had played:

> I was among those people employed by LHDA to convince them that resettlement would bring them a better life...[So] I must stand all the torture because it is through my tongue that these people ended up here.
>
> Now these people are angry with me, they are always telling me that I helped LHDA to lie to them...It is painful because I did not create what I said; neither did I pluck those things from the air. I read them from a formally written paper that had the stamps and signatures of the officials.

The cruel twist, she said, was that some LHWP staff "are now blaming us representatives, saying...that it is us who gave out wrong information, because we are not educated. Now, one asks if we are the ones who wrote those papers? Is it us who put the stamps on?"

Makuena Mohlomi understood how the compensation process had added to people's frustration. She cited in particular the decision to change the arrangements for compensation for communal assets.

> We knew that we were going to live a town life and we came here because we were promised that compensation for natural resources will be given to each individual household because we will have to buy everything, even medicine for a child who is suffering from common cold...What surprises us is that it is now said that the money that brought us here is no longer going to be given to an individual household, instead it is going to be used to make developments for us here in the village.

This money was now to be given to communities to make specific improvements, but the LHDA required them to produce a development plan. Makuena was resettled in 1997. She was interviewed in 2001. A report found that by the end of that year, community compensation for lost common resources still had not been dispersed, because of delays over establishing the institutional arrangements.[15]

It is not hard to see how changes like these, however well-intentioned, were unsettling and had contributed to a breakdown in trust between all concerned. Makuena added:

> These people [in LHDA] have used us to win over the resettled and now they are blaming us for their mistakes. That is how they are thanking us, and it is

us who are hurting, who are living with these people here, because we witness their suffering.

Compensation Is a Right, Not a Favor

As previously noted, 'Matsapane Tsapane had taken over the role of village chief before resettlement, and was on the people's committee attending negotiations with the LHDA. She had a good grasp of the compensation arrangements at the time, although she found some of the changes and options confusing. She mentioned that she had been unhappy with the quality of the materials to be used in the new homes, and with LHDA staff measuring fields in the farmers' absence:

> They had gone out to the fields with only one person from the village...I then asked why they were leaving the owners of the fields behind. They then told me that they were only testing...[But] after that they were no longer willing to come back. The people want them to come back, because they say there is no reason why they should be rushed to move when some things have not been settled.

She was also unhappy that LHDA had given so few local people jobs, most of which were part-time: "Those who are employed are very few and some are being laid off. Women are not employed at all."

Like Makuena Mohlomi, 'Matsapane felt that LHDA's policy changes sometimes made it seem that the community representatives were at fault:

> The Project should not turn away from agreements and promises they made to the communities; they should not make the people's committees look like liars...When [LHDA] turn away from agreements, they make it difficult for committees when they get back home, [where they are] accused of not fulfilling what they had been sent there to do.

Makuena Mohlomi had also pointed out: "We did not volunteer to come here...we came here with hurting hearts." Her reminder that relocation was involuntary is important. 'Matsapane, the village chief, pinpointed this as a source of much anger: "These people have never written letters to the Project, asking to be resettled. You are resettled whether you like it or not...[so] the Project should fulfill the resettled people's wishes."

At the heart of 'Matsapane's argument was the fact that the resettled had no choice but to accept being moved. Compensation was theirs by right and yet she and others felt they were put in a position of having to ask for and justify receiving the compensation they were entitled to in law. When asked what advice she would give to any other community faced with resettlement, 'Matsapane's reply is heartfelt: "When someone is resettled, he should be given everything that is his; no one should be a stumbling block [to this], saying that we will spoil our things. Is it your property then?"

Two Generations; Two Perspectives

For some, the relationship with LHDA staff had broken down completely. 'Maseipati Moqhali may have been resigned to living out her last years in the new settlement, but her grandson Tokiso, a 40-year-old father of six, was not:

> The Project has been lying to us; to date we are not working. Now our live-stock are dying of hunger. We were satisfied with our original place...we did not struggle like this to make ends meet. We don't even have fields to plough here.

With his extra skills in roofing and radio repair, Tokiso Moqhali would appear to have been in a better position than some to make a new life, but he found the lack of work totally demoralizing. His rejection of their new life extended to the cement block housing.[16] He mocked his grandmother's gratitude for her new home in Likalaneng:

> She is happy with it because she is old. This give-away house of theirs is not good. Now it is cracking and we are not able to fill the cracks because we don't know these things. It would be no problem if it was not cemented. It doesn't help to be given a modern house...the roof is leaking too. This thing will eventually fall down upon us because we are not able to mend it.

Tokiso was no longer able to contain his anger or to negotiate with the authorities. He refused to go to the LHWP office to find out why their food ration had been delayed for months: "So who should I ask? When you go there and talk to them, they tell you lots of stories."

In contrast, although some of the changes she feared had come to pass, such as the collapse of her burial society, Tokiso's grandmother 'Maseipati Moqhali had adjusted significantly better than she anticipated. She regretted losing touch with old neighbors: "We became separated because we choose different places. Some of us are at Ha Makotoko, others are at Ha Matala while we are here [in Likalaneng]. We became scattered like little chicks." She acknowledged that life in the new location had not been easy, but indicated that she was adapting to the new situation: "My heart is being used to this place."

Significantly, she was positive about the way they were accepted into the new community. When reflecting on her earlier concerns about becoming "a *molopitsi* [beggar] in other people's villages," she laughed and said she had become resigned

Figure 8.2 'Maseipati Moqhali, whose original home in Ha Tsapane was submerged by the Mohale Dam reservoir. Photo by Paul Middleton.

to her fate: "I realized that there is no use thinking that one day I will go back to Molika-liko. I am old now and I am clear that I will never go back—as a result I have accepted."

"That Man Who Just Sits"

The narrators featuring in this and the previous chapter present evidence that shows that their material assets have been largely replaced by money, in arrangements that involve much oversight by the LHDA. Many of their social assets, such as supportive networks and relationships, have been strained by separation and increased vulnerability. It has also been shown that resettlement has resulted in a sense of diminution, because the traditional knowledge and "wisdom" so important in the previous location were no longer relevant or in demand. In addition few of the promised employment and training opportunities had materialized.[17] This has long-term implications, for without training for adults and better education for their children, it is hard for the resettled to seize the initiative, create their own livelihoods and become independent of the authorities.

Quite apart from the lack of income, the lack of occupation had far-reaching effects on people's morale. In the pre-resettlement interviews, the specter of unemployment and being idle haunted the people of Molika-liko, who were so used to providing for themselves. Tokiso Moqhali expressed his fear that if he had no occupation in the new location, he would be tempted to steal: "And then it will be that I am that man who just sits... I am just sitting. And then it will happen that I will change and will end up stealing."

Tokiso's fear of turning to crime did not materialize, but demoralization appeared widespread. One of the younger people interviewed, 'Malibuseng Mosotho's 17-year-old daughter 'Mathabang, was still at school. The interviews drawn on for this book as a whole showed that people of her age generally welcomed the improved educational opportunities and modern facilities that resettlement brought, but 'Mathabang expressed a preference to return to her remote village and old way of life, which she associated with happier times. As her interview progressed, she revealed one way resettlement had changed her father for the worse: "My father drinks heavily since he arrived here... Sometimes my father shouts at my mother, especially when he has been drinking." She referred several times to the enforced idleness among the resettled: "Those who have been removed from their homes come to sit here without jobs."

There was sadness in her interview, and she implied that other children of resettled families shared her concerns: "The children say ever since they arrived here life is difficult in their families [because] life here depends on money and their parents do not have it."

'Mathabang's father, Makibinyane Mosotho, was also interviewed. In this chapter, we have already learned from his wife that he invested the family's savings in a car that had been off the road for most of the time. When interviewed, he made no mention of this but was clearly extremely worried about the lack of work and the fact that "we have not had any training... They said we would live a good life here... They would take us 'out of the furrow' [improve our lives] but instead we are sinking."

Makibinyane Mosotho had had three months' work with the LHWP in the three years since relocation. He said he had been offered no training. His account suggested that he felt at a loss and was scared by the rate that money was being spent: "Life here is heavier than it was there in the mountains. When anything runs short, you go to the shop... Money does not stay with you... In the rural areas children are able to fetch wild vegetables... [and there] is much milk in summer and money is saved."

His greatest anxiety was that he no longer had land to leave his children, and with no jobs available, he feared all the compensation money would be spent. He thought their lives would improve with resettlement, but for him the reality has been a loss of purpose and confidence: "I do not have the cleverness for here," he admitted sadly.

"Forced to be lazy"

Since resettlement, women's responsibilities and occupations had changed in a number of ways. Today, said Makuena Mohlomi, women lack occupation: "They are just seated here and they are becoming dull." 'Matokelo Motseki, 42, agreed: "Life here is boring. We are forced to be lazy because things that we used to do are not easy to do now since this place is so different from Molika-liko." She described how reduced access to natural resources affected women:

> It has changed my routine because at Molika-liko I used to go gathering fire-wood at least twice a week. But here...we no longer go out for wood; instead we go to the chief over there and ask [to buy it]...wild vegetables are also scarce and it is a waste of time to go out to the fields to collect them. Here we are bored, because even for washing we have to draw water from the well over there instead of going to the river to do the washing with running water.

'Matokelo appreciated the less labor-intensive routine in her new home, but rued a certain lack of substance in her life, believing there was little now to gave her a sense of achievement or pride. She spoke of their diet being far less varied, of the new concrete houses that could not be decorated with *litema,* the traditional drawings that women did on their rondavels, the fact that they no longer cared for their children's health by gathering local herbs and roots, and finally that the grasses to make mats, bags, baskets, and brooms were in scarce supply. She also regretted no longer washing the clothes by the river, an activity that provided a welcome opportunity for women to get together and exchange news. The literature of resettlement shows that women can be particularly at risk from resettlement when much of their work and status in the family depends on access to natural resources and common land. Many of these women's skills, customs, and knowledge were no longer relevant and they feared they were, as Makuena put it, "becoming dull."

"A wonderful thing"

Despite the perceived failures of communication and implementation, it is important to note that the narrators did give the LHDA credit for many things, notably improved transport facilities, increased access to clinics, schools, and markets, and eventually piped water supplies. The interviews also reveal that the LHDA handled a highly emotive issue with considerable success. The relationship with one's ancestors is an important part of Basotho cultural and spiritual life. When the narrators were interviewed prior to resettlement, they were very concerned about leaving their family graves behind; the LHDA undertook to move the dead to the various new sites and pay for ceremonies to honor their reburial.

Moving the graves was clearly going to be a painful process for the resettled, fraught with emotional tension and the potential for things to go wrong. But almost every narrator voiced satisfaction with the way it was implemented: "They did a wonderful thing really. LHDA people exhumed their graves and resettled them here where we are," said 'Matokelo. Motseki Motseki concurred: "[It] was done properly, because coffins were bought for them. They were carried by the project authorities to this place...Although the exercise was painful, we were satisfied because they were now with us, and that pain has since left us."

Fears for the Future

If I were still near that field of mine, I would still plough it, maybe until I die. It would be left for my children, but now I no longer have it—and its compensation seems to be of no good to us.

—'Malibuseng Mosotho

The interviews discussed in this chapter revealed widespread concern about what the future would hold for the resettled as they adapted to their new situation. Certainly the loss of land and the sense of security their fields brought has been the cause of considerable anxiety. The former residents of Molika-liko described feeling adrift in the new locations, unable to satisfactorily control the flow of events or to influence those in authority. The continuing negotiations over compensation seemed to have done little to restore a sense of participation or involvement. Shortfalls in the resettlement process and the failure to properly value lost assets, to pay individuals on time, or to trust the villagers to use their compensation monies productively made these men and women feel that they were no longer able to determine their own futures or, crucially, that of their children.

The resettled voiced concerns about their immediate prospects, but more so about their ability to look after future generations when there was no land to pass on and few tangible replacement assets. 'Matsoiliti Mohajane's view of the difference between land and money mirrored that of almost every narrator: "They are not comparable because money is used for many purposes and it cannot sustain us for the rest of our lives. But we know that if one has a plot of land, that one will be able to grow [food] as long as one lives."

Makibinyane Mosotho—the owner of the broken-down car—seemed to have made a shift from believing land ownership was the key to a future, to seeing education as the route to a better life: "There are many [opportunities] for both boys and girls because here...there is a school for sewing, I take [a daughter] there; I give her an inheritance that lasts...I take a son to a building school and he gets certificates...It is his future." Makibinyane had managed to pay their school fees by selling his remaining sheep and cows, one by one. But as he described his dwindling resources and his days spent without occupation, his growing anxiety was evident. He was not alone in wanting to turn the clock back: "At present we would be single-voiced if it could be said, 'Men, go back to your [old] place.' We would be single-voiced and go back up there."

The sudden involuntary immersion into the market economy; competing for mostly scarce and insecure wage labor; finding that everything had a price; and lacking trust in the formal institutions, the banks, and government offices through which the market operated daunted many of the narrators. Although there were undoubted benefits, such as improved access to health care facilities and schools, the cultural losses so poorly understood by those engaged in resettlement planning held back the livelihood and societal rebuilding that was so vital. For some interviewees, the color had gone out of their lives, their houses remained undecorated, they struggled to maintain the informal institutions that provided both sociability and insurance now that people were separated, and they found it hard to reestablish strong bonds in the new locations when it was money rather than trust that mediated the relationships between them.

CHAPTER 9

Conclusion

The experiences detailed in this volume, drawing on a wide range of displacement events (as a consequence of mega dam projects, the creation of game parks and conservation areas, and large-scale agriculture and mines) across two continents and over a 30-year time period, reveal the ways in which displacement and resettlement trigger far-reaching change for individuals, families, and cultural groups. This process of change takes place not in isolation from other events that are occurring at the local, regional, and international levels, but rather it intermeshes with those events in complex ways. For example, land acquisition for development projects emerges out of and takes place alongside a wider set of development policies in Kenya, Pakistan, India, and Botswana that are built around land-reform initiatives, privatization, sedentarization of mobile populations, and economic liberalization. It is clear from the interviews that affected populations are fully aware of these wider political-economy dynamics. Quite understandably, however, the conversations among the displaced that provide most of the data for the analysis contained in this book reflect mainly on the immediacy of their displacement and resettlement experience. As such, their concerns are predominantly about coping with upheaval and its associated trauma, with asset loss and compensation, and with the threats to social stability brought about by a weakening of bonds and relationships that formerly shaped the sense of community and belonging in a place.

On the Margins

However, beyond these immediate concerns, the interviews conducted some years after the initial event reveal other concerns among the displaced, with their vulnerability to higher-scale changes such as urbanization and integration into a monetized economy. What is revealed is a form of what Cernea describes as "social marginalization,"[1] manifested in a general sense that displaced people experience contemporary "development"—that is, both the immediate development project and the wider political economy—from the margins of events. Their status in society before their displacement and in their resettlement already placed them at some distance from the centers of power in their countries. Physically, the narrators were geographically remote from the administrative hub of the state, often speaking a different language from that of the dominant population, following a different faith, and engaging only partially in the formal economy. Most of the narrators belonged to societies that practiced livelihoods that emphasized this separateness from the mainstream (pastoralism, mountain farming), and had a dependency on common property resources.

What the interviews suggest, however, is that the development process—which, it has been argued, is a process of "standardization" designed to make visible and countable those at the margins, precisely to permit the state to exercise governance over them—at least in the early phase actually serves to further distance and marginalize the displaced. The interviews go some way to helping us understand why and how this might occur. The American anthropologist James C. Scott describes the kind of projects that the narrators are witness to in this volume as examples of high modernist state planning, based on misguided assumptions that planners and planning can engineer social change with rational, accountable outcomes.[2] So often the hubris of the state, as discussed in Chapter 1, leads to failure on a massive scale, as happened in Nyerere's Tanzanian villagization. Planning fails because targets are unattainable. The pursuit of standardization is frequently ignorant of history, it stifles innovation and creativity, and it meets resistance from people who quickly identify state hubris, but more keenly see also injustice and unfairness in the process.

Being Displaced by Development

The Lesotho chapters in particular capture what it must have been like to be a statistic in the planning documents prepared by the Lesotho Highlands Development Authority when they were calculating the size of the dam wall and shading in the area to be inundated by the reservoir. On paper, the relocation of villages and their inhabitants to neighboring areas or, more distantly, to the fringes of the capital Maseru must have appeared a straightforward exercise in asset valuation, compensation, and relocation. In reality, as the testimonies confirm, it was far more complex—a "puzzling game." Chapters 7 and 8 draw on two collections of interviews. The first collection was with the villagers prior to relocation; the second collection was done three or four years after displacement.

The first interviews reveal how misunderstandings punctuated the process as the technical form of language preferred by planners trampled over local understandings of space, ownership, and value, creating mistrust and confusion. The affected villagers from remote settlements, already struggling with higher prices and a troubled engagement with the market that was now on their doorstep as a result of the new roads built to accommodate heavy construction machinery,[3] and coping also with the loss of labor opportunities in the South African mines, had fallen back on profitable though precarious cannabis production to make up for lost income.

We learn from Lipholo Bosielo and other narrators how the Lesotho Highlands Water Project (LHWP) officials failed to grasp the significance of the soil, land, vegetation and rivers as essential components of the villagers' ontological security. Leaving the land, being uprooted from the soil, was described as breaking a relationship of trust, one that bound the farmer and his or her family to one another, and to other mountain communities, through tending, planting, and harvesting. The villagers had engaged with the market and understood how cash was temporary, how it slipped through the fingers like quicksilver, and they knew that without land ("the land that keeps giving"), resettlement meant that the displaced were uncertain about their ability to fulfill their obligations to the next generation. Retrenchment (layoffs) from the South African mines had been a shock, coming home was difficult because Lesotho was anyway fast-changing, as the market and the state encroached further into the lives of the villages they had left behind. But the dam and the inundation was different again, the land that cushioned their return from the mines was to be taken from them, and with it went existential as well as economic security and a repositioning in relation to the state.

Land in the Lesotho highlands was the foundation upon which informal arrangements between households were made, and these arrangements provided an opportunity for those who were landless, or who could not draw on labor, to share the land and labor of others. Those whose crops failed, or who illness or misfortune kept from the field or market, were able to call on others for produce or for small loans to tide them over. Sharing arrangements with varying degrees of institutionalization exist in urban areas also, but in the absence of land ownership, the relocated villagers expressed concern that the land-based institutions that had for generations helped to define social relations were in many respects ineffective for those who relocated to towns. And moreover, to build such relationships in a new place, whether rural or urban and where people are separated by distance and by concrete walls, takes considerable time; trust must develop and people must prove their integrity. When the narrators talk about not having "the cleverness" for the new place, the concern is real that familiarity with the new location is in itself insufficient to establish supportive networks.

The distancing and marginalization of displaced people occurs also because of the internal fragmentation created within families and communities. Such fragmentation, we can observe from the interviews, has multiple causes. It is in part a consequence of the unraveling of the kinds of social networks we have discussed in relation to Lesotho, where the strength of the household or family unit is weakened by the fact that they no longer play a crucial role in networks that rely on and help build trust. But the resettlement process itself creates divisions and conflict within and across generations.

Those displaced by coal mining in Jharkhand experienced firsthand how officials from the local subsidiary of the Coal India Limited selected the village headmen to "represent" the interests of the villagers scattered throughout the Damodar Valley. Certainly there were acts of resistance and active campaigning, particularly by women, against what they perceived as injustices in the distribution of jobs, the valuing of lost assets, and the payment of compensation. But the complexity of the policies and the inconsistencies of their application meant that the community representatives, who were ill-prepared and poorly supported by local officials, could not be expected to manage complicated negotiations in an adversarial system where the need to prove asset ownership fell to the displaced who were largely illiterate and from India's poorest strata of society.

Resettlement specialists have argued for some time that cash compensation for lost land and other assets, particularly for rural populations, cannot on its own guarantee that people will have the chance to establish a sustainable livelihood in the new location.[4] As an alternative, it is frequently argued that some sort of resettlement with development is more appropriate, offering not just land for land compensation plus cash for lost assets, but also employment, training, education, and access to business loans.[5] And this should mark a longer term commitment to those affected on the part of the state or the company involved. At present the resettlement commitment mostly ends when people step off the bus and first arrive in the new place, or when the final compensation payments have been made. Indeed it was a feature of virtually all the collections drawn on in the volume that the resettled identified a failure on the part of the responsible authorities to provide meaningful training and to assist them in finding employment. To their credit, Central Coalfields Limited, which is responsible for the open-pit mines that displaced the Jharkhand villagers, made provisions for selected jobs in, or associated with, the mines to be available to individuals from families who qualified to receive such a benefit. However, the qualification criteria were overly complex and relied on evidence of ownership that could not easily be provided. Dissatisfied families turned for help to their *neta* or headman, who had usually been appointed to negotiate on their behalf, but as the interviewers recall, these representatives were often incapable of conducting the negotiations or, at worst, they were corrupted by the process and put their own interests ahead of those of the community. Within families, siblings competed among themselves for any available job. One villager was of the view that the company identified and exploited these weaknesses; promises were made then changed or simply not kept.

This loss of internal cohesion among the Jharkhand villagers was exacerbated by the fractured nature of the mine development itself. Open-pit mines spread slowly like ink on blotting paper, encroaching on forests and agricultural land in stages. It is similar to road construction and other linear projects in the sense that different groups of people are affected at different times and in different ways, depending on whether they lose a home, some land, all land, or access to common property such as forests, rivers, or grazing land. Under these conditions, community action is difficult to organize, because people have different interests and rarely come together as a political grouping for collective action. It would be hard to argue that the *adivasi* communities living in the Damodar Valley were able to exercise their formal rights before the arrival of the mines; however, the transformation of the environment and the social change brought about by the mining operations appears to have further disenfranchised the villagers.

This process of disenfranchisement arises in part from the deficit of trust displaced people have in the state and in state bodies that are responsible for land acquisition, removals, and resettlement. In his classic volume, *The Anti-Politics Machine: "Development," Depoliticization, and Bureaucratic Power in Lesotho*, James Ferguson was interested to observe what actual impact a development intervention, in this case the Thaba Tseka Development Assistance Program, had in the mountainous area of central Lesotho in the 1980s. He concluded that the most significant effect of the project was not poverty alleviation or increased agricultural output, but rather it was to significantly strengthen the presence of the Lesotho government in the area. It is understandable that in thinking about their upcoming displacement from Molika-liko, the villagers featured in Chapter 7 are cautious and are concerned about increased intrusion by the state in their new lives. Makibinyane Mosotho reflects that the protective cover of the mountain village enabled them to grow and sell cannabis without police interference. However, in the new location, this essential livelihood activity would not be possible; moreover, town life would inevitably bind them into the formal institutions of the state, including the banks, an outcome that it was feared would restrict their freedoms, rather than opening new possibilities. This causal link between state-mandated resettlement and the fear of greater government control over the lives of the displaced can be heard through the testimonies of the Boran and Orma pastoralists in Chapter 4, who describe the seizing of their former rangelands for large-scale agricultural production and settlement as not only restricting their mobility but also bringing their commercial activities, and indeed their very movements, much more closely under the control of the government.

This nexus between displacement, resettlement, and disenfranchisement arising out of the resettlement process, the impoverishment that so often follows, and the loss of status and citizenship rights comes through strongly in the interviews conducted with the San in Botswana. The narrators describe a set of policies, ostensibly designed to conserve the land and promote agricultural production and tourism, as having the effect of barring their access to traditional hunting and gathering territories, forcibly resettling them on inappropriate land, and bringing them into conflict with non-San farming communities. And in a similar way to the *adivasi* communities in India's coal belt, the San also described losing power over their lives and being unable to alter or even influence the course of events. Activities they formerly pursued, such as hunting game, had become illegal. Forced off the land, the displaced San had no option but to seek work on farms as laborers or to drift into surrounding towns. The children were sent far afield to state boarding schools. In political terms, what the San describe is once again an example of political disenfranchisement and systematic marginalization. What community cohesion existed before resettlement was weakened; with no formal independent voice in Parliament, the San were dependent on non-San chiefs or on international human rights advocacy groups to represent their interests, which neither did satisfactorily.

Interlocking Disadvantage

The academic literature on development-created population displacement and resettlement argues that for the majority of involuntarily resettled people the outcome is one of increased impoverishment.[6] Attempts at explaining why impoverishment occurs have by and large been concerned with the process of resettlement itself and have sought solutions by identifying risks that arise from the process and ways to address those risks.[7] In recent years, for example, Cernea has identified planners' fixation with monetary compensation as a key weakness in resettlement operations.[8] Elsewhere, Scudder and Colson[9] have drawn on a longitudinal analysis of the displacement created by the Kariba Dam on the Zambia/Zimbabwe border to show how the resettlement process can be understood as occurring in predictable phases. Within each phase there are stresses, and the people and communities affected respond to those stresses, moving eventually to the incorporation of the displaced into the wider society. These approaches can been criticized for being somewhat narrow, mechanistic, and even apolitical in the sense that they do not question the rationale of the original decision to proceed with a project of a certain size and in a certain location that is going to have largely predictable impacts on the people who live on land, the use of which is going to be changed. And neither do these approaches overtly question the manner in which the resettlement takes place; the power relations involved; and the role of the state, private capital, and powerful groups in society. McDowell[10] has sought to reintroduce the question of power by applying the sustainable-livelihoods approach[11] to understanding rural poverty, an approach that has emerged in recent years out of Development Studies and which has, in turn, been influential in international development operations. The sustainable-livelihoods turn in the study of involuntary resettlement helps us to understand that poverty—or rather impoverishment—is not just about what assets people have or lose, as with displacement and resettlement, but rather, as a recent IFAD report[12] makes clear, it is about "interlocking disadvantages" that limit people's opportunities to improve their livelihoods, undermine their assets and capabilities, and increase the risks they face. Moreover, this approach recognizes that these disadvantages can include a variety of forms of exclusion, discrimination, and disempowerment, which in turn determine people's ability to access those resources (natural resources, cash, social networks, education, etc.) that are essential to securing livelihoods and overcoming poverty.

The deprivation that arises out of these forms of exclusion are embedded in social and political relations and affect different groups of people (e.g., indigenous people, pastoralists, women, the landless) in different ways. We have seen from the interviews discussed above that displaced people are in many senses a special category of people who, by virtue of their displacement and resettlement, enter a different realm of social and political relations and who face a particular set of interlocking disadvantages. It is possible to further explore these disadvantages through the interviews.

"Disadvantage" is perhaps not the noun that Roba Dokota, formerly an Orma pastoralist from Kenya's Coast Province, was reaching for to describe the devastation of losing to disease and starvation 195 of his 200 cattle as a consequence of being barred access to traditional grazing grounds on the floodplains of the Tana River in the early 1990s (see Chapter 4). The land had been compulsorily seized by the Kenyan government and passed over to a state-owned development authority for large-scale internationally funded irrigated rice production—an endeavor that proved unsuccessful. As Dokota's interview so vividly describes, the loss of water and pasture and the subsequent death of cattle for those pursuing a pastoralist livelihood is not merely a set back or a technical risk that can be remedied through some compensatory intervention, but rather it has deep seated sociocultural and psychological consequences as well as economic consequences, including crises of identity, a detrimental impact on health, and in turn exacerbated intracommunity and intergenerational tensions.

Pastoralists in East Africa are used to drought; they have developed survival strategies to keep animals alive during the worst periods by, for example, moving them over the rangelands to find alternative sources of water, by investing during the good times in anticipation of bad times to come, and by drawing on humanitarian assistance. Drought does not necessarily have to be a crisis. For this to occur, there have to be other problems. Typically, these involve disrupted migration patterns and an inability to access main or reserve pastures and water sources (a situation that is often made worse by conflict that makes movement too dangerous) and distorted market conditions that make it difficult for pastoralists to trade their cattle. What is so tragic about the Tana River, and indeed the Tsavo East National Park displacements (here we are using the term "displacement" to refer to a loss of access to a particular resource) is that they did not occur at a time of drought or heightened conflict; they became crises for those affected precisely because migration patterns were deliberately disrupted by government actions designed to bar livestock access to rangelands, actions that were conducted in such a way and with such haste and, reportedly, violence that the pastoralists' resilience was undermined. It is also the case that in some senses the displacements described in Chapter 4 have even more serious consequences than humanitarian crises brought about by drought, precisely because the displaced pastoralists have been permanently excluded from their rangelands with no possibility of return. In drought conditions, it is known that the rains will at some point return, as will the mobility needed by pastoralists.

For Dokota and many of the Orma and Boran pastoralists who feature in this book, the actions of the state have so severely diminished their opportunities to pursue a pastoralist life that they have been forced to adopt practices such as security work, charcoal burning, and settled agriculture, which to them are foreign and undesirable. The successful ownership and management of cattle brings high prestige; ownership translates into political influence and children inherit both the wealth and the good name. Haji Kuno Galgalo, a pastoralist displaced by the Tsavo East National Park who lost many of his cattle and was unable to restock during the period covered by the interviews, describes his own decline in status, no longer participating in important community decision making. The impoverishment he is concerned with is not primarily material; rather, it is social and cultural. It is the inability to ensure marriage among the Orma and to have to stand by and watch as the fabric of the society that was built on the rangelands gradually unravels. Migrations over centuries across the territories of southern Ethiopia and Kenya have bound pastoralist communities through a shared identity that is described in ethnic terms but also through a shared religion. It is the threat to his faith by his no longer participating in the hajj or educating his children in the Islamic texts that Haji Kuno Galgalo fears as one of the consequences of a settled, nonpastoralist life.

The multidimensionality and interlocking nature of impoverishment is revealed in the experiences of the so-called "tribal" communities displaced by the Jharkhand mines. It is clear that as a result of the mining operations, the villagers lost access to resources (in the forests and rivers and on commonly owned lands) that were vital to their livelihood strategies; in addition, they lost assets in the form of physical capital such as their homes and fields. For most people, the compensation monies, the replacement housing, and the few "company" jobs that were available to eligible households in exchange for land were insufficient to replace those lost assets or to provide a foundation on which new and sustainable livelihoods could be built. Instead we read in Chapter 6 about people who formerly lived in rather remote rural areas, whose life was hard and should not be romanticized as some traditional rural idyll, who were transformed into laborers eking out a precarious and dangerous living on the margins of industrial mines feeding India's mainly urban economic growth. It is understood that impoverishment affects different groups of people in different ways; displacement and resettlement-induced impoverishment amplifies this dynamic. This is illustrated in the Damodar Valley, where women were by practice excluded from employment and did not qualify for jobs because their names did not appear on land title documents. Women were in many cases more disadvantaged by the resettlement polices and their implementation than were their husbands and sons.

Each displacement and resettlement situation is different. The multiple factors that affect how individuals, households, and communities cope with loss, and in many cases the trauma of loss, have to be identified and understood. Arguably, an entire village relocated as one to a location close to a newly constructed reservoir should be able to maintain a sense of collective identity and retain the institutions that bind the village together into a unit, with leadership structures that can represent the interests of its members; it can demand assistance from the responsible authorities. If that is done, the trauma of resettlement may be reduced. For the Damodar Valley residents, however, the situation was different. It has already been described how the displacement occurred in a fractured and, to the residents, unknown way over a number of years, and we have seen that the compensation package and the process of implementation were divisive, resulting in a situation where much of the preexisting cohesiveness was lost, thus reducing the capabilities of the affected villagers to adjust and manage the new situation. This was exacerbated by the fact that for many remaining behind in the valley, once the mining had started and environmental conditions began to deteriorate, farming was no longer an option and people drifted away, moving even to Kolkata (Calcutta) in West Bengal.

It is common in involuntary resettlement that those with assets and connections, often those better educated, who frequently are community leaders, are able to take advantage of resettlement benefits,; this is sometimes termed "social decapitation."[13] These are the people who are the first to leave an affected area and begin making a new life elsewhere. Those who are left behind are likely to be the poorer and less educated people, who struggle to survive in the new environment as they seek income-earning opportunities or government assistance. In the Damodar Valley, as the competition between the villagers intensified, hostility towards those who were able to secure jobs in the mines increased and families themselves fractured, increasing out-migration. A picture emerges of interlocking disadvantages that have been carried over since before the mines caused such upheaval: low levels of education and skills that are not readily tradable in the modern economy, a subordinate role for women, a superficial understanding of the fast-changing political economy in India, and low status in Indian society. These then intermesh with new disadvantages created by the displacement itself and the resettlement process: insufficient and inappropriate compensation for lost assets and policies applied in a manner that further divides a weakened community. These disadvantages are then compounded by the post-resettlement economic, political, and environmental context of greater livelihood insecurity, deteriorating health, a poorer diet and, for most of the women, a diminished status that limits their opportunity to improve their family's situation.

The Damodar Valley residents who remained behind, watching helplessly over a number of years as the forested slopes were scraped away to reveal the coal beneath, saw their familiar landscape and their important sites disappearing as each day passed.

For the residents of the Tarbela area in Pakistan, as described in Chapter 3, it was known for some years that eventually the dam would be completed and the waters of the reservoir would rise inexorably, inundating their hamlets and communities. Yet still people would not admit to themselves that such a dramatic event was going to befall them and their communities. Ejaz Ahmed Khan recalled that the government of the day, through its implementing agency the Water and Power Development Authority (WAPDA), failed to properly inform the local residents of what was to occur. A WAPDA official admits that they themselves were in the dark for much of the time, uncertain about how to handle the evacuation or to help people build lives once they had been moved to specially constructed townships in neighboring districts or much further afield in the Punjab. When trying to piece together the socioeconomic and cultural impacts of displacement and resettlement, the Tarbela case is interesting because it enables us through the interviews to reflect on these impacts some 30 to 40 years later. It is in the testimony of the Tarbela displaced that we hear perhaps the most striking claim contained in this volume. A number of respondents claim that the upheaval from the construction of the dam and reservoir, the sudden loss of land and homes, and the trauma of the resettlement resulted in the premature deaths of some of the older villagers. In the 1990s, Michael Cernea then working as a social scientist for the World Bank, reviewed evidence on resettlement outcomes in World-Bank-funded projects in the developing world in a number of key sectors, including the water and hydropower sector. With this evidence base, he developed a model to predict and overcome resettlement-related impoverishment risks.[14] One of the seven risks he identified was that of increased morbidity and mortality. The precise causality for early death was not delineated; however, the model proposes that the risks occur with differing degrees of intensity and in differing combinations in given settings. In this way, one could hypothesize that premature death among resettlers might happen because people's health status declines because of changed environmental conditions and susceptibility to new diseases in new locations; a changed and inferior diet; or perhaps as a result of poor housing conditions. There is insufficient evidence to draw any firm conclusions from the Tarbela interviews, but the fact of the statements is significant, as is the belief that these deaths may be attributable to the increased stress and worry brought about by the loss of the familiar, the upset of disrupted family life, and—a common theme throughout this volume—despair at not being able to secure a future for the narrators' children. The psychological impact of that perceived failure on the part of the resettled seems significant.

The impact of resettlement on the Tarbela families in the early 1970s was studied by the World Commission on Dams (WCD) in the late 1990s and was reported on in 2000.[15] The commission, established to undertake a broad cost–benefit analysis of large dams that weighed the economic advantages against the environmental and social costs, found hundreds of outstanding compensation and land claims among the Tarbela "affectees." Even where alternate land had been allotted, many of the displaced had still not taken possession of those lands, and the conditions in the resettlement townships were described as "poor," with an air of abandonment. The interviews in Chapter 3 were gathered some years after the commission visited the same areas. However, the complaints remained very similar; the narratives provided a reflective consideration of the impact of resettlement on the lives of the Tarbela displaced that complements the WCD report.

The oral history field methods that were used to collect the interviews in this book encouraged the displaced and their relatives to take stock of the changes that had occurred over the previous three decades. What emerged was a strong nostalgia for Tarbela and what it stood for, compared to post-resettlement life. For many people, Tarbela was still home. They lamented the loss of neighborliness, the sense of community and order, and described a natural environment that was giving and generous. Tarbela remained with them as their real home, as opposed to the resettlement locations, where they were strangers and outsiders, imposed on people who sometimes did not welcome their presence, and detached from the natural environment. In these testimonies, one can read a romanticizing of the past and of the social order in which people knew their place, abided by the rules that governed the political life of villages and respected—up to a point—the hierarchy and system of authority, which saw local land-owning families wield considerable power over the landless villagers, although countered with largesse. Although some of the interviewees were highly critical of this system, and of the court system that passed judgment on disputes, there is a sense in which the past, despite its iniquities and injustices, presented a balanced, disciplined, and predictable order, in contrast to their more unpredictable lives in Khallabat Township or Karachi.

The ill discipline and chaos of the present time, they described linked in important ways to the failures of the state to fulfill their side of the resettlement contract. Promised jobs did not materialize, leaving the young men, in particular, with few choices: to accept uncertain and low-paid casual labor, to seek work overseas, or to remain in the resettlement townships, waiting for employment but being overwhelmed with despondency (as if "in a deep well") and finding solace in heroin and hashish. The scattering of families, a number of narrators argued, contributed to the restlessness, because family traditions were no longer observed and role models were absent. And where land was provided, as the WCD found, the quality was often poor and compensation money was quickly used up trying to coax crops from barren soil, adding to families' financial difficulties.

This examination of some of the interlocking disadvantages identified by the interviewers has overlooked another side to the "conversations" into which we have had the opportunity to listen. For some, the changes brought about by or hastened by "development" have been viewed more positively. Eighty-year-old Maqsoodan Jan, from a family of musicians and entertainers in a valley inundated by the Tarbela Reservoir, missed the colorful celebration of religious and family events that featured in her previous life, but she felt liberated in the resettlement location, owning her own home and no longer at the beck and call of her land-lords. In all the chapters, there is the acknowledgment that material progress in the form of electricity, clean water, and, in particular, education improved their lives. Gul Bibi, also displaced by the Tarbela Dam, believed that the education of girls and women in particular has helped to liberate them from repressive relationships with men. Tetri Kisku, who described struggling to come to terms with the impact of mines in the Damodar Valley in India, observed that for some *adivasi* girls, even a few years of formal education and some grasp of the Hindi language opened new opportunities and widened their horizons.

Whether one is discussing the negative or the positive outcomes of resettle-ment as identified by the narrators, it is always difficult analytically to disentangle causation. The changes that the displaced have experienced will have arisen as the result of dynamics that have been created by the displacement and resettlement process, but always in relation to "background" changes that affect displacees and nondisplacees alike. The Tarbela Dam and Kenyan rice and conservation project present particularly difficult challenges, as the events occurred some years previ-ously and both societies have undergone far-reaching changes in their economy, demography, and social relations and the respondents understandably relate their current situation to an event that for them is both political and formative.

Lessons about Process

The narrators are keen observers of the displacement and resettlement process, and their experiences provide an insider's evaluation of success or failure. There is a substantial amount of publicly available material evaluating involuntary resettlement. The scores of reports prepared by the Inspection Panel of the World Bank, investigating complaints from individuals and communities about what they perceive to be the harmful effects of World-Bank-funded projects, are a rich source of information.[16] Many of these reports are concerned with failings related to involuntary resettlement; they reveal repeated weaknesses in the process and in implementation, not just on the part of the World Bank, but also by its implementing partners: governments, private contractors, parastatals, and even other lending bodies. Those weaknesses tend to revolve around the lack of consultation with or disclosure to affected communities; the failure to fully anticipate the impacts of particular investments; the failure to identify and respond to the needs of all people who are likely to be affected (including those without title to land and those who are affected indirectly or "downstream" from a project); weaknesses in compensation (inappropriate, insufficient, late or partial payments); failure to identify and provide alternative, appropriate, and sufficient replacement land; and corruption and malpractice. The interviews contained in this volume tend to concur with these panel investigation findings, but they add new dimensions to our knowledge about involuntary resettlement practice. What is remarkable is that the same mistakes were made back in the late 1970s in creating Pakistan's Tarbela Dam, and yet lessons about participation, sensitivity to the disproportionate negative impact on women and the landless, and the need to secure alternate land long before resettlement takes place appear not to have been learned. The same mistakes are being repeated today. In Chapter 3, a WAPDA (Water and Power Development Authority) official puts those failings down to inexperience. Evidence presented elsewhere in this volume and summarized above, however, suggest that the real source of such repeated failure can be found in the model of development and the exercise of power by governments and agencies granted eminent domain rights over local landowners and users.

An important critique that emerges from the interviews is a dimension that is not highlighted in the inspection panel reports. It is a critique that returns us to Scudder and Colson's emphasis of the psychosocial stress related to losing one's home and being moved to somewhere alien, where a longing for what has been left behind remains a dominant emotion. Once again in Tarbela, we learn how psychologically ill-prepared people were for the waters to rise and for the trucks to arrive to take them and their possessions to the new location. This is frequently the case in resettlement operations, where for a variety of reasons timetables slip, sometimes by years, legal obstacles are put in the way of the excavators moving in, finances are not in place, and the disbelief and scepticism of communities grows. Rumors abound that the project has been canceled or that the line of the road, the airstrip, or the borders of the conservation park have been changed and will bypass people's lands. However, the projects do go ahead, the heavy moving vehicles do arrive, perhaps early in the morning, unannounced, and people are caught unprepared. Resistance then follows and, as we have heard from the witnesses in this volume, force is likely to be used. During field work in China, author Christopher McDowell was told of agonizing choices made by women clambering on to flat-bottomed boats that were removing them from their homes on the banks of the Yangtze River in advance of the rising of the waters brought about by the near completion of the Three Gorges Dam. As in Tarbela, a project that had been decades in planning and years in construction had come down to last-minute decisions about which things could be taken and which would be left to the waters.

A more substantive critique of resettlement that permeates the testimonies is the inability of resettlement planners and the agencies that were given the responsibility of initiating this process of change to anticipate and fully understand what it means to dismantle communities of people and to understand how, once disentangled, the ties that bind people together cannot simply or easily be rewoven in a new setting. Where the bridging and bonding across and between individuals and families have been undermined, people predictably feel cut adrift. They feel less able to cope with the challenges that resettlement brings. It is perhaps unreasonable to place all the blame on resettlement planners for failing to understand the complexities of social change and for lacking the means and knowledge to rebuild long-established communities. Arguably, the reality is that collectively we do not have the human knowledge to manage such dramatic processes of changes. Where governments and international humanitarian organizations are confronted with other displaced people, in times of conflict, drought, or of a natural disaster, the priority is to keep the time in which people are in a state of displacement, in a camp or sheltering in the homes of others as short as possible. Indeed, the reaction of displaced people is to independently return home as soon as they deem it safe. For those under the care of the international community, the most eagerly pursued "durable solution" is repatriation, recognizing that the best option for the future is to piece together shattered communities. In the case of development-created involuntary resettlement, the preferred option of return is not available as a policy option.

The Value of Oral History in Resettlement Research

Chapter 2 outlined the strengths of the oral testimony approach as a complement to other research methods, and noted how such personal accounts remind readers of the complexity and variety of people's experiences and of the importance of the nonquantifiable responses—in this case, descriptions of the psychological distress caused by grieving for lost places and the sense of having lost control over so much in one's life beyond simply the physical location where it is being played out. They show how grief and a sense of powerlessness are exacerbated when they are not acknowledged or, in the case of the latter, are not addressed by actions that could go some way to restoring a sense of agency and independence. They reveal the frustration felt by the resettled when their perception is that they have to ask for their compensation as though it is a favor, not a right. Studded with personal detail, these accounts also show how individuals and families do not fit neat categories for the purposes of asset valuation and compensation. An alcoholic uncle is unable to take up the job offered as compensation for his land, for example, but the extended family loses the desperately needed employment because the rules are too inflexible to accommodate a reasonable solution.

Even well-meaning policies that are carefully thought through by experts and professionals are only as good as their implementation in the field, where often poorly trained and supported local staff are trying to put them into practice among distressed and anxious families. They prove that even where implementation is generally agreed to be inadequate, the authorities also get things right at times, as when the Lesotho Highland Water Project staff arranged for the reburial of the villagers' ancestors in their new locations in a way that was sensitive to the emotions and traditions involved, and which the resettled universally acknowledged with gratitude. They provide a realistic picture of the positive, negative, and unexpected outcomes that emerge when families start to rebuild lives and a sense of community—for example, the dispute with a neighboring village that had been inadequately prepared for the new population settled alongside them, or the tensions developing between generations as the reality of the old "home" recedes into the past and lives on only in people's memories.

Making the Resettled Count

In the preparation of this volume, the authors have eavesdropped on conversations held among people who have been displaced in the name of progress. It is a privileged insight into how those people experienced, understood, and offered a critique of events and decisions that changed their lives in dramatic ways. The big picture is that the displaced and resettled whose views are aired in these chapters had no choice but to make sacrifices for what was termed the national good. The resettlement described was in all cases involuntary. As economic growth, industrialization, and the push for natural resource conservation grows, ever larger numbers of people will also be resettled against their will in the coming decades. It remains an open question as to whether or not governments, development funding bodies, and civil society can together work towards improving the legal, policy, and operational framework within which future resettlement will be undertaken. Scudder, a leading authority on involuntary resettlement, has reflected on more than 50 years of writing about and evaluating the social and environmental effects of large dams. He remains unconvinced that affected populations, both in the immediate area and downstream, can become benefi-ciaries of such projects. If the political will is there to ensure the rights of the resettled, if the legal framework is strengthened and proper financing is in place, the improvement of people's lives may be possible. For Scudder, what is key is that populations who are to be displaced and resettled be not only involved in the resettlement planning and decision making, but that the process must involve their consent.[17] At present, the standard to which the funders and implementers aspire is "informed consultation;" they argue that consent cannot be sought for a process that is ultimately involuntary and imposed. The power of the testimo-nies contained in this volume, however, suggests that a process of negotiated and informed consent with affected communities is not only desirable but essential, if people are to be granted autonomy and given back the control that involuntary resettlement takes from them. The interviews inform us that it is the individuals, families, and communities themselves who have the knowledge to understand how resettlement, where it is necessary and unavoidable, can be conducted in a lawful and democratic manner, achieving change that is desired by all in society.

Notes

Preface

1. For more on Panos London see www.panos.org.uk and for oral testimony work, see http://panos.org.uk/our-work/our-methodologies/voice/
2. H. Slim and P. Thompson, *Listening for a Change: Oral Testimony and Development* (London: Panos, 1993).

I Moving People: States, Displacement, and Resettlement

1. See T. C. Bisht, *Displacement, Resettlement and Everyday Life: An Ethnographic Study of People Displaced by the Tehri Dam in India* (PhD thesis, La Trobe University, Victoria, Australia).
2. T. Scudder and E. Colson, "From Welfare to Development: A Conceptual Framework for the Analysis of Dislocated People," in A. Hansen and A. Oliver-Smith, eds., *Involuntary Migration and Resettlement: The Problems and Responses of Dislocated People* (Boulder, CO: Westview Press, 1982). C. McDowell, ed., *Understanding Impoverishment: The Consequences of Development-Induced Displacement* (Oxford: Berghahn, 1996). M. Cernea and C. McDowell, eds., *Risks and Reconstruction: The Experiences of Refugees and Resettlers* (Washington, D.C.: The World Bank, 2000). T. Scudder, *The Future of Large Dams: Dealing with Social, Environmental, Institutional and Political Costs* (London: Earthscan, 2006). M. Cernea and H. M. Mathur, eds., *Can Compensation Prevent Impoverishment?* (Delhi: Oxford University Press, 2008).
3. A. Applebaum, *Gulag: A History* (New York: Doubleday, 2004)
4. J. C. Scott, *Seeing Like a State: How Certain Schemes to Improve the Human Condition Have Failed* (New Haven, CT: Yale University Press, 1998).
5. G. Hyden, *Beyond Ujamaa in Tanzania: Underdevelopment and an Uncaptured Peasantry* (London: Heinemann, 1980).
6. M. Cernea, "Risks, Safeguards and Reconstruction: A Model for Population Displacement and Resettlement," in M. Cernea and C. McDowell, eds. *Risks and Reconstruction,* 33–35.
7. D. E. McMillan, *Sahel Visions: Planned Settlement and River Blindness Control in Burkina Faso* (Tucson: University of Arizona Press, 1995).
8. E. Colson, *The Social Consequences of Resettlement* (Manchester: Manchester University Press, 1971). C. McDowell, *Understanding Impoverishment.* M. Cernea, "Risks, Safeguards and Reconstruction: A Model for Population Displacement and Resettlement," in M. Cernea and C. McDowell, *Risks and Reconstruction.* E. Ferris, *Natural Disaster and Conflict-Induced Displacement: Similarities, Differences and Interconnections* (Washington, D.C.: The Brookings Institute, 2008). W. Kaelin, "The Role of the Guiding Principles in Internal Displacement," *Forced Migration Rerview,* Vol. 23 (2005), 8–9. C. McDowell and G. Morrell, *Displacement beyond Conflict: Challenges for the 21st Century* (Oxford: Berghahn, 2010).

9. C. McDowell, "Involuntary Resettlement, Impoverishment Risks and Sustainable Livelihoods," in *Australasian Journal of Disaster and Trauma Studies*, 6, No. 2, 2002, http://www.massey.ac.nz/~trauma/

10. Ferris, E. *Natural Disaster and Conflict-Induced Displacement*; also Cernea and McDowell, *Risks and Reconstruction*.

11. Cernea and McDowell, *Risks and Reconstruction*; McDowell and Morrell, *Displacement Beyond Conflict*.

12. Cernea and McDowell, *Risks and Reconstruction*; T. E. Downing, "Mitigating Social Impoverishment when People Are Involuntarily Displaced," in C. McDowell, ed., *Understanding Impoverishment: The Consequences of Development-Induced Displacement, 33–48* (Oxford: Berghahn, 1996).

13. Personal correspondence from Professor Frank Pieke, University of Leiden, June 2009.

14. E. Lahiff, *Land Reform and Poverty in South Africa* (Cape Town: University of the Western Cape, Programme for Land and Agrarian Studies, 2007).

15. B. McDonald and M. Webber, "Involuntary Resettlement in China: a Model of Good Practice," *Forced Migration Review*, Vol. 14 (2002), 38–39.

2 The Individual Voice: The Challenges and Benefits of Listening to Personal Narratives

1. For more on this, see H. Slim and P. Thompson, *Listening for a Change: Oral Testimony and Development* (London: Panos, 1993).

2. Personal communication to O. Bennett, 1998.

3. See http://panos.org.uk/oral-testimonies/ for other Panos oral testimony projects.

4. Slim and Thompson, *Listening for a Change*, 88–89.

5. R. Kalshian, ed., *The Caterpillar and the Mahua Flower: Tremors in India's Mining Fields* (New Delhi: Panos South Asia, 2007), and *Alchemy of Iniquity: Resistance and Repression in India's Mines, a Photographic Enquiry* (New Delhi: Panos South Asia, 2008).

6. See, for example, work by Kuntala Lahari-Dutt cited in Chapter 6.

7. H. Brody, "Taking the Words from Their Mouths," in *Tribes: Battle for Lands and Language,* Index on Censorship, Vol. 28, Issue 4, 1999, 42–47.

8. Project communication, Panos London, 1999.

9. See, for example, *The Khwe of the Okavango Panhandle: The Past Life* (P. O. Box 344, Shakawe, Botswana: Teemacane Trust, 2002); *The Khwe of the Okavango Panhandle: The Use of Veld Plants for Food and Medicine (Part 1)* (Shakawe, Botswana: Letloa Trust Lands, Livelihoods and Heritage Resource Centre, 2007); and W. le Roux and A. White, eds., *Voices of the San: Living in Southern Africa Today* (Cape Town, South Africa: Kwela Books, 2004).

10. From S. Warrington, "Voices, Voices Everywhere, But How Much Learning Is Going on?" in *Participatory Learning and Action 63: How Wide Are the Ripples? From Local Participation to International Organisational Learning*, K. Newman and H. Beardon, eds., 31–38 (London: International Institute for Environment and Development, 2011).

11. J. Gaventa, "The Powerful, the Powerless, and the Experts," in *Voices of Change: Participatory Research in the United States and Canada*, P. Park, M. Brydon-Miller, B. Hall, and T. Jackson, eds., 22 (Westport, CT and London: Bergin & Garvey, 1993).

12. Ibid., 29.

13. T. Downing, *Avoiding New Poverty: Mining-Induced Displacement and Resettlement*. Mining, Minerals and Sustainable Development Working Paper No. 58 (London: International Institute for Environment and Development, 2002), 19.

14. D. Narayan, with R. Patel, K. Schafft, A. Rademacher, and S. Koch-Sculte, *Voices of the Poor: Can Anyone Hear Us?* (New York: Oxford University Press, 2000), 3.

15. R. Chambers, "Power, Knowledge and Policy Influence: Reflections on an Experience," in K. Brock and R. McGee, eds., *Knowing Poverty: Critical Reflections on Participatory Research and Policy* (London: Earthscan Publications, 2002), 153.

16. R. Chambers, *Who Counts? The Quiet Revolution of Participation and Numbers,* Working Paper 296 Institute of Development Studies (University of Sussex, 2007), 34.

17. U. Kothari and D. Hulme, *Narratives, Stories and Tales: Understanding Poverty Dynamics through Life Histories,* Global Poverty Research Group Working Paper No. 11 (University of Manchester, 2004), 3.

18. Ibid., 33.

19. Ibid., 35–36.

20. Ibid., 5.

21. International Fund for Agricultural Development, *Rural Poverty Report 2011* (Rome: International Fund for Agricultural Development, 2010), 8.

22. As well as oral testimony, for example, Panos London now uses digital storytelling and participatory video to record and communicate individual voices.

23. See Warrington, "Voices, Voices Everywhere."

24. Much has been written on this issue. See, for example, P. Thompson, *The Voice of the Past; Oral History* (Oxford: Oxford University Press, 1988), 68–71; and for a retrospective view of the debates, A. Thomson, M. Frisch, and P. Hamilton, "The Memory and History Debates: Some International Perspectives," *Oral History,* Vol. 22, No. 2 (Autumn 1994), 33–43.

25. A. Faraday and K. Plummer, "Doing Life Histories," *Sociological Review,* Vol. 27, No. 4 (1979), 777.

26. B. R. Sorenson, *Relocated Lives: Displacement and Resettlement within the Mahaweli Project, Sri Lanka* (Amsterdam: VU University Press, 1996), and "The Experience of Displacement: Reconstructing Places and Identities in Sri Lanka," in K. F. Olwig and K. Hastrup, eds., *Siting Culture: The Shifting Anthropological Object,* 142–164 (London: Routledge, 1997).

27. Faraday and Plummer, "Doing Life Histories," 777.

28. One collection of 45 interviews with the Tonga in Zimbabwe and Zambia, who were displaced by the Kariba Dam in the late 1950s, informed our book, but was not included because we could not do justice to the wealth of material in the six case studies that form the heart of this book if we had included this collection as well.

29. P. Read, *Returning to Nothing: The Meaning of Lost Places* (Cambridge University Press, 1996), 197.

30. Thompson, *The Voice of the Past,* 10.

3 "We had a set way of life. All that has been disturbed": Tarbela Dam, Pakistan

1. Information and figures in this section are from *Tarbela Dam and Related Aspects of the Indus River Basin, Pakistan* (Cape Town, 2000), the World Commission on Dams case study prepared as input to the World Commission on Dams.

2. There are several references within interviews to tribal areas being *Ilaqa Ghair,* meaning they are not under the direct control of the administration.

3. Panos's partners in Pakistan were SUNGI Development Foundation and Samaji Tanzeem Mutasireen Tarbela (SMT) in Haripur. SMT works on behalf of the resettled, seeking justice and resolution on compensation issues. Sixty interviews were gathered between 2001 and 2003, predominantly in Khallabat Township, but also in the Punjab, Karachi, and other more remote locations. This chapter is based on the 40 translated into English from the Urdu transcriptions of the Hindko interviews (see note 12).

4. "It is presumed that this [decision] was because of the non-acceptance of non-Sindhi population in Sindh interior [and] fears of the law and order situation." From *Tarbela Dam and Related Aspects,* 80.

5. For more on this see Yousaf Rafiq, "Settlement of Tarbela Dam Affectees' Claims," *Pakistan Economist,* Karachi, issue 30 (1999).

6. Interview with WAPDA official, 2002.

7. Three former gold panners were interviewed at the village where they settled. Once highly skilled workers, they now compete for laboring jobs and have not been able to educate their children, all of whom are unemployed.

8. In May 2011, for example, SMT representatives met WAPDA and government officials to push forward the implementation of the Peshawar High Court decisions on outstanding claims.

9. *Tarbela Dam and Related Aspects,* 73.

10. Ibid., 84.

11. For example, Tameel Begum was married to a man who became a heroin addict: "I did embroidery, then I did crochet work [at home], but...I had three children and was unable to meet their needs. So I started a small canteen at the girls' school and I sold toffees, biscuits, and other small items." Her lack of education prevented her from getting better-paid work.

12. Most of the displaced were Hindko speakers, a language related to Punjabi. Some Pathans spoke Pushto, or were bilingual in Pushto and Hindko. Many older narrators expressed concern about distance growing between generations over use of language. "The [next generation] will forget their original language with time. Already the Hindko they speak is no longer pure; it is adulterated with Sindhi, Punjabi, and Urdu words" (Rafaqat Ali Khan).

13. Several other interviewers say that those working in the cotton mills develop lung problems or "TB" (tuberculosis).

4 "I have lost status in my community": Conservation and Agricultural Production in Kenya

1. Pastoralism is a form of animal husbandry practiced in environments characterized by high seasonal variability in pastures and water, where mobility and negotiated access to resources are key strategies to maintain high productivity.

2. See Helen de Jode, ed., *Modern and Mobile: The Future of Livestock Production in Africa's Drylands* (London: International Institute for Environment and Development, 2009).

3. *Arid Waste? Reassessing the Value of Dryland Pastoralism,* IIED Briefing Paper (London: International Institute for Environment and Development, 2009), 1.

4. Sessional Paper No. 3 of 2009 on Land Policy (Ministry of Lands: Kenya, 2009).

5. Draft National Land Policy, National Land Policy Secretariat (Ministry of Lands: Kenya, 2007), 21.

6. Panos London and Panos Eastern Africa worked with Intermediate Technology Development Group (now renamed Practical Action) Eastern Africa, to gather 18 interviews with Boran and Orma men and women, in those languages, between 1999 and 2001. Mursal Galgalo and Sophia Duba were crucial to the project. Some of the interviewees, and almost all the women, were primarily displaced by conflict or political intervention; their experience of resettlement involved interventions that were not available to the narrators for whom development was the key cause of displacement. This chapter therefore draws on the stories of the latter group.

7. Tsavo was long the homeland for Orma and Maasai pastoralists and Wata hunter-gatherers. The colonial government gazetted it as a national park in 1948. At that time, some local people were relocated. Following Kenyan independence in 1963, management of Tsavo was turned over to the authority that became the Kenya Wildlife Service.

8. The project involved the conversion of approximately 2,000 hectares of fertile floodplain for commercial rice production between 1991 and 1999. The El Niño floods of 1997 destroyed a large area and the project was never relaunched. In 2010 the government revived controversial plans for the area's development. See www.tanariverdelta.org

9. It appears no compensation was offered; conversation with Sofia Duba, 2011.

10. See note 8 above. For more on development schemes, see "Development, Conservation and People's Livelihood at Crossroads: The Proposed Sugarcane Project in the Tana River Delta," Kenya Wetlands Forum (Nairobi: The East African Wildlife Society, 2005).

11. The Wata (hunter-gatherers) have no cattle, so the pastoralists regarded them as poor, with no prospects for wealth, and did not allow their daughters to marry them.

12. The Shifta War (1963–1967) was a secessionist conflict in which ethnic Somalis in Kenya's Northern Frontier District attempted to join with their fellow Somalis in a Greater Somalia, encompassing north-eastern Kenya and eastern Ethiopia. The Kenyan government named the war "shifta," after the Somali word for "bandit." A cease-fire was signed in 1967 but the conflict and violent clampdowns left a legacy of disorganized banditry in the area for several decades and caused significant disruption to the pastoralist way of life.
13. Galana Ranch is a "private protected area," defined by the IUCN as areas owned by institutions or individuals that are registered game ranches in which wildlife conservation is the primary aim.

5 "The people's place became the animals' place": Resettlement Policies and Conservation in Botswana and Namibia

1. There is no universally acceptable terminology, with the use of San and Bushmen disliked by different groups, so where possible we have referred to the specific group, for example the Khwe in Botswana. "Bushmen" derives from the first Dutch settlers in the Cape in the 1600s, who associated the San with the African equivalent of the orangutan or "forest man" they knew from Indonesia, and christened them *bosjesmans*. The origin of the name Basarwa, used for the San by the Batswana (the Tswana people of Botswana), is associated with the San lack of cattle ownership, thus defining them in negative terms and implicitly implying poverty by Tswana standards.
2. For more on the oral history project, see Chapter 2.
3. According to the Working Group of Indigenous Minorities in Southern Africa (WIMSA), San populations in Botswana and Namibia number 46,000 and 38,000 respectively. In Angola there are 7,000; in South Africa, 6,000. In Zambia and Zimbabwe, San communities number a few hundred.
4. See, for example, The First Peoples of the Kalahari (FPK), an indigenous human rights organization, and WIMSA, a nongovernmental regional network that coordinates and represents the interests of San peoples throughout southern Africa.
5. Kuru Family of Organisations: www.kuru.co.bw See also Ditshwanelo: The Botswana Centre for Human Rights: www.ditshwanelo.org.bw
6. World Directory of Minorities and Indigenous Peoples, accessed March 2011, http://www.unhcr.org/refworld/docid/49749cdac.html
7. Ibid.
8. Panos worked with the then Kuru Development Trust to gather an initial 48 testimonies in Botswana and Namibia between 1999 and 2001. WIMSA and the Trust for Okavango Cultural and Development Initiatives were also involved. The interviews were conducted in Khwe, ||Anikhwe, Hai||om and Ju|'hoansi; the spelling of Khwe names in this chapter is according to the orthography developed by researchers from the University of Cologne. Willemien le Roux and Sue Armstrong played crucial roles in the project.
9. "Report on the Review of the Remote Area Development Programme" (Gaborone: Botswana Institute for Development Policy Analysis, for Ministry of Local Government, December 2003), xiv–xvii.
10. Patricia Draper and Marion Kranichfeld, "Coming in from the Bush: Settled Life by the !Kung and Their Accommodation to Bantu Neighbors," *Human Ecology*, Vol. 18, No. 4 (December 1990): 363–384.
11. "Report on the Review of the Remote Area Development Programme," 2003, xvi.
12. *Pula* ("rain") is the currency of Botswana.
13. "Report on the Review of the Remote Area Development Programme," 2003, xvi–xvii.
14. A German colony until 1915, Namibia remains a favorite destination for German tourists.

15. Namutoni and Okaukuejo are rest camps within Etosha; Outjo is 114 kilometers (70.5 miles) south of Okaukuejo.
16. No land has yet been given back, but there has been some affirmative action towards giving the Hai‖om jobs as wardens. Negotiations have begun about limited access to certain zones for gathering purposes.
17. Other groups called it "peppercorn hair," because it differed from their Bantu hair, and grew in more discrete tufts.
18. As Namibia does not yet have a national San organization, WIMSA supports and coordinates its San community-based organizations and initiatives.
19. All the points made by narrators about the education system are borne out by the "Report on the Review of the Remote Area Development Programme."

6 "Our fields have gone, our lifestyle has changed": Coal Mining in India

1. Panos London and Panos India worked with Prerana Resource Centre of Hazaribagh, Jharkhand. Prerana was a local community organization working on the social and environmental impact of the mining industry. Mitu Varma, Bulu and Justin Imam, Kuntala Lahiri-Dutt, and Father Tony Herbert were key contributors to the project. Forty interviews were recorded in the *adivasi* languages of Santhali, Mundari, Khorta and Oraon in 2001 and 2002 and later translated into Hindi. Twenty-nine were translated into English. For more on ways the interviews were used, see Chapter 2.
2. See Kuntala Lahiri-Dutt, "Illegal Coal Mining in Eastern India: Rethinking Legitimacy and Limits of Justice," *Economic and Political Weekly*, Vol. 42, No. 49 (December 8–14, 2007), 57–67. Reprinted in 2009 as a chapter in *Key Texts on Social Justice in India: State of Justice in India, Issues of Social Justice*, edited by Sanam Roohi and Ranabir Samaddar, 294–323 (New Delhi: Sage, 2009).
3. From Kuntala Lahiri-Dutt, Radhika Krishnan, and Nesar Ahmad, "Private Coal-mining Companies in Jharkhand, Land Acquisition and Dispossession: A New Paradigm of Mining in India," *Economic and Political Weekly* (Mumbai, India: forthcoming 2012), 10 of draft.
4. See *India's Childhood in the 'Pits': A Report on the Impacts of Mining on Children in India* (New Delhi, India: Dhaatri Resource Centre for Women and Children-Samata and HAQ: Centre for Child Rights, March 2010), especially "Part 11, State reports, No. 6 Jharkhand."
5. See Lahiri-Dutt, Krishnan, and Ahmad, "Private Coal-mining Companies in Jharkhand," 3 of draft. [see Note 3 above]
6. Under the Constitution of the Republic of India of 1950, tribal peoples along with so-called "untouchables" became subject to special protective provisions, although problems of remoteness, poverty, and prejudice continue to mitigate against *adivasis* exploiting these provisions. The vast majority of tribes were classified as "Scheduled Tribes," but this is a legal term, which differs from area to area and therefore excludes some groups who might be considered tribal. Source: World Directory of Minorities and Indigenous Peoples, accessed March 2011, http://www.unhcr.org /refworld/docid/49749d14c.html
7. Tribal peoples have been disproportionately affected by development-induced displacement throughout India. They represented 8% of the population (2001 census) but of the 60 million people internally displaced in India since 1951, 24 million are *adivasis*. Source: Adivasi Development Network, accessed March 2011, http://www.adivasinetwork.org
8. Source: www.coalindia.in (accessed March 2011).
9. See Michael Cernea and Hari Mohan Mathur, eds., *Can Compensation Prevent Impoverishment? Reforming Resettlement through Investments* (New Delhi: Oxford University Press, 2008).
10. It is the World Bank's Inspection Panel Report No. 24000—*Investigation Report/India: Coal Sector Environmental and Social Mitigation Project* (Credit No. 2862-IN) (Washington D. C.: World Bank, 2002).

11. *No Action to Be Taken: Tracking Down the World Bank's Inspection Panel Report and Management Reponse, Coal Mining Project Parej East, India* (Heidelberg: FIAN International, 2006), Document G52e. [FIAN = FoodFirst Information and Action Network]

12. Ministry of Home Affairs, *Report of Committee on Rehabilitation of Displaced Tribals Due to Development Projects* (New Delhi: Government of India, 1985).

13. For more on Coal India's policy, see Kuntala Lahiri-Dutt and Nesar Ahmad, "Considering Gender in Social Impact Assessments," in *New Directions in Social Impact Assessments: Conceptual and Methodological Advances,* edited by Frank Vanclay and Ana Maria Esteves (Cheltenham: Edward Elgar, 2012).

14. See Lahiri-Dutt and Ahmad, "Considering Gender in Social Impact Assessments."

15. See Lahiri-Dutt, Krishnan, and Ahmad, "Private Coal-mining Companies in Jharkhand," 8–9 of draft. [see Note 3]

16. See Tribal Women's Artists Collective: http://sinclairenvironmental.com/sanskriti/twac.htm

17. *India's Childhood in the 'Pits,'* 22 and 119.

7 "The wisdom of living in this place will be lost": Mohale Dam, Lesotho, before Resettlement

1. Thirty-six interviews were recorded in 1997 and 1998, with the help of Transformation Resource Centre (TRC), the Lesotho Highlands Church Action Group and Sechaba Consultants; 28 were translated from Sesotho into English. The interview collection was coordinated by Dr Motlatsi Thabane of the National University of Lesotho, whose insights were invaluable.

2. Impact of the Lesotho Highlands Water Project, May 2005, accessed June 21, 2011, http://www.lhwp.org.ls

3. See Ryan Hoover, *Pipe Dreams: The World Bank's Failed Efforts to Restore Lives and Livelihoods of Dam-Affected People in Lesotho* (Berkeley, CA: International Rivers, 2001), 17.

4. See Thayer Scudder, "Assessing the Impacts of the LHWP on Resettled Households and Other Affected People 1986–2005," in *On the Wrong Side of Development: Lessons Learned from the Lesotho Highlands Water Project,* edited by M. L. Thamae and L. Pottinger, 39–87 (Lesotho: Transformation Resource Centre, 2006); and LHDA, *Lesotho Highlands Water Project Phase IB Environmental Impact Assessment: Executive Summary* (May 1997), 21, as cited in Hoover, *Pipe Dreams,* 24.

5. "In late 2004, the project was granted a loan extension by the World Bank, which reported that while engineering works are complete, there are major concerns about the social and development work to improve the lives of affected people." Source: *A Brief History of Africa's Largest Water Project* (Berkeley, CA: International Rivers, 2001, updated 2005). See also Scudder, "Assessing the Impacts of the LHWP."

6. See Motlatsi Thabane, "Shifts from Old to New Social and Ecological Environments in the Lesotho Highlands Water Scheme," *Journal of Southern African Studies,* Vol. 26, Issue 4 (December 2000), 633–654.

7. When interviewed three years later, she and her family had not yet been relocated. Neither of her three sons had jobs anymore, though her husband had had some piecework with LHDA.

8. See, for example, Thabane, "Shifts from Old to New," and M. L. Thamae and L. Pottinger, eds., *On the Wrong Side of Development: Lessons Learned from the Lesotho Highlands Water Project* (Lesotho: Transformation Resource Centre, 2006).

9. Burial societies provided 23.4% of the available credit, along with local moneylenders (35%) and relatives (25.5%), followed by neighbors (11.7%) and friends (4.4%). See S. Sets'abi and V. Mashinini, "The Livelihood Patterns of the People Relocated from the Mohale Dam Area: Data Analysis and Interpretation," in Thamae and Pottinger, eds., *On the Wrong Side of Development,* 115–145.

10. For more on this see the reports, especially 1995–2001, of the independent Panel of Experts (POE), which reported to the LHWP on environmental and social issues on a regular basis from 1989, as cited in Scudder "Accessing the Impacts of the LHWP"; also Hoover, *Pipe Dreams.*

11. For more on compensation and changes, see Hoover, *Pipe Dreams*, 25–33, and Rachel Slater and Matseliso Mphale, *Compensation, Welfare and Development: One-off Lump-sum and Regular Transfers in the Lesotho Highlands Water Project* (London: Overseas Development Institute, 2009).

12. Letsie III of Lesotho.

8 "I do not have the cleverness for here": Mohale Dam, Lesotho, after Displacement

1. See, for example, Thayer Scudder, "Assessing the Impacts of the LHWP on Resettled Households and other Affected People 1986–2005," in *On the Wrong Side of Development: Lessons Learned from the Lesotho Highlands Water Project,* edited by M. L. Thamae and L. Pottinger (Lesotho: Transformation Resource Centre, 2006) 39–87; and K. Horta and L. Pottinger, "The Role of the World Bank: The Perspective of International NGOs," in *On the Wrong Side of Development: Lessons Learned from the Lesotho Highlands Water Project,* edited by M. L. Thamae and L. Pottinger (Lesotho: Transformation Resource Centre, 2006), 23–38.

2. World Bank, *Project Performance Assessment Report (LHWP Phase 1B)* (Washington, D.C.: The World Bank, May 2010).

3. This second collection in Lesotho took place in 2001 and 2002 with 11 women and 7 men. Five men and four women were traced to their new locations. The new interviewees were largely chosen to increase the range of experience represented and to correct the gender imbalance in the first set of interviews. All interviews were translated from Sesotho into English. Panos's partner was Lesotho's Transformation Resource Centre; J. M. Lenka coordinated the project.

4. Molika-liko was particularly fertile land (see Chapter 7). See also M. Thabane, "Shifts from Old to New Social and Ecological Environments in the Lesotho Highlands Water Scheme," *Journal of Southern African Studies,* Vol. 26, Issue 4 (December 2000), 633–654.

5. See Thamae and Pottinger, eds., *On the Wrong Side of Development,* 121.

6. For more on this, see Ryan Hoover, *Pipe Dreams: The World Bank's Failed Efforts to Restore Lives and Livelihoods of Dam-Affected People in Lesotho* (Berkeley, CA: International Rivers Network, 2001), 26–27.

7. See Motlatsi Thabane, "Shifts from Old to New Social and Ecological Environments in the Lesotho Highlands Water Scheme," *Journal of Southern African Studies,* Vol. 26, Issue 4 (December 2000), 633–654.

8. For more on this see Scudder, "Assessing the Impacts of the LHWP," 80–82.

9. Thamae and Pottinger, eds., *On the Wrong Side of Development.*

10. See Hoover, *Pipe Dreams,* 28–29.

11. Rachel Slater and Matseliso Mphale, *Compensation, Welfare and Development: One-Off Lump-Sum and Regular Transfers in the Lesotho Highlands Water Project* (London: Overseas Development Institute, 2009).

12. In 2000, concerned villages sent representatives to an NGO-convened workshop, where they discussed their fears about the resettlement process. They drew up a declaration, which included the following: "We want transparency . . . We want to see how much money we have been compensated and how much interest that money is earning—We want to be in charge of our own assets and to invest our money as we see fit" (Berkeley, CA: International Rivers Network Newsletter, June 2000).

13. Thamae and Pottinger, eds., *On the Wrong Side of Development,* 35–90.

14. De Wet notes that "the translation of policy into practice is an essentially problematic and often messy process." See Chris de Wet, ed., *Development-Induced Displacement: Problems, Policies and People* (Oxford: Berghahn Books, 2006), 3–4.

15. See Scudder, "Assessing the Impacts of the LHWP," 67.

16. Most women liked the new houses, though many reported leaking roofs and cracked walls and said that they felt colder than in their traditional rondavels (circular buildings with pointed roofs) and

the new houses had to be heated with expensive paraffin stoves. Two women interviewed had built small rondavels beside their project house, where they could have an open fire.

17. Thamae and Pottinger, eds., *On the Wrong Side of Development,* 60.

9   Conclusion

1. M. Cernea, "Risks, Safeguards, and Reconstruction," in M. Cernea and C. McDowell, eds. *Risks and Reconstruction: The Experiences of Refugees and Resettlers* (Washington D.C.: The World Bank, 2000), 11–55.

2. James C. Scott, *Seeing Like a State: How Certain Schemes to Improve the Human Condition Have Failed* (New Haven: Yale University Press, 1998).

3. J. Ferguson, *The Anti-Politics Machine:"Development," Depoliticization, and Bureaucratic Power in Lesotho* (Minneapolis: University of Minnesota Press, 1994).

4. M. Cernea and H. M. Mathur, eds., *Can Compensation Prevent Impoverishment?* (Delhi: Oxford University Press, 2008).

5. See for example B. McDonald and M. Webber, "Involuntary Resettlement in China: A Model of Good Practice," *Forced Migration Review,* Vol. 14, 38–39, 2002.

6. See C. McDowell, ed., *Understanding Impoverishment: The Consequences of Development-Induced Displacement* (Oxford: Berghahn, 1996).

7. M. Cernea, "Risks, Safeguards, and Reconstruction, 2000.

8. M. Cernea and H. M. Mathur, eds., *Can Compensation Prevent Impoverishment?* 2008.

9. T. Scudder and E. Colson, "From Welfare to Development: A Conceptual Framework for the Analysis of Dislocated People." In A. Hansen and A. Oliver-Smith, eds., *Involuntary Migration and Resettlement: The Problems, and Responses of Dislocated People* (Boulder, CO: Westview Press, 1982).

10. C. McDowell, "Involuntary Resettlement, Impoverishment Risks and Sustainable Livelihoods," in *Australasian Journal of Disaster and Trauma Studies,* Vol. 6, No. 2, 2002, http://www.massey .ac.nz/~trauma/

11. I. Scoones, *Sustainable Rural Livelihoods: A Framework for Analysis* (Sussex: Institute of Development Studies Working Paper 72, 1998).

12. International Fund for Agricultural Development (IFAD), *Rural Poverty Report 2011* (Rome: IFAD, 2011).

13. O. Bennett, "Breaking the Threads," *Oral History,* Vol. 27, No. 1 (Spring 1999), 38–46

14. M. Cernea, "Risks, Safeguards, and Reconstruction," 2000.

15. World Commission on Dams, *Tarbela Dam and Related Aspects of the Indus River Basin, Pakistan,* Final Report (Cape Town, South Africa: World Commission on Dams: 2000).

16. See http://web.worldbank.org/website/external/extinspectionpanel/

17. T. Scudder, *The Future of Large Dams: Dealing with Social, Environmental, Institutional and Political Costs* (London: Earthscan, 2006).

Select Bibliography

Applebaum, A. *Gulag: A History*, New York: Doubleday, 2004.

Armstrong, A., and O. Bennett. "Representing the Resettled: The Ethical Issues Raised by Research and Representation of the San." In *Conservation and Mobile Indigenous Peoples: Displacement, Forced Settlement and Sustainable Development*, edited by Dawn Chatty and Marcus Colchester, 188-202. Oxford: Berghahn Books, 2002.

Barker, R., and N. Cross. *At the Desert's Edge: Oral Histories from the Sahel*. London: Panos, 1992.

Bennett, O. "Breaking the Threads." *Oral History*, Vol. 27, No. 1 (Spring 1999), 38–46.

Bennett, O., J. Bexley, and K. Warnock, eds. *Arms to Fight, Arms to Protect: Women Speak Out About Conflict*. London: Panos, 1995.

Bisht, T. C. "Displacement, Resettlement and Everyday Life: An Ethnographic Study of People Displaced by the Tehri Dam in India," PhD thesis, La Trobe University, Victoria, Australia, 2008.

Brody, H. "Taking the Words from Their Mouths." In *Tribes: Battle for Lands and Language. Index on Censorship*, Vol. 28, Issue 4 (London, 1999), 42–47.

Cernea, M. "Risks, Safeguards and Reconstruction: A Model for Population Displacement and Resettlement." In *Risks and Reconstruction: The Experiences of Refugees and Resettlers*, edited by M. Cernea and C. McDowell, 11–55. Washington, D.C.: The World Bank, 2000.

Cernea, M., and H. M. Mathur, eds. *Can Compensation Prevent Impoverishment?* Delhi: Oxford University Press, 2008.

Cernea, M., and C. McDowell, eds. *Risks and Reconstruction: The Experiences of Refugees and Resettlers*. Washington, D.C.: The World Bank, 2000.

Chambers, R. "Power, Knowledge and Policy Influence: Reflections on an Experience." In *Knowing Poverty: Critical Reflections on Participatory Research and Policy*, edited by K. Brock and R. McGee, 135–65. London: Earthscan Publications, 2002.

Chambers, R. *Who Counts? The Quiet Revolution of Participation and Numbers*. Working Paper 296, Institute of Development Studies, University of Sussex, 2007.

Colson, E. *The Social Consequences of Resettlement*. Manchester: Manchester University Press, 1971.

de Wet, C., ed., *Development-Induced Displacement: Problems, Policies and People*. Oxford: Berghahn Books, 2006.

Downing, T. E. "Mitigating Social Impoverishment when People Are Involuntarily Displaced." In *Understanding Impoverishment: The Consequences of Development-Induced Displacement*, edited by C. McDowell, 33–48. Oxford: Berghahn, 1996.

Downing, T. E. *Avoiding New Poverty: Mining-Induced Displacement and Resettlement*. Mining, Minerals and Sustainable Development Working Paper No. 58, International Institute for Environment and Development, London, 2002.

Ferguson, J. *The Anti-Politics Machine: "Development," Depoliticization, and Bureaucratic Power in Lesotho*. Minneapolis: University of Minnesota Press, 1994.

Ferris, E. *Natural Disaster and Conflict-Induced Displacement: Similarities, Differences and Interconnections*. Washington, D.C.: The Brookings Institute, 2008.

Gaventa, J. "The Powerful, the Powerless, and the Experts." In *Voices of Change: Participatory Research in the United States and Canada*, edited by P. Park, M. Brydon-Miller, B. Hall, and T. Jackson, 21–40. Westport CT and London: Bergin & Garvey, 1993.

Hyden, G. *Beyond Ujamaa in Tanzania: Underdevelopment and an Uncaptured Peasantry.* London: Heinemann, 1980.

Internal Displacement Monitoring Centre. *Internal Displacement: Global Overview of Trends in 2010,* Geneva: IDMC, 2011.

International Federation of the Red Cross, *World Disasters Report 2010,* Geneva: IFRC, 2010.

International Fund for Agricultural Development (IFAD). *Rural Poverty Report 2011.* Rome: IFAD, 2011.

Kaelin, W. "The Role of the Guiding Principles in Internal Displacement." In *Forced Migration Review,* Vol. 23, 8–9. 2005.

Kothari, U., and D. Hulme. *Narratives, Stories and Tales: Understanding Poverty Dynamics Through Life Histories,* Global Poverty Research Group Working Paper No. 11. Manchester, UK: University of Manchester, 2004.

Lahiff, E. *Land Reform and Poverty in South Africa.* Cape Town: University of the Western Cape, Programme for Land and Agrarian Studies, 2007.

McDonald, B. and M. Webber. "Involuntary Resettlement in China: A Model of Good Practice." *Forced Migration Review,* Vol. 14, 38–39. 2002.

McDowell, C., ed. *Understanding Impoverishment: The Consequences of Development-Induced Displacement.* Oxford: Berghahn, 1996.

McDowell, C. "Involuntary Resettlement, Impoverishment Risks and Sustainable Livelihoods," *Australasian Journal of Disaster and Trauma Studies,* Vol. 6, No. 2, 2002, http://www.massey.ac.nz/~trauma/

McDowell, C., and G. Morrell. *Displacement beyond Conflict: Challenges for the 21st Century.* Oxford: Berghahn, 2010.

McMillan, D. E. *Sahel Visions: Planned Settlement and River Blindness Control in Burkina Faso.* Tucson: University of Arizona Press, 1995.

Narayan, D., with R. Patel, K. Schafft, A. Rademacher, and A. Koch-Sculte. *Voices of the Poor: Can Anyone Hear Us?* New York: Oxford University Press, 2000.

Painter, T. *Getting It Right: Linking Concepts and Action for Improving the Use of Natural Resources in Sahelian Africa.* Dryland Networks Program Issues Paper No. 40. International Institute for Environment and Development, London, 1993.

Read, P. *Returning to Nothing: The Meaning of Lost Places.* Cambridge: Cambridge University Press, 1996.

le Roux, W., and A. White, eds. *Voices of the San: Living in Southern Africa Today.* Cape Town, South Africa: Kwela Books, 2004.

Scoones, I., *Sustainable Rural Livelihoods: A Framework for Analysis,* IDS Working Paper 72. Sussex: Institute of Development Studies, 1998.

Scott, J. C. *Seeing Like a State: How Certain Schemes to Improve the Human Condition Have Failed.* New Haven, CT: Yale University Press, 1998.

Scudder, T. *The Future of Large Dams: Dealing with Social, Environmental, Institutional and Political Costs.* London: Earthscan, 2006.

Scudder, T., and E. Colson. "From Welfare to Development: A Conceptual Framework for the Analysis of Dislocated People." In *Involuntary Migration and Resettlement: The Problems, and Responses of Dislocated People,* edited by A. Hansen and A. Oliver-Smith, 267–287. Boulder, CO: Westview Press, 1982.

Slim, H., and P. Thompson. *Listening for a Change: Oral Testimony and Development.* London: Panos, 1993.

Sorenson, B. R. *Relocated Lives: Displacement and Resettlement within the Mahaweli Project, Sri Lanka.* Amsterdam: VU University Press, 1996.

Sorenson, B. R. "The Experience of Displacement: Reconstructing Places and Identities in Sri Lanka." In *Siting Culture: The Shifting Anthropological Object,* edited by K. F. Olwig and K. Hastrup, 142–164. London: Routledge, 1997.

Thompson, P. *The Voice of the Past; Oral History.* Oxford: Oxford University Press, 1988.

World Commission on Dams (WCD). *Tarbela Dam and Related Aspects of the Indus River Basin, Pakistan.* Cape Town, South Africa: WCD, 2000.

Index

Page numbers in bold face denote figures.